At the Nexus of Philosophy and History

AT THE NEXUS
OF PHILOSOPHY AND HISTORY

EDITED BY BERNARD P. DAUENHAUER

The University of Georgia Press
Athens and London

© 1987 by the University of Georgia Press
Athens, Georgia 30602
All rights reserved
Designed by Mary Mendell
Set in 10 on 13 Trump Mediaeval with Eurostile display
The paper in this book meets the guidelines for permanence
and durability of the Committee on Production Guidelines
for Book Longevity of the Council on Library Resources.
Printed in the United States of America
91 90 89 88 87   5 4 3 2 1
Library of Congress Cataloging in Publication Data
At the nexus of philosophy and history.
1. History—Philosophy. 2. Philosophy—History.
I. Dauenhauer, Bernard P.
D16.9.A88 1987   901   86-7134
ISBN 0-8203-0893-5
British Library Cataloging in Publication Data available

Contents

Acknowledgments

This book as been made possible by many people, each of whom deserves, and has, my gratitude. On the one hand, and obviously, there would have been no book without the contributors. Their spirit of cooperation and their encouragement, in addition to their essays, have been invaluable. On the other hand, and crucially if not obviously, there would have been no book without the support of several of my colleagues here at the University of Georgia. Lester Stephens, head of the history department, provided indispensable advice both for this volume and for the conference on philosophy and history out of which it developed. Frederick Ferré, head of the philosophy department, gave the necessary initial endorsement to the project and cooperated fully at every stage of its execution. William Jackson Payne, dean of the University's Franklin College of Arts and Sciences, contributed both much-appreciated interest and absolutely essential funding. And Thomas Dyer, associate vice president for academic affairs, in his capacity of director of the University's Bicentennial program, generously injected the final funds necessary to complete the task. To all of these people, I am very grateful. Likewise I am indebted for their expert editorial advice to my colleagues at the University of Georgia Press: Karen Orchard, Malcolm Call, and Ellen Harris.

Introduction

Bernard P. Dauenhauer

What is the relation between philosophy and history? In an often cited passage of the *Poetics*, Aristotle says:

> The distinction between historian and poet . . . consists really in this, that the one describes the thing that has been, and the other a kind of thing that might be. Hence poetry is something more philosophic and of graver import than history, since its statements are of the nature rather of universals, whereas those of history are singulars.[1]

History, then, would be relatively distant from and substantially inferior to philosophy.

This passage from Aristotle can be taken to typify what I will call the philosophical strand of the Western intellectual tradition concerning the connection between philosophy and history.[2] According to the philosophical strand, the subject matters of history and philosophy are fundamentally discrete. The subject matter of history is the set of contingent, transient human performances. The subject matter of philosophy, on the other hand, is the "eternal verities," or at least the universal laws and conditions in conformity with which all permanence is constituted and which regulate all change. Whereas human performances are all bound by the spatial and temporal constraints within which they transpire, these laws or verities are essentially independent of the peculiarities of any particular time or place. The distinctive and noble task of the philosopher is to peer beyond the vagaries of the particular and the contingent and to catch sight of the divine, of the permanent universal and necessary principles of all that is.

This philosophical strand has had a long and honored career. It continues to have vigorous, able proponents today. But needless to say, it has hardly gone unchallenged. The depreciation of history in favor of philosophy has never totally dominated the Western intellectual scene. The philosophical strand has regularly been opposed by what might be called, with admitted imprecision, the rhetorical strand. The rhetorical strand emphasizes the establishment and maintenance of the community. It is the community which gives sense and worth to both history and philosophy. History, on the rhetorical view, is not concerned with just any human performances. It is concerned with singular human achievements—whether words, or deeds, or works—of substantial importance for the community. As Heraclitus, well before Aristotle, had put it: "The best men choose one thing rather than all else: everlasting fame among mortal men. The majority are satisfied, like well-fed cattle."[3]

These distinctive achievements, of course, belong to a particular era and locale. The task and glory of the historian—or encomiastic poet, for that matter—is to identify important instances of these achievements, to report them, and, if possible, to relate them to one another or to their context in a coherent narrative or story.[4] Philosophy's importance, for the rhetorical strand, is relative to its contribution to the establishment and enhancement of the concrete, historical community.

It is easy to see how history, according to the rhetorical strand, could give rise to the Ciceronian claim that history is *magistra vitae,* teacher of and for life. History, then, can and should be a moral discipline, a discipline providing guidance for human life. This view too, and the rhetorical strand in which it is embedded, has always had its proponents.

The ways in which these two strands have appeared in the works of various thinkers has obviously been quite variegated. Indeed, it would be barbarous to reify these two strands, to think of them as fixed components which individual thinkers worked upon. But if one understands these strands to be clusters of emphases and of issues, then the usefulness of distinguishing them becomes apparent.

The proximate intellectual context for this collection of essays has been set by nineteenth- and twentieth-century challenges to the apparent ahistoricality of the philosophical strand. One sort of challenge to the philosophical dissociation of history from philosophy is to be found in the work of Hegelians and Marxists. History for them has its own rationality. Philosophy's task and glory is to give voice to that rationality.

Another sort of challenge springs from a skepticism about whether either history or philosophy, as construed by the philosophical strand, could ever legitimately claim to achieve their stated purpose of articulating the truth about their respective subject matters. Nietzsche's work, at least in some of its parts, gives rise to doubt about whether the pursuit of truth, in its usual sense, by any discipline ultimately makes sense.

These sorts of challenges, coupled with the persistence of the rhetorical strand, have by no means routed the philosophical strand. But the discussions they have provoked are numerous and prominent in contemporary research in the humanities. It is difficult, and perhaps impossible, neatly to characterize just what is at stake in these contemporary investigations. But the following questions point to some of the most salient features of the present problematic concerning the relation between history and philosophy. These are the questions that prompted this collection of studies.

Starting from the side of philosophy, there is on the one hand the question of the relation between philosophy, understood as an ensemble of concepts and judgments, and the history of philosophy, namely, the previously articulated ensembles of the same sort. On the other hand, there is also the question of the relation between philosophy and the multiple extraphilosophical manifestations of cultural life. Starting from the side of history as historiography, one finds much the same sort of questions, namely, the question of the connection between historiography and its own history and the question of the connection between historiography and the other dimensions of cultural life.

One especially topical dimension of this latter pair of questions is the confrontation between the "New History" and the "Old History." The New History, relying heavily upon quantified data and theoretical models, stresses abstract, ideal types rather than the particular entities and events upon which old history—political or traditional history—habitually focuses. Where the old history dealt with what happened and how it happened, the New History asks why things happened as they did and what consequences follow upon their occurrence. Where the old history emphasized the interruptions that specific people introduced into the flow of "natural" processes, the New History emphasizes the continuity and durability of these processes.

At least one more substantial question confronts both philosophy and history—as well, perhaps, as every discipline in the humanities. What is the point of the study of either philosophy or history? Do these studied improve those who study them? If so, how? And if not, then just what is the point of pursuing them? And should they be pursued by everyone? Could it be that the study of one of these disciplines, either philosophy or history, would make the study of the other insignificant?[5]

None of the essays collected here pretends to deal with this entire skein of issues. But when taken together, they not only reveal more fully the scope and depth of the philosophy-history problematic but also constitute a substantial response to it.

These essays can be divided, with only occasional and mild violence, into two parts. Part 1, "Historical Aspects of Philosophical Thought," deals with the implications of the widely accepted claim that all philosophical thought, like all thought of any sort, bears the mark of its development within some determinate historical context. If both the way in which its questions are framed and what counts as evidence are conditioned by specific historical contexts, then how should one understand the claims which philosophy makes for the validity or binding force of its answers? Part 2, "On History and Its Uses," is concerned with the closely related but distinct matter of how one is to assess the study of history. What is there to study? And what can its study illuminate?

The lead essay of Part 1, and of the collection as a whole, is that of the philosopher Richard Bernstein. Its objective is to explore the ways in which an appeal to history, and not only to the history of philosophy, can and has performed a critical function in the contests among philosophers and their philosophies. After examining several ways in which contemporary philosophical thought, both Anglo-American and Continental, has used appeals to history to establish critical theses, Bernstein argues that philosophy must in-

clude what he calls a "double gesture." That is, it must attend both
to tradition, to the past, and to the requirement of criticism. Philosophy is impoverished, he claims, if it either forgets its past or
simply reiterates the tradition. Without the tradition whence it
springs, philosophy is a paltry affair. But one must also preserve the
Enlightenment insight that, in dealing with tradition, "we never
escape the demand to warrant our validity claims, to defend them
by the best possible arguments and reasons which are available to
us."

Louis Dupré's study concentrates on philosophy's relationship to
its own history. He begins by noting that, in the context of the strong
historical consciousness of the nineteenth century, two distinct attitudes toward philosophy emerged. One attitude reduced philosophy to a branch of cultural history. The other attitude, to counter
this relativist historicism, confined philosophy to purely formal
issues in logic and conceptual-linguistic analysis. Against this background, Dupré asks: "Is an acquaintance with past philosophy on its
own terms necessary or even useful for philosophical self-understanding?" Would not such a study sacrifice philosophy's basic
claim to definitiveness? Dupré's reply is that, "if temporality forms
an essential dimension of being, the study of former reflection constitutes an essential task of man's ultimate self-understanding."
The historical consciousness is itself acutely aware of the tension
between the permanent and the transient. Philosophy, in its own
turn, must deal with this tension. To make his case, Dupré studies a
specific issue, namely the shift in the philosophical understanding
of the Immanence-Transcendence relation. This examination yields
the conclusion that "each philosophy sheds a new and definitive
light on man's self-understanding as meaning-giving and being in
the world."

The positions of both Bernstein and Dupré are in effect, if not by
name, challenged by Richard Winfield. Drawing on Kantian and
Hegelian resources, Winfield claims that "philosophy appears in
history but presents what is eternally valid. Neither the history of
institutions nor the history of philosophy plays any role in determining philosophical problems or their proper resolution." In
short, there is a total disjunction between the task of philosophy
and that of history. As Socrates saw, in his quest for wisdom the

philosopher can be guided by only two things: the recognition of his own ignorance and of the radical difference in meaning between truth and opinion. "Today and tomorrow," Winfield concludes, "only by reasoning in freedom from history can we determine whether the routes of the past are paths we must follow."

Bowman Clarke's contribution was not written to rebut Winfield, but it presents an apparent counterexample to Winfield's general thesis. Clarke examines Kant's claim in the *Critique of Pure Reason* that logic is a closed and complete body of doctrine. In Kant's view, logic is a science that has its own subject matter. No form of logical truth or rule of inference has had to be revised since Aristotle. And logic has made no advance beyond Aristotle. Therefore, logic is essentially ahistorical. Though this claim was of great importance to Kant's own position, Clarke shows that Kant himself makes several improvements in logic precisely in this first *Critique.* Thus "ironically . . . the *Critique of Pure Reason* is rather pivotal in this . . . evolution of logic." This examination of Kant's position butresses Clarke's own thesis that logic is instrumental to our needs and purposes, which are unquestionably "historically conditioned and culturally relative."

The final essay in Part 1 is Nancy Streuver's "Philosophical Problems and Historical Solutions." Streuver builds upon the reflections of R. G. Collingwood on the relation between philosophy and history and defends on the one hand the ineradicable pertinence of history and philosophy to one another and on the other hand the propriety of claiming that historical inquiry is edifying. To make her case, she adopts the thesis of "social realism," namely "that the reality that is both topic and context of an investigative action is social action. All the evidence, the only evidence we have, is linguistic and semantic evidence of exchange, of communicative activity." This thesis holds for all philosophical inquiry as well as for all historical inquiry. All available evidence is not only discursive but also temporal. Since it is discursive, it is essentially dialogical. Since it is temporal, there is no readily available way to distinguish between present and past contributions to the evidence. Given this condition, what historical inquiry can bring to philosophy are the premises and procedures of social realism. What philosophy can bring to historical inquiry are ways of preventing the reification of historical constructs. The adoption of the thesis of social realism leads, on the one hand, to the conclusion that "not the past, but investigating the past is edifying." On the other hand, it indicates that although philosophy and history benefit each other, "philosophy has more to gain by becoming historical, than history has to gain by becoming philosophically kosher."

The essays which make up Part 2 are concerned, each in its own way, with one or both of the following questions: (a) What is the proper topic or object of historiographical efforts? and (b) What fruit should be sought from these efforts? These questions are matters of concern for both philosophers and historians.

Nietzsche, whose contemporary influence throughout the humanities is increasingly strong, is one major philosophical figure who exhibited a lifelong occupation with these topics. In her piece, Ofelia Schutte presents a careful analysis of three successive stages in Nietzsche's reflections on philosophy and history. In his first stage, Nietzsche, in opposition to Hegel, insisted upon keeping history, understood as knowledge of the past, distinct from philosophy, which searches for eternal wisdom. Later, Nietzsche argued in favor of integrating philosophy and history. In his words: "There are no eternal *facts*, nor are there any absolute truths. Thus *historical philosophizing* is necessary henceforth, and the virtue of modesty as well." Still later Nietzsche focused less on history as a branch of knowledge and more on the human potential for historical transformation. Nietzsche's thought about history and its relation to philosophy may not be totally consistent. But in his own way he has successively espoused most of the major positions on this issue. Nonetheless there is, Schutte finds, a distinct unity to his reflections. In all stages he gave voice to an apparently irreconcilable tension between what is and has come to be in human history and what could transform human life in the future.

The fame and reputation of Bertrand Russell as a philosopher is secure, at least in the English-speaking world. But his interest in and treatment of history and its purposes is not well known. Kirk Willis's contribution sets forth a clear account of Russell's doctrine concerning what the study of history can and should accomplish. Though history is, in Russell's view, necessarily subjective and imperfect, it is nonetheless the most indispensable of intellectual endeavors. It can and should enlarge the imagination, temper arrogance, teach tolerance, and show the place of the individual in the larger human family. Russell's view was that "the primary impetus for change both within and between civilizations . . . comes from the activities of exceptional individuals." Accordingly, historiography should embody the threefold recognition that dominant individuals define the characters of each particular civilization, no nation can flourish unless it tolerates exceptional individuals, and intelligence is a cause of historical change. If historiography respects these conditions then history can do what it should, namely, be a crucial force for moral education.

Ernst Breisach's contribution is focused upon the historiographical questions of what the proper "unit" is for historical research and how the historian is to deal with temporal succession. He critically examines two influential alternatives to the widely criticized traditional or political history. These two alternatives, namely, that of the turn-of-the-century American New Historians and that of the pre-1950 French New Historians, the *Annalistes*, both opposed political history in favor of economic and social history. Both aimed to make history scientific. But whereas the American New Historians espoused progressivism, the *Annalistes* held no such notion. In the final analysis, though, for Breisach the success of any version of the New History, like the success of any history, depends on its ability to handle the problem of time, "the issue of continuity in the midst of change." Thus far, no version of the New History has successfully established "a clear dynamics of history that could fuse together the past, the present, and expectations for the future." Until such a dynamics is fashioned, Breisach concludes, no historiography can be counted a complete success.

The outright dismissal or rejection of political history is surely excessive. Drawing extensively upon Martin Heidegger's *Being and Time* and Paul Ricoeur's recent studies of history and narrativity, in my own contribution to this volume I argue that if the study of history is to be a senseful enterprise, then one must acknowledge the enduring possibility of efficacious, deliberate human agency. This claim does not imply that every senseful product of historical scholarship must refer explicitly to events or actions brought about by identifiable human agents. It holds rather for the corpus of historical scholarship taken as a totality. One major consequence of this thesis is that neither political history nor social history can make complete sense without the other. A second major consequence is that, though just what the content of the lesson is remains open to debate, history is ineluctably *magistra vitae.*

Thomas Flynn, in an essay which is directly relevant to the controversy between the new history and traditional history but which has wider implications, examines Michel Foucault's historiography. He does so by concentrating upon Foucault's concept of an event. Foucault, who is in Flynn's view more Nietzschean than structuralist, understands an event to be a chance occurrence which, nonetheless, gets its specificity through its differential relation to other events in a series. A series is a discontinuously systematized discursive or nondiscursive practice. Foucault's historiography, then, requires a "search for the 'forces of domination' operating in history by a painstaking and inventive analysis of innumerable heterogeneous events." Though Flynn sees Foucault's achievement to be an important moment in the history of historiography, he finds it flawed by nominalism, aestheticism, and, perhaps, nihilism. Its flaw is a consequence of Foucault's attempt to disregard people as responsible historical agents.

A. Anthony Smith's contribution, the last in this collection, sets forth Jurgen Habermas's "account of the historical processes which have brought about our contemporary situation and his argument for the direction future development ought to take." He criticizes the goal Habermas sets for historical praxis and then defends an alternative historical praxis which he says is more faithful to Habermasian principles than is Habermas's own proposal. Habermas seeks to insure rational historical development through a specific type of discourse that anticipates what he calls the ideal speech situation. This type of discourse both includes all who are affected by any proposed course of action and excludes the use of coercion against any of the participants. He seeks to have this sort of discourse institutionalized in what he calls counterinstitutions to prevailing economic and political institutions. Smith argues that Habermas's proposal is doomed to be inefficacious. The *Lebenswelt* cannot be rationalized, Smith contends, unless political administration and economic action are subordinated to the actually expressed desires of the men and women who inhabit it. To achieve this subordination, according to Smith, "the institutionalization of discourse must involve the organizational structure of council democracy defended in the classical Marxist tradition." On his own grounds, Smith claims, Habermas should seek this form of institutionalized discourse.

This collection of essays, taken as a whole, obviously does not develop a elaborate theory of history. It was not meant to do so. But it does bring to light the principal aspects of the question of the relation between history and philosophy. It presents the current state of the question in its amplitude and variegation. And this is what it is meant to do. Even though agreement among contributors was not sought, at least two general, related elements of what might be labeled a majoritarian view do emerge in this collection. First, though emphases differ, neither philosophy nor history can make full sense without the other. Each needs the other to supply what may not be a deficiency but surely is a lack in its own resources and achievements. Both the historian and the philosopher must acknowledge the need for what Bernstein calls the double gesture. That is, there must be recognition of and respect for the past, but there must also be a critical moment, a moment in which the past and what it brings is assessed. Second, and correlatively, most contributions either explicitly claim or at least suggest that the study of history bears upon present or future human conduct. History is not the mere record of the past entertained simply for its own sake. History then bears upon and is related to the open present and future. It does not merely recall what has been. It also suggests both what might have been and what might yet come to be. History deals with the possible as well as the actual. Insofar as it deals with the possible, history is like poetry. Therefore Aristotle's judgment concerning the relative proximity of history and poetry to philosophy stands in need of emendation.

Notes

1. Aristotle, *Poetics*, 1451 B1–8.
2. As H.-G. Gadamer, among others, has shown, Aristotle's own position is much more complex than is suggested by this quotation. Evidence of this complexity

is found in his concern for practical as well as speculative philosophy. See especially Gadamer, *Truth and Method,* trans. Garrett Barden and John Cumming (New York: Seabury Press, 1975).

3. Heraclitus, Fragment 29 in Kathleen Freeman, *Ancilla to the Pre-Socratic Philosophers* (Oxford: Basil Blackwell, 1956), p. 26.

4. For a good account of this view of history, see Hannah Arendt, "The Concept of History," in her *Between Past and Future* (New York: Viking Press, 1968), pp. 41–90. Pindar exemplifies the poets who took up something of the same task. See, for example, Nancy F. Rubin, "The Epicinian Speaker in Pindar's First Olympian," *Poetics Today* 5, no. 2 (1984): 377–97.

5. Questions of this sort have been raised by Plato and ever since. See, for example, Thomas L. Pangle, "Socrates on the Problem of Political Education," *Political Theory* 13, no. 1 (1985): 112–37.

PART 1 Historical Aspects of Philosophical Thought

History, Philosophy, and the Question of Relativism

Richard Bernstein

In her preface to *Between Past and Future,* Hannah Arendt imaginatively interprets a parable by Franz Kafka. Kafka's parable reads as follows:

> He has two antagonists: the first presses him from behind, from the origin. The second blocks the road ahead. He gives battle to both. To be sure, the first supports him in his fight with the second, for he wants to push him forward, and in the same way the second supports him in his fight with the first, since he drives him back. But it is only theoretically so. For it is not only the two antagonists who are there, but he himself as well, and who really knows his intentions? His dream, though, is that some time in an unguarded moment—and this would require a night darker than any night has ever been yet—he will jump out of the fighting line and be promoted, on account of his experience in fighting, to the position of umpire over his antagonists in their fight with each other.[1]

Arendt's interpretation of this parable illuminates the gap in which the activity of thinking takes place—thinking that is situated in "a battleground on which the forces of the past and the future clash with each other." It is in this gap that the experience of thinking occurs—thinking that must be practiced and exercised over and over again but which knows no finality.

Kafka's parable is sufficiently rich so that it can be interpreted as a parable of the relation of philosophy to its past, to its history. For just as the "He" of the parable gains his identity in the battle with the two antagonists, so I want to suggest that this is the situation of philosophy. While it may dream of jumping out of the fighting line and achieving the position of a neutral umpire, it is an illusory dream. And like Kant's analysis of dialectical illusion, and Wittgenstein's Tractarian understanding of the limits of language, even when we are dimly aware that we cannot break out of these limits, that we cannot "jump out of the fighting line," we are still tempted to try. We never escape the battlefield in which there is always uneasy resolution and unresolved tension. It is a battle that is fraught with different types of dangers and illusions. For there is the illusion that philosophy can once and for all cut itself off from its past, jump out of its own history—something it never succeeds in doing. If it could, it would simply disappear and lose its identity. And there is the illusion of imagining that it can completely identify itself with its past, an illusion which if it could be realized would also mean a loss of its identity. For its proper place, its *topos* is always in the gap, and in fighting the battle between past and future.

When the danger is perceived as being overwhelmed by its past, philosophy fights back. We see this moment exemplified by Descartes, Kant, Nietzsche, Husserl, and more recently by logical positivists and analytic philosophers. At such moments philosophers are prone to make a sharp distinction between "doing philosophy" and the history of philosophy, with the confidence that once we hit on the right method, discover the way of making philosophy into a rigorous discipline, then we can simply abandon to antiquarians what appears to be the "dead weight" of the past. At such moments the history of philosophy is viewed with extreme suspicion, a repository of confusions and obscurities, an endless battleground of competing opinions with no resolution, a trap that can ensnare us. We need to make a break with the past; we need to forget in order to get on with the serious endeavor of philosophizing. And there are times when there is a backlash against the pretensions of the ahistorical character of philosophy, when we realize that even the boldest attempts to break with history fail, when we see how even those philosophers who thought that they were laying entirely new foundations for philosophy are themselves deeply marked by prejudices and biases which they have inherited from the very past that they have been battling. At such moments there is sometimes the temptation to claim that philosophy itself is nothing but the history of philosophy—a stance which ironically is itself unhistorical insofar as it tends to forget that there would be no history of philosophy unless philosophers themselves (who make this history) thought of themselves as breaking with the past.

I do not think that this unstable, in-between status of philosophy is a cause for despair, but rather that it is the *topos* in which philosophy always dwells. It would only be a cause for despair if we had reason to think that there can be an end to the battle, that philosophy could and should achieve the position of a neutral umpire. The quest for certainty, the search for an Archimedian point which can serve as a foundation for philosophy, the aspiration to see the world aright *sub specie aeternitatis*, the metaphysics of presence where we desire to break out of the endless process of signification and interpretation and face reality with immediacy and directness, are all variations on the dream of "He" to jump out of the fighting line. And even if we judge these attempts to fail in their ultimate objective, we do a serious injustice to philosophy if we fail to realize how much is achieved and illuminated in these failed attempts. Philosophers—especially since the beginnings of modern philosophy— have been plagued by the anxiety that unless we can discover fixed, indubitable foundations, we are confronted with intellectual and moral chaos, radical skepticism, and self-defeating relativism—a situation that is metaphorically described by Descartes when he says it is "as if I had all of a sudden fallen into very deep water [and] I am so disconcerted that I can neither make certain of setting my feet on the bottom, nor can I swim and so support myself on the surface."[2] In another context I have labeled this anxiety "the Cartesian Anxiety" and have argued that it is an anxiety that needs to be exorcised, that can only be cured by a type of philosophic therapy.[3] But here I want to focus on the critical space of this unstable gap between philosophy and its past. For the theme that I want to explore is the way in which an appeal to history (and not just the history of philosophy) serves a critical function in the battle of philosophy. It is not simply that we locate the critical function of philosophy in those moments when philosophy fights back and seeks to push back its past, but also in those moments when this process is reversed, when we appeal to history and the history of philoso-

phy in order to uncover, challenge, and criticize current prejudgments and prejudices—prejudices that can run so deep that we are
not even aware of them as uncritical biases. I do not want to suggest that this is the only function which the study of history of
philosophy can serve, but it is a function which I think has not
always been fully appreciated. So let me turn to several attempts
and several different ways in which the appeal to history has been
used critically in our contemporary situation.

The two major philosophic movements of the twentieth century
have prided themselves on their ahistorical thrust, and both initially helped to foster a deep suspicion of the positive role that the
study of history might play for philosophy. In this respect, both
analytic philosophy and phenomenology were true heirs of the Cartesian bias. Both in very different ways sought to rid us once and for
all from what they took to be the dangers of historicism and to delineate ways in which philosophy might "finally" become a rigorous
discipline that would no longer be burdened by past errors and dead
ends. This antihistorical animus was no less fundamental for Frege
and Husserl than it was for later logical positivists and conceptual
analysts. To the extent that either movement showed an interest in
the history of philosophy, it was motivated by the desire to show
how what was valuable and viable in this tradition could be interpreted as seeing through a glass darkly what now was supposedly
seen so perspicuously—to show how the task of philosophy, properly understood, could correct the mistakes and confusions of the
past.
    Although I think parallel stories can be told about the break-
down of the antihistorical bias of analytic philosophy and phenomenology, a breakdown which can be seen as a "return of the
repressed," I want to focus on the development of analytic philosophy and some of its recent critics. Analytic philosophy as a style of
philosophizing has undergone many internal transformations from
its early origins in logical positivism and the writings of Russell
and Moore. But even when we follow its sometimes tortuous paths
and its diverse currents from positivism to ordinary-language analysis to the philosophy of language and formal semantics, the anti-

historical bias of this style of philosophizing has persisted. Recently, however, there are many signs of the breakup of the hegem-
ony of analytic philosophy. Even a generation ago there seemed to
be an optimistic confidence among many analytic philosophers
that philosophy had finally discovered its proper subject matter, its
problems, and its procedures, so that genuine progress could be
made in solving or dissolving philosophic problems. But even
among the staunchest defenders of analytic philosophy this confidence is now seriously questioned. Recently there have been a
growing number of critiques of the presuppositions, unquestioned
assumptions, and metaphors that have characterized so much of
contemporary analytic philosophy.

Two of the most forceful and controversial critics of analytic philosophy have been Richard Rorty and Alasdair MacIntyre. Philosophers are frequently insensitive to the criticisms of "outsiders," but
what has disturbed (or delighted) so many philosophers is that both
Rorty and MacIntyre are "insiders." I do not simply mean that they
have established their credentials as professional philosophers, but
more specifically that each has contributed to discussions which
have been in the foreground of analytic philosophy. But the distinctive feature of their recent critiques is the use that they make of
history in carrying out these critiques. Rorty, in *Philosophy and the
Mirror of Nature*, not only "goes after" the pretentions of analytic
philosophy, he seeks to deconstruct what he calls the "Cartesian-
Lockean-Kantian" tradition, and the obsession with epistemology
and foundationalism that he takes to be characteristic of so much of
modern philosophy. Rorty typically begins his critiques with a
"softening-up" strategy in which he shows his dexterity in picking
apart the typical argumentative strategies that have been valorized
by analytic philosophers. But the subversive quality of his critique
soon becomes evident, for he is calling into question just this ad-
versarial, argumentative style of philosophizing. He wants to dig
deeper and come to some understanding of why philosophers engage
in the language games that they do. And this requires a historical
critique, a type of genealogical unmasking where we become aware
of the historical accidents and contingencies that shape what we
frequently take to be intuitive and self-evident.

One of the many spinoffs of Rorty's reflections is a distinctive (and controversial) interpretation of how the history of philosophy has developed.[4] He rejects the view that there are perennial problems of philosophy which arise as soon as we reflect. He is equally relentless in his criticism of a variant of this, where we take the more charitable and self-congratulatory attitude that our philosophic ancestors were dealing with basic problems, but the trouble is that they lacked the proper conceptual tools for solving them. His alternative, which can be seen as a novel blending of themes suggested by Heidegger, Derrida, Foucault, Kuhn, and Feyerabend, may be stated as follows. There are moments in history when, because of all sorts of historical accidents—like what is going on in some part of culture such as science or religion—a new set of metaphors, distinctions, and problems is invented and captures the imagination of followers. For a time, when a particular philosophic language game gets entrenched, it sets the direction for "normal" philosophizing. After a while, because of some other historical accidents—like the appearance of a new genius or just plain boredom and sterility—another cluster of metaphors, distinctions, and problems usurp the place of what is now a dying tradition. At first the abnormal talk of some new genius may be dismissed as an emanation of the lunatic fringe or as not being "genuine" or "serious" philosophy. But sometimes this abnormal talk will set philosophy in new directions. We must resist the Whiggish temptation to rewrite the history of philosophy in our own image—where we see our predecessors as "really" treating what we now take to be fundamental problems. The crucial point for Rorty is to realize that a philosophical paradigm does *not* displace a former one because it can better formulate the legitimate problems of a prior paradigm; rather, because of a set of historical contingencies, it nudges the former paradigm aside. This is what happened in the seventeenth century when within a relatively short period of time the entire tradition of scholasticism collapsed and no longer seemed to have much point. After such a revolution or upheaval occurs, philosophers have a difficult time figuring out the point of the elaborate language game that had evolved. While Rorty refuses to make predictions, he certainly suggests that this is likely to happen again with modern philosophy and its offspring, analytic philosophy. To understand a historical movement such as analytic philosophy, we must uncover the metaphors, distinctions, and problems that characterize its form of normal philosophizing, and this requires historical digging into how a distinctive type of problematic was invented.

I do not want to suggest that I uncritically accept Rorty's understanding of how the history of philosophy develops, or rather moves by fits and starts. And I think there is plenty to criticize in the specific genealogies that he elaborates. But I do want to highlight the seriousness (and playfulness) of Rorty's critique, for if he is right then many analytic philosophers are self-deceived in what they think they are doing—solving and dissolving the "genuine" problems of philosophy. In this context the most important point to emphasize is that Rorty's forays into the history of philosophy and the normal philosophizing of analytic philosophers is primarily critical in its intent. His historical analyses are intended to uncover prejudgments and prejudices, to expose their historical contingencies. At the very least, he forces us to ask new sorts of questions about just what analytic philosophers are doing, and these critical questions could not even be raised without a historical perspective on the present.

MacIntyre, who has been critical of Rorty's historical interpretations and more generally Rorty's conception of the history of philosophy, makes an even more ambitious use of history in his critique of contemporary moral philosophy in *After Virtue*. In the main, Rorty restricts himself to the history of philosophy. But in a quasi-Hegelian manner, MacIntyre thinks that if we want to understand philosophy and its history, we can only properly make sense of it in terms of more pervasive themes in culture and society. This is evidenced in the way in which he examines emotivism. For emotivism is not just a curious minor chapter in the history of moral philosophy. We can argumentatively show why an emotivist theory of meaning is mistaken, but this does not yet touch what MacIntyre takes to be a more fundamental issue. For he claims that

> to a large degree people now think, talk, and act *as if* emotivism were true, no matter what their avowed theoretical standpoint may be. Emotivism has become embodied in our culture. But of course in saying this I am not merely contending that

morality is not what it once was, but also and more importantly that what once was morality has to a large degree disappeared . . . and that this marks a degeneration, a grave cultural loss.[5]

MacIntyre seeks to show us that emotivism has become embodied in our culture and sketches a historical account of just how this came to be—a historical account which is not meant to be neutral but rather has the critical intent of showing us why this is a degeneration and a cultural loss. A degeneration from what? From what MacIntyre calls the "tradition of the virtues"—a tradition that began long before Aristotle, but where Aristotle's ethical and political writings are the canonical texts, a tradition which according to MacIntyre continued to develop creatively through the Middle Ages. If MacIntyre is to complete his narrative argument, it is not sufficient simply to describe and evoke the memory of this tradition. He must also defend it. To use his own words, he seeks to make "the rational case" for a tradition in which the Aristotelian ethical and political texts are canonical. The Aristotelian tradition of the virtues must be "rationally vindicated." According to MacIntyre's narrative it was the Enlightenment project of seeking to justify moral principles that bears a great deal of the responsibility for the "catastrophe" of the collapse of the tradition of the virtues. This Enlightenment project, when unmasked—as it was by Nietzsche—ineluctably leads to emotivism. According to MacIntyre we are confronted with a grand Either/Or.

> *Either* one must follow through the aspirations and the collapse of the different versions of the Enlightenment project until there remains only the Nietzschean diagnosis and the Nietzschean problematic *or* one must hold that the Enlightenment project was not only mistaken, but should never have been commenced in the first place. There is no third alternative.[6]

Once again, in citing MacIntyre, my main point is not to endorse what he is claiming, but to highlight another variation of the way in which the appeal to history can serve a critical philosophical function.[7] To anticipate a point that I want to emphasize later in this essay, MacIntyre's own historical critique of contemporary morality and moral philosophy itself demands a close critical examination of his "rational vindication" of the Aristotelian tradition. To return to Kafka's parable, both Rorty and MacIntyre help us to see how "He" uses one antagonist in his fight with the second, how the appeal to history can enable us to think critically in the gap between past and future. But "He" must give battle to both antagonists. Rorty and MacIntyre are not just telling us likely stories that are intended to make sense of our present predicament. They are making claims to validity, claims which have an implicit future reference and which must themselves be subjected to careful scrutiny and evaluation. In carrying out this critical task, an appeal to the past, to the history of philosophy, or to a more general cultural and social history is never sufficient. But before dealing more explicitly with the doubly critical character of the fight of philosophy, I want to extend the horizon of the ways in which the appeal to history has served a critical function in recent philosophy.

One of the most dramatic consequences of the appeal to history in recent philosophy has been the appeal to history in the understanding of the nature of science. Kuhn was certainly prophetic when he opened *The Structure of Scientific Revolutions* with the following claim:

History, if viewed as a repository for more than anecdote or chronology, could produce a decisive transformation in the image of science by which we are now possessed. That image has been previously drawn, even by scientists themselves, mainly from the study of finished scientific achievements as these are recorded in the classics, and more recently, in the textbooks from which each new scientific generation learns to practice its trade. Inevitably, however, the aim of such books is persuasive and pedagogic; a concept of science drawn from them is no more likely to fit the enterprise that produced them than an image of a national culture drawn from a tourist brochure or a language text. This essay attempts to show that we have been misled by them in fundamental ways. Its aim is to sketch a quite different concept of science that can emerge from the historical record of research activity itself.[8]

If we place Kuhn's remarks in their historical context we can grasp why *The Structure of Scientific Revolutions* had such an impact on our understanding of science and also influenced many other areas of inquiry. For Kuhn gave expression to a new emerging orientation—to emphases and concerns that were being fed by a wide variety of sources. By 1962, the "received" or "orthodox" view of the structure of scientific theory and explanation was coming under increased attack.[9] Not only was there a questioning of the fundamental dogmas of logical empiricism, including a sharp analytic-synthetic distinction, the observational-theoretical distinction, the dichotomy between the context of discovery and the context of justification, and the primacy of the deductive-nomological analysis of scientific explanation, there was a growing sense that there was something artificial and distortive about the very way in which problems in the philosophy of science were formulated. Hanson, Feyerabend, Toulmin, Lakatos, and even Popper emphasized how a sensitivity to science as a historical, ongoing activity transformed our "image of science." The appeal to history was not anecdotal, it was critical. I do not want to underestimate the differences among those who transformed our understanding of scientific inquiry, but this should not blind us to the common themes and affinities that emerged in these debates and controversies.[10] Although Kuhn's slippery and ambiguous term 'paradigm' has been seriously challenged for clarifying the character of scientific development, Kuhn helped to initiate a "paradigm-shift" in the philosophy and history of science. The new sensitivity to the relevance of the history of scientific inquiry for gaining a philosophical perspective on science was itself fraught with dangers. For there was the danger of displacing the "epistemological myth of the given" with a "historical myth of the given," where we falsely imagine that global interpretations of the nature of science can be resolved by direct appeals to history.[11] But the appeal to history is not sufficient to bear this weight. The history of science has served a powerful critical function in our understanding of science, but the diverse appeals to history themselves demand careful critical scrutiny.

Thus far, in discussing Rorty, MacIntyre, and Kuhn, I have been focusing on diverse uses of history in criticizing some of the anti-historical biases of analytic philosophy, but I have already suggested that we can find affinities with what has happened in continental philosophy since the early days of phenomenology. To illustrate what I mean, let me briefly consider some of the contributions of Hans-Georg Gadamer and Michel Foucault.

The transition from Rorty, MacIntyre, and Kuhn to Gadamer is an easy and natural one. Rorty himself appropriated the expression 'hermeneutics' from Gadamer. (The penultimate chapter of *Philosophy and the Mirror of Nature* is entitled "From Epistemology to Hermeneutics.") Kuhn, too, recognizes the affinity of his approach to understanding scientific inquiry and hermeneutics.[12] There are many family resemblances between MacIntyre's own understanding of the role of narrative and tradition—and especially his appeal to Aristotle—and Gadamer's own appropriation of Aristotle. (Indeed, I think one of the most exciting aspects of recent philosophy is the increasing crisscrossing that is taking place between Anglo-American and Continental philosophy.)

Gadamer not only is constantly making a critical use of the history of philosophy, he is a thinker who has sought to challenge the Enlightenment's prejudice against prejudice. He has defended the centrality of tradition and rightful authority in all human understanding. We are beings thrown into the world who are always shaped by and shaping the traditions that form us. Tradition for Gadamer is a repository of truth, and in the dialogical conversation with tradition our task is to recover this truth. This is not the occasion for a full-scale explication and assessment of Gadamer's claims, but I would like to focus on one dominant theme in Gadamer which exemplifies what he means by hermeneutics, and how it can enable us to gain a critical perspective on our contemporary situation: his interpretation of Aristotle's conception of *praxis* and *phronesis*.[13] All understanding for Gadamer involves appropriation; and this is what he seeks to do with Aristotle's texts. Appropriation itself for Gadamer requires what Aristotle called *phronesis*, where knowledge is not detached from our being but is determinative of what we are in the process of becoming. Hermeneutical understanding for Gadamer is itself a form of *phronesis*, a judgmental mediation between the universal and the particular. And Gadamer himself has sought to delineate the ways in which the practical wisdom of *phronesis* differs from *episteme* and *techne*. But Gadamer's interest in Aristotle's ethical and political writings is not merely philological or antiquarian. He tells us: "When Aristotle, in the sixth book of the *Nicomachean Ethics*, distinguishes the manner of 'practical' knowledge . . . from theoretical and technical knowledge, he expresses, in my opinion, one of the greatest truths by which the Greeks throw light upon 'scientific' mystification of modern society of specialization."[14]

He spells out what he means when he writes:

> In my own eyes, the great merit of Aristotle was that he anticipated the impasse of our scientific culture by his description of the structure of practical reason as distinct from theoretical knowledge and technical skill. By philosophical arguments he refuted the claim of the professional lawmakers whose function at that time corresponded to the role of the expert in the modern scientific society. Of course, I do not mean to equate the modern expert with the professional sophist. In his own field he is a faithful and reliable investigator, and in general he is well aware of the particularity of his methodical assumptions and realises that the results of his investigation have a limited relevance. Nevertheless, the problem of our society is that the longing of the citizenry for orientation and normative patterns invests the expert with an exaggerated authority. Modern society expects him to provide a substitute for past moral and political orientations. Consequently, the concept of 'praxis' which was developed in the last two centuries is an awful deformation of what practice really is. In all the debates of the last century practice was understood as application of science to technical tasks. . . . It degrades practical reason to technical control.[15]

Here, too. we witness still another subtle and powerful critical encounter with the present—an encounter informed by the appropriation of Aristotle's reflections on *praxis* and *phronesis*. But again there is double movement in this critique. If Gadamer is right about what he takes to be "one of the greatest truths" found in Aristotle, then this needs to be rationally vindicated. It is here that the "He" of Kafka's parable needs to fight back. If we accept Gadamer's analysis of the problem of our scientific civilization, it cannot be simply because when compared with the classical Greek understanding of *praxis* and *phronesis* we judge our society to be deficient and deformed, but rather because we are *now* prepared to defend and argumentatively justify what we take to be the "truth" in the tradition of practical philosophy. Such an argumentative defense always makes an implicit reference to the future, to the openness of critical examination of validity claims. It is a bad or degenerate form of historicism to think we can justify such validity claims by the appeal to tradition and inherited authority. In this respect, I am in complete agreement with Habermas, who has forcefully argued against Gadamer that in any critical encounter with tradition we never escape the demand to warrant our validity claims, to defend them by the best possible arguments and reasons which are available to us. This is the "truth" in the Enlightenment tradition that still needs to be preserved and defended.[16] This is the "truth" in Kant's call for "the freedom to make public use of one's reason at every point."[17]

Before returning explicitly to the double gesture—the dialectical tension—between philosophy and its history, I want to consider how we can enlarge our appreciation of the critical function of the appeal to history by briefly considering the work of Michel Foucault. At first glance Foucault is problematic in several respects. Whereas Gadamer seeks to show continuities and affinities between the past and the present, to enable us to fuse alien horizons, Foucault's characteristic emphasis is on epistemological ruptures and radical breaks of *episteme* and discursive practice. He has an uncanny ability to make the familiar appear strange and alien. His histories, archaeological excavations, and genealogical unmaskings strike us as antihistories.[18] Moreover, his texts defy any easy genre classification. Are they history, philosophy, sociology, fictions? Transgression is not only a constant theme in Foucault, it is embodied in his rhetorical style—a style that makes us acutely aware of the exclusionary tactics of all forms of discourse, including the discourse of philosophers. Just as he is an antihistorical "historian," he sometimes appears to be an antiphilosophical philosopher. When he asks the question, How is a given form of knowledge possible? he is not searching for transcendental conditions but for an analysis of these micropractices and "unthought" rules embedded in what seems so marginal—the substructure of our discourses.

Foucault is always throwing us off-center, forcing us to ask new sorts of questions and engaging in new sorts of inquiries to write a "history of the present." Consider his *Discipline and Punish*, which strikingly begins with a description of the brutal public execution of Damiens, a description juxtaposed with the "timetable"—the rules for "the house of young prisoners in Paris" which was drawn up eighty years later by Léon Faucher.[19] What does any of this have to do with philosophy? What concern for philosophers is there in a study which announces itself as "The Birth of the Prison?" And yet, as Foucault's own "narrative" unfolds, we gradually become aware that such themes as "knowledge," "power," "truth," "subjectivity," the nature of "man," "the character of the human sciences"—themes which have been central for philosophy—come obliquely into the foreground. He concludes with a chilling analysis of the "Panopticon society," "the disciplinary society," "the carceral city"—which turns out to be our society. In short, Foucault presents us with nothing less than a radical critique of our present condition, radical not only in the sense of holding up to us a mirror of what we have become, but radical in the sense of getting at its archaeological underpinnings: "the historical background to various studies of the power of normalization and the formation of knowledge in modern society." Foucault frequently leaves us with more questions than he resolves. His analyses force us to raise new questions about freedom, power, knowledge, and emancipation.[20] We witness a penetrating critique that could only be achieved by "historical" digging—a digging not into the history of philosophy but the "history" that makes philosophy itself possible.

My brief discussions of Rorty, MacIntyre, Kuhn, Gadamer, and Foucault are intended to be a series of reminders—signposts—of some of the diverse ways in which the appeal to history serves the critical function of philosophy. Not only are there different conceptions and kinds of history which are used, but also different ways in which they serve a critical function. But for all their differences, they share in common the intent to expose prejudgments, prejudices, and illusions. They seek to provide us with an understanding that goes below the surface. Each manifests a negative moment which calls into question what has been unquestioned. In this respect they share in the *ethos* that is perhaps the deepest and most persistent theme in the tradition of philosophic reflection. There is a double character, a double gesture in all these "historical" critiques. For the more seriously we take them, the more seriously we must critically evaluate them, exploring their ramifications, testing their validity, pursuing the questions that they raise. We are not only thrust backward, but forward. "He" must always engage in a double battle. Philosophy becomes thin and is in danger of losing its identity when it forgets its past, when it gives up trying to grapple with both the strangeness and familiarity of what is "other" and alien. But it also becomes thin when it is seduced into thinking that the appeal to tradition is sufficient to answer its questions. It should be clear that I reject foundationalism in its multifarious forms. I not only reject the idea that philosophy itself can be grounded on permanent foundations but that philosophy itself is a foundational discipline, an arbitrator for the rest of culture. But I also reject the idea that history—in any of its forms—is or can be a foundational discipline, that it can answer the questions we ask in philosophy. I do not believe that there are perennial problems in philosophy or philosophical intuitions which are so deep that they escape historical contingencies. But there is another way of understanding the perennial character of philosophy, for there is a perennial impulse of wonder that can take a variety of forms. There is a deep impulse to understand, to make sense of, to comprehend "that articulated and integrated vision of man-in-the-universe—or shall I say, discourse-about-man-in-all-discourse—which has traditionally been its goal,"[21] even when this discourse seeks to unravel what has been taken to be intelligible. And this impulse and the task it sets for us—although it may be suppressed or repressed—has itself an uncanny way of reasserting itself, even when it appears most moribund.

Let me conclude with a passage from John Dewey. For the interpretation of Kafka's parable that I have sketched above might well be taken as commentary on what Dewey wrote:

There is current among those who philosophize the conviction that, while past thinkers have reflected in their systems the conditions and perplexities of their own day, present-day philosophy in general, and one's own philosophy in particular, is emancipated from the influence of that complex of institutions which forms culture. Bacon, Descartes, Kant each thought with fervor that he was founding philosophy anew because he was placing it securely upon an exclusive intellectual basis, exclusive, that is, of everything but intellect. The movement of time has revealed the illusion; it exhibits as the work of philosophy the old and ever new undertaking of adjusting that body of traditions which constitute the actual mind of man to scientific tendencies and political aspirations which are novel and incompatible with received authorities. Philosophers are parts of history, caught in its movement; creators perhaps in some measure of its future, but also assuredly creatures of its past.[22]

Notes

1. Cited in Hannah Arendt, *Between Past and Future* (New York: Viking Press, 1961), p. 7.
2. René Descartes, *The Philosophical Works of Descartes*, trans. Elizabeth S. Haldane and G. R. T. Ross, 2 vols. (Cambridge: Cambridge University Press, 1969), 1:149.
3. See *Beyond Objectivism and Relativism* (Philadelphia: University of Pennsylvania Press, 1983), pp. 16–20.
4. The following paragraph is based upon my critical study of Rorty's *Philosophy and the Mirror of Nature*. See "Philosophy in the Conversation of Mankind," *The Review of Metaphysics* 33 (June 1980): 748.
5. Alasdair MacIntyre, *After Virtue* (Notre Dame: University of Notre Dame Press, 1981), p. 21.
6. Ibid., p. 111.
7. For my critique of MacIntyre, see "Nietzsche or Aristotle? Reflections on Alasdair MacIntyre's *After Virtue*," *Soundings* 47 (Spring 1984).
8. Thomas Kuhn, *The Structure of Scientific Revolutions* (Chicago: University of Chicago Press, 1962), p. 1.
9. For a detailed elaboration of the "received view" and the criticisms brought

against it, see the foreword to Frederick Suppe, ed., *The Structure of Scientific Theories*, 2d ed. (Urbana: University of Illinois Press, 1977).

10. I have analyzed this historical shift in the understanding of science in *Beyond Objectivism and Relativism*, part 2.

11. See my discussion of this danger in *Beyond Objectivism and Relativism*, pp. 71 ff.

12. See Kuhn's preface to *The Essential Tension* (Chicago: University of Chicago Press, 1977). See also my discussion of hermeneutics and the philosophy of science in *Beyond Objectivism and Relativism*.

13. See my discussion and critique of Gadamer in *Beyond Objectivism and Relativism*, part 3.

14. Hans-Georg Gadamer, "The Problem of Historical Consciousness," reprinted in *Interpretive Social Science: A Reader*, ed. Paul Rabinow and William Sullivan (Berkeley and Los Angeles: University of California Press, 1981), p. 107.

15. Hans-Georg Gadamer, "Hermeneutics and Social Science," *Cultural Hermeneutics* 2 (1975): 312.

16. I have developed this theme more fully in *Beyond Objectivism and Relativism*. See especially pp. 150 ff.

17. Immanuel Kant, "What is Enlightenment?" in *Foundations of the Metaphysics of Morals*, trans. Lewis White Beck (New York: Library of Liberal Arts, 1959), p. 87.

18. See Hayden White, "Foucault Decoded: Notes from Underground," in *Tropics of Discourse* (Baltimore: Johns Hopkins Press, 1978).

19. Michel Foucault, *Discipline and Punish* (New York: Viking Books, 1979), pp. 3–7.

20. For a penetrating critique of Foucault's critique, see Charles Taylor, "Foucault on Freedom and Truth," *Political Theory* 12 (1984).

21. Wilfrid Sellars, *Science, Perception and Reality* (New York: Humanities Press, 1963), p. 171.

22. John Dewey, *Philosophy and Civilization* (New York: Monton, Balch & Company, 1931), pp. 3–4.

The Paradox of History in Philosophy

Among all the branches of learning, philosophy and history appear to be most seriously concerned with their own past. In the physical sciences, historical questions have such a low priority that only few universities possess a chair in the history of science. A study of the various, often misguided attempts that have resulted in the present state of physics, chemistry, or biology is generally held to offer little assistance toward achieving respectable results in those disciplines. The past of a science hardly continues to belong to the science as such. Whatever is not eliminated is assimilated—often in theories that remain only marginally related to the original concepts. Hence students are not required to read the "classics" of science as they are in philosophy and, to a lesser degree, in history. Semianonymous, continuously adjusted textbooks provide all the information an average scientist will ever need about the history of a current problem; in most cases they provide it more effectively. To return to the past for other than historical reasons may merely result in reinventing the wheel, or, more commonly, in failing to reinvent it. The names that survive stand enshrined in a hall of fame erected according to the norms and demands of the present generation. The concerns of the past appear to matter very little; what counts are the past contributions to the present concerns.

In philosophy the situation looks very different. Here the new never destroys the old. Even when it appears to absorb the past, it leaves its integrity intact. A new philosophy never simply surpasses an older one. It may abandon certain of its problems, because it finds them poorly articulated, or because they no longer excite its interest. But such a shift never entirely replaces the older philosophy in the manner in which a heliocentric replaces a geocentric cosmology. This is particularly true for the great philosophers who gave a new impetus to methodic thought. Plato's and Aristotle's methods and fundamental insights remain ours—to a point where even their formulations have survived in our philosophical language. The distance that separates their writing from our time appears to have had no decisive impact upon their message. Metaphysical thought seems possessed of an ultimacy that makes intelligible the Greek claim that in "theology" humans acquire the status of the immortals. There are, and probably always will be, Neoplatonists. It is still possible today to philosophize *ad mentem divi Thomae,* and in some areas (ethics and metaphysics come immediately to mind) Thomist philosophy has yielded remarkable fruits. Even John Locke's philosophy, so closely connected with the scientific methods and political theories of a former age, two centuries later still inspired Whitehead's daringly new speculation. Nor should the impact of one philosophy upon another be envisaged as the kind of free association whereby an old idea serendipitously leads to a new one. The link between the two often proves so tight that one cannot be understood without a substantial knowledge of the other in its own right.

An analogy with the "progressive" absorption of older scientific theories by new ones is profoundly misleading. Nor is our present fascination with models and paradigms likely to provide much insight into the permanent quality of philosophical reflection. For to speak of models and paradigms in a sense that aims beyond the justified exclusion of mutual compatibility implies that philosophical systems are liable to the same kind of historical relativity as scientific theories. However much a philosophical system may seem time-bound, it cannot abandon its claims of definitiveness without betraying the nature of the enterprise itself. All major philosophers have expressed the concerns of their age while surpassing their historical limitations in the very act of expressing them. Collingwood clearly perceived the dialectical relation between the two.

In part, the problems of philosophy are unchanging; in part, they vary from age to age, according to the special characteristics of human life and thought at the time; and in the best philosophers of every age these two parts are so interwoven that the permanent problems appear *sub specie saeculi*, and the special problems of the age *sub specie aeternitatis*. Whenever human thought has been dominated by some special interest, the most fruitful philosophy of the age has reflected that domination; not passively, by mere submission to its influence, but actively, by making a special attempt to understand it and placing it in the focus of philosophical inquiry.[1]

Nevertheless, while presenting its claims of truth, philosophy has always remained acutely aware of the irreducible differences among its various theories. Whereas the history of science was, until recently, conceived as a rectilinear progress, the straightness of which was preserved by regular excisions of aberrant (that is, from the present point of view, unsuccessful) theories, philosophy's unregenerate pluralism has, from the start, prevented the development of a single line of progress. Socrates alone counted among his disciples the founders of the cynical and skeptical schools as well as Plato and, indirectly, Aristotle. All of these and other schools have, in some way, survived without merging with one another. Until recently this universally accepted pluralism rarely spawned relativism.

In the strong historical consciousness of the nineteenth century two attitudes emerged. One reduced philosophy to a branch of cultural history. The practice of philosophy came thereby to consist in the history of philosophy. The other, intent upon avoiding this kind of relativism altogether, concentrated instead on purely formal problems of logic, or conceptual and linguistic analysis in which the historical element plays no decisive role. A positivistic, analytic, or phenomenological approach would enable philosophy to become "scientific" and finally liberate itself from centuries of irreconcilable metaphysical squabbles. The price paid for this simplification was a refusal to deal with matters of existential concern. Wherever the history of philosophy was still granted any room, a severely truncated version of it emerged leaping from selected writings of Plato and Aristotle directly to Locke and Hume in order to come to rest in Kant.

These developments leave us with a question. Is an acquaintance with past philosophy on its own terms necessary or even useful for philosophical self-understanding? Can philosophy afford to devote even part of its own enterprise to the knowledge of past reflection without sacrificing its most basic claim of definitiveness? Should not the history of philosophy, as being devoid of intrinsic philosophical significance, be relegated to the shady realm of the history of ideas, while philosophers should feel free to borrow from their predecessors what they find useful without much concern for original context or meaning? How can a definitive claim to truth tolerate historical alternatives? And, on the opposite end, how but by abstaining from any judgment based upon one's own perception of truth could a historian treat other people's ideas fairly? In the following pages I submit the thesis that, if temporality forms an essential dimension of being, the study of former reflection constitutes an essential task of humanity's ultimate self-understanding. Without it, the definite character of that understanding is not safeguarded but distortingly empoverished.

We must, of course, admit the cultural conditioning of all philosophical reflection. Ideas develop within a socioeconomic context and this context may have a decisive impact upon their development. The gradual destruction of the Roman Empire by the invading barbarians may in itself have little philosophical significance, yet it brought a particular mode of thinking to an abrupt halt. Similarly, the acceptance of the Christian faith, another non-philosophical fact, initiated a wholly new development in ideal philosophy. Neither one of these factors can claim the kind of intrinsic necessity that would allow us to deduce them from equally ideal premises. One might go farther and, with the nineteenth-century philosopher R. H. Lotze, describe philosophy itself as a fact, the particular rational form of which is unique to the Western world and firmly embedded in its social and cultural structures. Most civilizations have been able to dispense with the sort of systematic or analytic thought that we call philosophy altogether. In that sense, at least, each philosophical achievement displays a purely contingent quality: its existence has depended on external elements which clearly lack the ideal necessity characteristic of philosophical reflection. Similar restrictions surround its alleged universality. For all its general claims, Western philosophy finds it difficult to enter into dialogue with Eastern wisdom. Even philosophical systems developed in one cultural province of Europe show only a remote resemblance to those elaborated in another one. The difference between French and British philosophy includes far more than a different mode of expression. And yet the efforts of French existentialists as well as those of British analysts aim at establishing a truth that presumes to be intrinsically independent of the cultural circumstances in which each one was conceived and to impose itself by argument rather than by cultural affiliation. Ancient culture is gone, yet the philosophies it produced, even more than its works of art, survive its demise. They continue to compel our reflection and often our assent.

The seeming opposition between the cultural-historical conditioning of all philosophical systems and the lasting quality of their arguments cannot be reconciled merely by separating an eternal content (the truth value) from the temporal form of its discovery. Such a view is bound to an adequation theory of truth which, at least in that naive formulation, shows a distinctly historical context. The historical nature of philosophy reaches far deeper than the *ordo inventionis:* it is rooted in the condition of the human being—the one being for which truth exists. Though most philosophers have accepted both the permanent and the transient aspects of their predecessors' thought, few have directly confronted the historical character of truth itself and even fewer the historical quality of what is ultimately real. Hegel first clearly formulated both. He was followed by Marx and a few other, orthodox or unorthodox, disciples. In the twentieth century Whitehead and Heidegger, by very different roads, approached a similar position.

In the introduction to his *Philosophy of History* Hegel has shown how the two meanings of the term 'history'—happening and narrative—are intrinsically related. "The narrative of history and historical deeds and events appear at the same time; a common inner principle brings them both together."[2] Hegel here suggests that history becomes a distinct order of reality only through a new stage of reflection. Those who live before the writing of history remain "without objective history, because they lack subjective history."[3] Raymond Aron translates this into modern language: "Man has in fact no past unless he is conscious of having one, for only such consciousness makes dialogue and choice possible. Without it, individuals and societies merely embody a past of which they are ignorant and to which they are passively subject; they merely afford to the outside observer a series of transformations, comparable to those of animal species, which can be set out in a temporal series."[4] Only a developed sense of freedom which unites consciousness to reality gives rise to a historical awareness. The story of ancient Israel strikingly illustrates the connection between objective history and the development of a historical consciousness. A group of rather disparate tribes "constituted itself by recording its own genesis as a people, as an event with a special meaning in history."[5] Israel acquired a real identity by attributing to an amalgamation of tribes a common past. Narrative form here clearly shaped objective reality. The "historical" books of the Bible allow us to witness the genesis of a people in its gradual separation from an undistinguished cosmic order. Israel's case may be better documented than others, but all historiography influences the course of history. People act according to their understanding of their own past, however distorted or unsupported that understanding may be. Hitler's fantasy of a millennial empire had its roots in a particular interpretation of Germany's past. Such an interpretation never reaches completion: historiography itself constantly revives its own, symbolically articulated reading of events and processes. The critique of earlier texts transforms the impact of the texts themselves. The new Christocentric reading of the Bible by New Testament writers played an essential role in the birth of a new religion. In the opposite direction, Valla's exposure of the Donation of Constantine definitively invalidated all papal titles to imperial power.

The Ontological Meaning of History

All of this supports Hegel's thesis about the link between objective history and historical consciousness. Yet we should avoid equating historical consciousness with historiographical concerns. Heidegger rightly distinguishes periods marked by a geniune awareness of new possibilities of Being from others that are mainly preoccupied with the methods and problems of history-writing.

The Renaissance presents a case of the former, while the nine-teenth century instantiates the latter. Some epochs that see them-selves as innovating are mainly more self-conscious, while others introduce genuine novelty without being fully aware of it. Nev-ertheless behind all historical consciousness lies an awareness of a past that, through its affinity with the present, opens up new pos-sibilities for the future. The historical consciousness is itself rooted in an acute awareness of a tension between the transient and the permanent "moments" of Being. It recognizes certain expe-riences of reality as no longer present yet still continuing to affect existence in the present.

For the same reason philosophy itself presupposes some con-sciousness of history. Since to exist—our vantage point for all re-flection on being—is itself to be-in-time, philosophy necessarily views itself as a historical event. It is a process as well, for at no stage can the reflection on, and through, an existence in time be considered exhaustive. From its very beginning philosophy has had to interpret and to convey meaning to the phenomena of tran-sitoriness and permanence. To the human mind Being appears only as emerging from a past and moving through the determining (but ungraspable) moment of the present into the future. The historical consciousness—whether in its historiographic or its philosophical mode—has always emphasized the past. Yet existence itself is never past. If it is at all, it is in the present. Hegel and Croce were undoubtedly right in asserting that all history consists ultimately of present history. Heidegger, the philosopher who has most thor-oughly investigated the significance of being-in-time without iden-tifying time with being, views existence as essentially resolutive and anticipatory, hence, even in dealing with the past, future-ori-ented. Its "fate" places it in a possibility which it has inherited yet which, at each moment of the present, it chooses, and chooses all the more authentically as it is more aware of that horizon of its future that renders all its possibilities insurmountably finite, namely, death. Death throws being-in-time back upon its original facticity, thus linking its future to its past. "If fate constitutes the primordial historicality of Dasein, then history has its essential importance neither in what is past nor in the 'today' and its con-nection with what is past, but in the authentic historizing of existence which arises from Dasein's future."[6] The "historicality" of existence is more than a mere temporality of individual existence. It also constitutes "history," that is, world-historical process (*weltgeschichtliches Geschehen*). For the past of existence consists not merely of its own past, but of what made that past possible as well. "Dasein has grown up both *into* and *in* a traditional way of interpreting itself: in terms of this it understands itself proximally and, within a certain range, constantly. By this understanding, the possibilities of its Being are disclosed and regulated."[7] Clearly, this historicity affects also the way in which *Dasein* interprets itself philosophically, that is, as a mode of Being. Thus the history of the inquiry determines the inquiry itself.

We know how in Heidegger's view the tradition in which the philosophical inquiry has taken place has, almost from the beginning, jeopardized the possibility of properly raising the question of Being. The ontology which it has created is one of "beings" in the world—in fact, a cosmology in which the meaning of Being has been forgotten. But this raises the question whether a theory that denies the meaningfulness of the entire available past of reflection and reaches beyond it to the earliest, undeveloped (and hence uncertain) roots of the tradition, is in a position to preserve concrete meaning in history. How much can we learn positively from a tradition that has been declared to be one prolonged misunderstanding? One hesitates to answer these questions, because it remains unclear whether Heidegger's theory of historicity also applies to philosophical reflection. More than any philosophy before him, Heidegger's thought is oriented toward the remote past. The aesthetico-religious character of his later attempts to point the way out of the historical crisis of Western thinking indicates in fact a return to an early (prephilosophical) vision of classical antiquity.

At the same time, in regarding historicality as essentially an *Entwurf* (project), he has, in principle, opened up a dimension which few thinkers in the past perceived, namely, the one that allows for the recognition of authentic novelty in history. Most Western thinkers so one-sidedly emphasized the past in their awareness of the historicity of philosophical thought that there was little room left for the originality which they nevertheless frequently claimed, at least for their own theory. Historicity in philosophical reflection has mainly consisted in integrating past with recent thought, rarely in granting definitive novelty to past, present, and future.

Plato described the mind's access to the ultimately real as a process of *anamnesis*—a remembering of the past. In doing so he may well have been the first to grant time (or, at least, a dimension of time) a metaphysical status. Parmenides regarded all becoming as illusory—a position that Hindu and Buddhist philosophies also appear to have consistently held. For Plato it is only through the essentially temporal process of recollection that the soul regains its natural habitat—the realm of eternal ideas. Yet the goal of this process, the absolute past, is itself atemporal. In it all succession ceases and Being regains its pristine permanence. Hence the genuine object of philosophical contemplation lies beyond time. Christian thinkers granted time a more decisive role. Heirs to the Hebrew sacred history, they attributed a lasting significance, indeed, an ontological quality to events in time. According to them, the eternal is permanently incarnated in time and the full meaning of existence consists in representing the past. The event of the Incarnation belongs to the past and bears no repetition. Yet in faith the believer becomes contemporary with this past and endows it with a transhistorical permanence. This past-oriented view of time, both under classical and under Christian influence, has dominated our conception of thinking.

The backward look appears as an essential moment in the process of reflection. Merleau-Ponty has written that the interrogation of the past begins in an age that has eaten of the tree of knowledge.[8] Not accidentally! For all reflection consists in a search for roots, the most obvious of which are the origins in time. If a concern with the past, then, belongs to all reflection, it forms an essential part of that self-justifying reflection for which we reserve the name of philosophy. To understand a philosophical problem requires a serious acquaintance with its origins and developments. As Jonathan Bennett wrote, we study philosophy's past because it may lead us straight to philosophical truths.[9] Exactly. Yet such a reflection upon past reflection requires more than a textbook summary of the positions any one philosopher or school of philosophy has held. The complexity characteristic of philosophical thought cannot be grasped in a survey, however balanced and accurate. It requires a constant return to the original text. Moreover, to command philosophical recognition, historians of philosophy must investigate the underlying assumptions, the basic, yet rarely acknowledged intuitions of the theories it presents. Only such "archeological" work will enable them to detect the signs of genuine novelty. Without it, they will fail to recognize new ideas under traditional concepts, or, when the new at last fully reveals its face (as it did in Descartes, for instance), it will remain as inexplicable as the fully armed Minerva leaping out of Jupiter's head.

But, of course, the idea of novelty has a history of its own. The full acceptance of it is of relatively recent origin. Thinkers and artists of the Renaissance were aware of the fact that they were breaking with a long tradition of the Middle Ages. Yet they still continued to view their own task as a restoration of an older way of thinking. Even a philosopher as revolutionary as Giordano Bruno considers his work a return of the *vetusta philosophia* (Pythagorean and Platonic). The idea did not become fully acceptable until the consciousness of human *self-making* in the eighteenth century shifted the general emphasis from past to future. Here the idea of unprecedented novelty emerges. It would, of course, be hazardous to accept this idea at face value. Though more self-conscious of its difference from the past, the eighteenth century introduced relatively few theories that were truly new, except the idea of novelty itself. But its importance must not be underestimated, for through it the past acquires a function wholly different from the one it had before. Then it was, as it still is in traditional cultures, what gave meaning to present and future. The future, the project, must henceforth decide which elements of the past remain useable and which should be discarded. Ever since the end of the *ancien régime* social reformers and politicians have tailored themselves highly selective representations of particular epochs to serve as models for their own projects. The idea of the Roman Republic cultivated during the years following the French revolution is about as far removed from the historical reality as David's pictorial representations of it are.

Speculative thought was much slower in reversing its direction from past to future. Not before the beginning of the twentieth century, with Whitehead and Bergson, can one speak of a genuine future-orientedness in philosophy. With Ortega y Gasset and the existentialist writers begins a general criticism of the tradition that identified the ontological with the past.

> If we speak of *being* in the traditional sense as a *being already* what one is, as a fixed, static, invariable, and given being, we shall have to say that the only element of being, of "nature," in man is what he has been. The past is man's moment of identity, his only element of the thing: nothing besides is inexorable and fatal. But, for the same reason, if man's only Eleatic being is what he has been, this means that his authentic being, what in effect he is—and not mere "has been"—is distinct from the past, and consists precisely and formally in "being what one has not been," in non-Eleatic being. . . . Man *is* not, he 'goes on being' this and that.[10]

There had been some anticipation of this in the nineteenth century, most notably in the work of August von Cieszkowski, a Polish disciple of Hegel. In his *Historiosophie* Cieszkowski set himself the task of completing Hegel's theory of history. Hegel's own principle, that only the totality contains truth, implies that the philosophical study of history must include the future as well as the past. Yet his philosophy of history only deals with the past. Can we know the future, and thereby establish a real historical totality? Cieszkowski thinks we can, on the same principle of *verum facere* on which Vico had once established our knowledge of the past. The thinking subject is also the one who shapes history, past and future. In the deed and the projects of our deeds the future reveals itself. In past ages such a knowledge was not attainable, because humans exercised insufficient control over nature to be master of their own destiny. Cieszkowski understood that more than a mere expansion of Hegel's theory of history was involved. At stake is a new, more voluntaristic concept of history. In achieving an identity of reality and thought, idealist thought has closed the circle. To proceed further means that philosophy must break out of the field of speculation into the unlimited domain of *praxis*. Only through this outward movement can consciousness regain the immediate union with the real which it had to abandon in order to attain a reflective one with it. From *Selbstdenken*, philosophy must move to *Selbsttun*.

Marx knew Cieszkowski and, via Moses Hess, adopted his notion of *praxis*. Though Marx's philosophical significance, as well as his impact upon later philosophies, tends to be exaggerated, he nevertheless played a vital role in preparing the acceptance of genuine novelty in history. In his work triumphs the idea, first formulated by Bruno, that in an infinite and hence perspectiveless universe, human beings impose whatever order they choose upon their physical and social environment. Henceforth an established idea no more than an established institution is justified by the sole fact of its existence. Nevertheless Marx continues to find some justification of the future in the past. For the future is never an arbitrary creation devised on the pattern of a purely ideal model, as it had been for Utopian thinkers. Even a revolutionary reversal of the past cannot be achieved at random, but only when the conditions created by the past are ready for it. Again and again Marx emphasized the actual presence of the seeds of the future. His predictions of a communist revolution are not born in a Utopian dream, he insists, but "merely express, in general terms, actual relations springing from an existing class struggle, from a historical movement going on under our eyes."[11] On the other side, Marx and, even more, his followers experienced serious problems in reconciling the so-called laws that determine history with the freedom whereby human beings shape their own destiny. Historical "conditioning" easily slides into social determinism.

But the philosopher faces the more intricate problems connected with the claims of permanent meaning. If one admits that, partly under the impact of reflection, reality changes, one is left with the alleged definitiveness of the ever-changing philosophical reflection. At this point the concept of philosophical novelty requires a precise definition. What does it mean when the new appears, or seems to appear, in a reflection that claims to be "ultimate"? The question is by no means the same as the one, previously discussed, on the relation between historical reality and reflection. There, only difference was at stake—between one stage of reflection and another. Here we ask how each different moment can possess more permanence than the changing reality which it reflects; how it can lastingly illuminate our being in the world. Metaphysical novelty discloses hitherto unknown aspects of our being in the world in such a manner that the disclosure will never again cease to reveal. To be sure, periods of forgetfulness may follow, but the text retains its revelatory power.

But how, one may wonder, can novelty gain entrance into the reflection on ultimate questions? Would its very emergence not imply that our questioning itself had failed to go to the roots? How could a reflection on the ultimate conditions of existence itself be subject to historical change? Only because the historical quality reaches down to the roots of that existence. As we constantly change our relation to Being as such, our understanding of that relation changes. Thus in the beginning of the modern age a basic shift took place in both. On a more obvious level, the self came to view itself at a distance from the surrounding cosmos, as a subject that grants meaning and value to all Being. On a less visible but more fundamental level, the relation immanence-transcendence changed in a way that would profoundly affect the ideas of God and of nature. The terms 'shift' or 'change' should not be understood to mean "difference" or "displacement," as if the old, having lost its relevance, had to yield to the new. Such was, undoubtedly, the manner in which most of those actively involved in a spiritual revolution understood it. To them certainly the conceptions of their immediate predecessors seemed inadequate and fit only to be permanently dismissed. The new understanding of reality appears destined to replace an older one. Yet if that were really the case, the history of philosophy would amount to no more than a succession of mutually exclusive systems of ideas that achieve progress only at the cost of sacrificing all previous stages of reflection. Past philosophy, then, would be the story of absurdities which Descartes *in toto* denounced and which Bertrand Russell in detail retold for our lasting amusement. In no event could it claim any measure of that permanence which philosophy holds as its distinctive characteristic.

The fact that innovation always takes place in the name of long-established principles and often covers itself with the spoils of an earlier philosophy should alert us to the deceptiveness of these appearances. Thus the philosophy of the Renaissance announced itself in part as a return to Plato and Neoplatonism, in part as a revival of the "real" Aristotle (as opposed to the one of Scholastic theology). In exploring the actual relation between the old and the new, the history of philosophy plays an indispensable role. Removed from the immediacy of the novel, it rises above the controversies which accompanied its arrival. The historian of philosophy, if he is a philosopher and not only a historian of ideas, must know to evaluate the novelty of a system on the basis of the definitive dimension it introduces in thought, rather than on its negative attitude toward the system it intends to replace. Philosophically, the task of the historian of philosophy consists in discerning the permanent significance of a new theory—as opposed to the exaggerated claims of originality which philosophers, especially since the eighteenth century, have made for their contributions. Next, the historian must "integrate" that novelty with older theories, not, however, by harmonizing different theories until they fit together in one coherent whole; any attempt at achieving a *philosophia perennis* which would overcome the oppositions among philosophical systems through the ages betrays its subject. A philosophical integration demands a study of that which gave rise to the contradictions. The form which this particular pursuit of truth takes consists neither in comparing the adequation of various theories, nor in introducing a new kind of coherence among them, but rather in showing the specific disclosure of Being in an irreducible yet ever growing (both intensively and comprehensively) complexity of philosophical reflection.

We might be inclined to think that Hegel, despite private preferences, historical inaccuracies, and plain ignorance, essentially succeeded in precisely such a philosophical reflection. He certainly conceived the history of philosophy as an irreducible totality in which each period and system occupies a definitive, irreplaceable position. Nor should we interpret the moving principle of his dialectic, the sublation (*Aufhebung*), as "replacing" a lower by a higher synthesis: the old is preserved in the new, as the term itself indicates. Nevertheless, his conception of the totality as a closed system forced Hegel to assign to each theory what often turns out to be a Procrustean bed, more devised for its function in his own thought than for the self-disclosure of the theory. So many other problems beset Hegel's approach that we would not mention him, had he not in more subtle ways been imitated by some of the very thinkers who criticized him. Neo-Kantian historians of philosophy such as Höfding and Windelband opposed Hegel's wide-spanning syntheses, yet forced philosophies within the narrow frame of their own epistemological problems. Only the most perceptive ones, among whom I count Dilthey, fully understood the high demands of history as a philosophical discipline.

A Case of Philosophical Novelty: The Shift in the Relation Immanence-Transcendence

Without feeling even as competent as those who failed most conspicuously, I shall nevertheless attempt to illustrate how the philosophy of one period brought genuinely new and definitive insight to the fundamental issue of the relation between immanence and transcendence of Being. In doing so I do not claim that the period I discuss is concerned only with that issue, nor that all of its problems can be reduced to it. Indeed, I explicitly hold the opposite. If I focus on the question of transcendence, I do so because I believe it to be a fundamental concern which that epoch, in not always obvious ways, reformulated. Moreover, in a transition period, such as the Renaissance, innovating thinkers present answers and hypotheses that remain open to multiple interpretations. They anticipate new positions often without fully realizing where they lead. The Renaissance is an "open" season during which no single philosophy (past or present) dominated the scene. Many dismiss it as a period of skepticism or eclecticism, at best an anticipation of the more rigorous philosophical systems that begin with Descartes and Locke. But to do so is to miss the more significant sense of novelty that pervades Renaissance thought. In it we witness the struggle of an age to give birth to new insight in what it means to be ultimately real. Confusion abounds and often we find ourselves unable to reconcile the rationalist (vaguely Pythagorean or Platonic) with the more mystical (most Neoplatonic) trends, occasionally present in the same thinker.

One of the main concerns at the beginning of the modern age is to replace the medieval division between a natural and a supernatural realm by a homogeneous picture of reality. The tendency to homogeneity had sporadically emerged in philosophers as early as Amaury de Bènes, Guillaume d'Auvergne, and David of Dinant. Eckhart's mystical doctrine had assumed it throughout. But repeated condemnations indicate that it had never been accepted in the mainstream of Christian thought. At the dawn of the new age it comes to dominate cosmological speculation, not only in such unorthodox writers as Patrizzi and Bruno, but even, I believe, in Nicolaus of Cusa. The new position had been made possible by the nominalist elimination of the divine as a principle of intelligibility which, until then, had formed an integral part of the cosmological structure. God, as the cause of the world, remained an essential principle, but one that fell entirely beyond the scope of human comprehension. This meant, for all practical purposes, that only a single object of cosmological knowledge remained, while the divine was relegated to a negative theology, important for moral and practical-religious purposes, but without cosmological significance. Ockham himself had criticized the distinction between an astronominal world order which, being more intimately linked to the divine, obeyed purely mathematical laws, and a wholly contingent sublunar sphere. There was only one cosmos and it was wholly natural.

A second element that significantly contributed to the relative independence of the cosmos with respect to its transcendent cause and, hence, to the homogenization of the order of nature, is the new meaning which the idea of nothingness adopts. Early Christian theories of creation had misinterpreted Plato's *chora* as a reality that preexisted the creation, and had therefore emphasized that the world had been created out of nothing (an idea that was conspicuously absent from the accounts in Genesis). Plato does not seem to have granted nonbeing more than the relative status of "diminished being"; in the Renaissance nothingness itself came to assume a positive meaning, as if it had been an absolute in its own right. Thus Cusa regards the *nihil* as an essential principle in the constitution of difference, multiplicity, and finitude. "Alteritas ex nihilo oritur." For Campanella it forms an integral "part" of the real, which accounts for chance and contingency. "Cuncta . . . a nihilo contracto componuntur."[12] Now the idea of nothingness thus conceived separates the created from the uncreated reality by an unbridgeable gap. This, as well as the nominalist distinction between God and the world, appears to reinforce the dual reality structure. But the new dualism differs from the early one in that it virtually eliminates one of the two terms from the field of knowledge. Henceforth the "supernatural" realm, being separated from "nature" by an epistemologically unbridgeable gap, ceases to count in cosmological speculation.

Still, the "detachment" of nature from its transcendent source must not be interpreted to mean an elimination of transcendence in favor of some kind of naturalism which simply transfers attributes of the divine sphere to the cosmos. What occurs is a shift in the relation immanence-transcendence, not an abrogation of one of the two terms. This appears most clearly in Cusa, who remained a metaphysician while most of his contemporaries turned to an experimental study of nature. For him the transcendent principle, though hidden from the mind, remains the inner motive of the cognitive process. It poses a limit which the mind is unable to cross, yet which determines the structure of the mind itself. In the coincidence of opposite qualities, when reduced to a minimum or when increased to a maximum, the mind becomes aware of a total immanence of the transcendent in each of its acts.[13] Indeed, in the new cosmology the link between transcendent and immanent nature becomes more intimate, even though the knowledge of its own essence has been withdrawn from the structure of reality. For Cusa the world is God's own infinity "contracted." It reflects the "absolute infinity" in its own relative infinity of time and space. The same divine essence which in itself rests in total simplicity, explicates itself in the multiplicity of the world. We know only the second mode of being, but we know it in such a manner that it could not be without the first.

The idea of the one absolute, lying beyond the grasp of human knowledge yet functioning as the source of cognitive attraction, entered most Renaissance thought. We recognize it most easily in Neoplatonists such as Pico della Mirandola. Renaissance Aristotelians seem to be much less concerned about the nature of the link between the transcendent and the immanent. They conceive the cosmos as ruled by its own eternal laws, and even as animated by its own "soul." Most of them, however, continue to assert the impact of a Prime Mover, which may be all the more intimate for giving the world more autonomy. Bruno brought these various trends in cosmological speculation to some conclusion by conceiving nature as fully autonomous and dispensing with any kind of external impetus. In him the relation to the transcendent, far from disappearing altogether, has become most intimate. God's power operates entirely from within, as an immanent presence. The cosmos must be understood through itself alone. Yet considered in itself, that divine essence remains totally transcendent—*totalmente infinito*, as opposed to the cosmos, *tutto infinito*—and, though the ground of all being, so totally beyond definiteness as to be unknowable. Bruno describes its immanent presence as "ubique et nusquam; infra omnia fundans, super omnia gubernans; intra omnia non inclusus, extra omnia non exclusus—in quo sunt omnia, et qui in nullo est ipse."[14] The content of the former idea of transcendence is divided: one part is attributed to the cosmos itself, the other is removed from it to a point where it ceases to grant meaning to the understanding of the cosmos.

In the medieval world picture cosmology and theology complemented each other. In the new era they follow an independent course. Already Bonaventure had claimed that the cosmos is not an image of God (as human beings are), but only bears God's traces (*vestigia*). Henceforth this distinction will become a fundamental principle almost universally accepted. For Cusa the creatures are "mute": they do not reveal the Creator, but only refer to him as to their "ratio et causa." Cusa's position is all the more significant since his whole thought, despite its radically negative theology, continues to move in the "image" tradition.[15] Bruno is even more emphatic. "From the knowledge of all dependent things we cannot deduce any other knowledge of the first cause and principle than by the inefficacious way of traces."[16] To know the universe is to know only a reflection of God—not to know his substance in any way at all. Thus the world ceases to be a mirror of the divine: instead it becomes a representation reflected in the mirror of the human mind, the sole principle of understanding.[17]

Nevertheless, in this universe accessible only to the human mind, the transcendent power retains its full force. Humans are capable of representing their own universe only insofar as they partake in God's creative power. Cusa formulated a rule that applies to most humanist philosophy. "As God is Creator of real entities and natural forms, so man is creator of rational entities and artificial forms which are nothing but similitudes of the divine intellect."[18] Hence the dominant role of the subject is from the beginning firmly attached to a transcendent pole which itself remains wholly beyond its reach. Even for Bruno a transcendent power motivates the cognitive process and the dynamism of knowledge can reach its completion only where it allows itself to be driven by a passionate response to the divine attraction.

Now all of this shows the clear impact of Platonic and Neoplatonic philosophy. Yet to see only the influence of the past is to remain blind to the far greater originality of Renaissance thought. Here a new relation between immanence and transcendence has been established that cannot be understood through its ancient sources alone, but that presupposes the intermediate Christian philosophy which it, in some respects, continues. In other respects it initiates a new tradition that would produce such diverse figures as Spinoza and Schelling. But here again, the later philosophies presuppose the older ones without replacing them. What matters is not the concepts that philosophies share, but the functions that such concepts fulfill in the total system. Thus the *monad* in Bruno answers the question of how much independence the manifold phenomena of nature can be granted with respect to its overriding unity, while in Leibniz its function consists in preserving a plurality of substances in a coherent, and hence united, universe. In one case the main concern is unity, in the other, multiplicity.

Conclusions

Philosophical systems, unlike scientific theories, resist assimilation, however strongly they may influence later systems. Philosophical reflection cannot be broken up into interchangeable parts. But to assert irreducible independence is not to deny the continuity of schools and traditions, or even the existence of the much vaguer family resemblances. Precisely by its ability to discern, beyond the influence and development of ideas, their irreducible uniqueness does philosophy distinguish itself most clearly from the history of ideas. As Bertrand Russell declared in the preface to his *Critical Exposition of the Philosophy of Leibniz,* the history of philosophy needs both. But it can only form an integral part of philosophy when, surpassing the methods of history, it knows how to find the permanent quality underneath the transient influences and critically to discuss its meaning and truth.[19] Nor, to repeat it, should one conceive the relation between the transient and the permanent as one between form and content. From a philosophical point of view such a distinction makes little sense, since the method here coincides with the content. The conceptual articulation is precisely what distinguishes philosophical theory from mere "insight," however profound. If this seems to leave the historian of philosophy at the mercy of all the errors and absurdities of the past, we should remember that students of past systems, if they are to fulfill their philosophical task, must be as critical of them as of their own reflections. This may, indeed, render their evaluation less neutral than that of the historian of ideas. But past philosophies teach negatively as well as positively. Part of the philosopher's task consists in showing the relativity of each system, the penalty of incompleteness and one-sidedness which the historically conditioned emphasis on a single aspect of our place in Being inflicts. Yet the critical awareness of this inevitable failure does not condemn a past philosophy to the rubbish heap of history, no more than it predestines present efforts to future obsolescence. Each philosophy sheds a new and definitive light on our self-understanding as meaning-giving being in the world. The medieval conceptions of transcendence have not simply been abolished by the different relation between transcendence and immanence established at the beginning of the modern age. We find ourselves so strongly in the latter tradition that the earlier has become inconceivable. Nevertheless the earlier tradition, itself dependent on Platonic, Aristotelian, Stoic, and Neoplatonic philosophies, is the one that has made the modern possible. It, far more profoundly than the philosophies of the Renaissance, discloses the very notion of transcendence. The variation of the modern concept could not have existed without the earlier, more profound reflection. Nor can the modern one retain its own meaning (however novel and definitive) without a constant reference to its past. It is the task of the historian of philosophy to show this living continuity.

Notes

1. R. G. Collingwood, "The Historical Imagination," in his *The Idea of History* (Oxford: Clarendon Press, 1946), p. 231.
2. G. F. W. Hegel, *Reason in History*, trans. Robert S. Hartman (Indianapolis: Bobbs-Merrill, 1953), p. 75.
3. Ibid., 76.
4. Raymond Aron, "The Philosophy of History" in *Chambers Encyclopedia* (Oxford: Pergamon Press, 1967), 7:150.
5. Eric Voegelin, *Israel and Revelation* (Baton Rouge: Louisiana State University Press, 1956), p. 124. Voegelin defines the significance of Israel as "a mankind striving for its order of existence within the world while attuning itself with the truth of being beyond the world" (p. 129).
6. Martin Heidegger, *Being and Time*, trans. John Macquarrie and Edward Robinson (New York: Harper & Row, 1962) p. 438.
7. Ibid., p. 46.
8. Maurice Merleau-Ponty, *Les Adventures de la dialectique* (Paris: Gallimard, 1955), p. 31.
9. Jonathan Bennett, "Critical Notice: *A Critical History of Western Philosophy*, ed. by D. J. O'Connor" in *Mind* 75, no. 299 (July 1966): 437.
10. José Ortega y Gassett, *Toward a Philosophy of History*, trans. Helene Weyl (New York: W. W. Norton, 1941), p. 212.
11. Karl Marx, "The Communist Manifesto" in *Werke* (Berlin: Dietz Verlag), 9:475; idem, *Selected Works* (Moscow: Foreign Languages, 1962), 1:46.
12. Tomasso Campanella, *Universalis philosophiae partes tres* (Paris: Philippe Burelly, 1638), p. 1.
13. Maurice de Gandillac, *Nikolaus von Kues* (Düsseldorf: L. Schwann, 1953), pp. 245–47.
14. Nicholas of Cusa, *De triplici minimo et mensura*, in *Schriften*, ed. Ernst Hoffmann (Leipzig: F. Meiner, 1936), 9:147.
15. Nicholas of Cusa, *De docta ignoranta*, in ibid., vol. 15a, bk. 2, concluding chapter.
16. Giordano Bruno, *De la causa*, in *Opere*, ed. G. Gentile (Bari: G. Laterza and sons, 1923–27), 1:173.
17. One should avoid making "trends" into laws. For Campanella nature remains a manifestation of God, though one that should be studied by empirical observation, not by symbolic interpretation, as had been done during the high Middle Ages.

18. Nicholas of Cusa, "De beryllo," in *Opera omnia,* ed. L. Baur (Leipzig: F. Meiner, 1940), 2:7.
19. Bertrand Russell, *A Critical Exposition of the Philosophy of Leibniz* (London: George Allen and Unwin, 1951), pp. xi–xii. My attention was drawn to this text by Paul Kuntz's interesting essay "The Dialectic of Historicism and Anti-historicism," *The Monist* 53 (Oct. 1969): 656–69.

Can Philosophy Have a Rational History?

Richard Dien Winfield

Philosophy's Embarrassment with History

Although few philosophers have ever denied that they reason as historical individuals, born to a specific age and members of a particular culture, only recently have so many judged reason to be historical in character. This embrace of history cannot come easily for philosophy. From the moment thinkers assume the mantle of philosophy by enjoining reason to advance beyond opinion to truth, they set themselves a task whose fulfillment is impossible, unless reason can legitimate the role of every factor that effects the course of its argument. If reason fails to validate each content and procedure it employs, and instead allows philosophical argument to be guided by any influence whose authority has not been philosophically justified, reason's quest for truth stands condemned by the very reliance on unexamined opinion it seeks to surmount. If philosophy is not to abandon all claim to wisdom unbiased by arbitrary grounds, how can it fail to seek an unconditioned, universal, timeless validity completely indifferent to every particular, conditioned circumstance that historical convention might produce? Hence, when philosophers relegate reason to history they seem to be eliminating the possibility of their own enterprise, as if fulfilling Socrates' warning that to do philosophy is to seek death, since eternal reason lies beyond human mortality.

Although philosophy's confession of its own historicity might seem to be the height of self-contradiction, it reflects just how great an embarrassment history can be for philosophical reflection. As much as philosophy's quest for truth may drive it to question the authority of all givens before the tribunal of autonomous reason, philosophy's own reality seems inescapably caught in the given frameworks of two parallel histories. As a cultural phenomenon, conceived in some time and place by living authors using some given language, philosophy is always situated within a world whose conventional practices and institutions have a history of their own that provides the background and linguistic medium for every effort of reason. This history of institutions and activities external to philosophy is not the only history framing philosophical investigation. From the very start, every philosophical inquiry stands equally within a history internal to philosophical thought: namely, the history of philosophy proper. Far from being an *ex post facto* construction, this latter history is reflected within the philosophies comprising it, as much by their own reference to their predecessor's argument as by the difference in contrast each must have simply to count as a philosophical development and not a mere restatement of past argument. Just as philosophy seems to incorporate the external history of nonphilosophical practices simply by employing the given language of its day, so it seems to direct its own course in reference to its internal history, finding its problems and approach by both rejecting and incorporating past theoretical achievements. On both counts, philosophy appears to be a child of its age, constitutively determined by the practical and theoretical heritage in, and in reference to which, it emerges.

Granted this predicament, there are three basic possibilities for philosophy's relation to the external and internal histories within which reasoning proceeds:

1. Philosophy is historically conditioned, and therefore unable to achieve the unconditioned universality it traditionally claims. Because it is relative to the historical development of factors external and/or internal to philosophical debate, philosophy can never rise above opinion and exercise autonomous reason.
2. Philosophy is historically determined, but history has an absolute development leading to an unconditioned standpoint from which philosophical reason can attain wisdom.
3. Philosophy appears in history, but presents what is eternally valid. Neither the history of institutions nor the history of philosophy plays any role in determining philosophical problems or their proper resolution.

Philosophy's Traditional Flight from History

Traditionally, philosophy has affirmed the third of these possibilities by appealing to some ahistorical foundation as the well-
spring of rational argument. Whether this foundation be characterized as a first principle of reality, the source of all being and
knowledge, the ego, the transcendental conditions of experience, or
the structure of communicative competence, it always provides a
timeless, privileged given on which objective truth is grounded.

Once the chosen foundation becomes characterized in cognitive
rather than ontological terms, the denial of the historical character
of reason readily carries with it a denial of the reality of history. For
if all discourse is rooted in some eternal framework, such as intentionality or the structure of narrative, it may well be doubted
whether history is any more than a meaning constituted by the
timeless foundations of reference. Far from determining rational
reflection, history would then be a product of the conditions of
discourse, representing a construct no more privileged than any
other object of knowledge.[1]

Needless to say, the growing acceptance of a historical reason has
largely resulted from critical recognition of the insoluble dilemmas of any foundational appeal to privileged givens. The moment
philosophers root objectivity in some foundation, they tie the justification of truth claims to a ground whose privileged role can never
itself be justified. Any attempt to argue for the chosen foundation
would undermine its supposed primacy simply by introducing
other reasons in support of it. If, on the other hand, the proffered
foundation be ascribed its privileged authority in virtue of its immediacy, there is no way to decide between it and any other competing candidate whose immediacy is similarly claimed. Hence,
the only account that can be given of any putative foundation is
one that explains how its given content has come to be granted its
privileged role. This explanation would not comprise a justification of the chosen foundation, but rather a deconstruction unravel-
ing the genesis of the conceptual scheme it grounds. If it be accepted that philosophical theory must advance some given content
as the standard and basis of argument in order to reason at all, there
is little else to do but undertake a deconstruction that turns to the

history of such a content's advance. In this way, the traditional appeal to ahistorical foundations has ended up inviting us to turn to history, where the ground of argument is no longer sought in some self-evident principle or privileged standpoint, but rather in the historically situated process wherein the fundamental terms of specific philosophies come to occupy their special place.

The Problem of Relativist Historicism

In considering the historical genesis of philosophical theories, contemporary thinkers have generally cast their gaze beyond the history of philosophy to the history of cultural practices and institutions distinct from the phenomena of philosophical inquiry. Accordingly, it is worth first considering the possible ways in which philosophy can or can not be determined by the history external to it.

To begin with, there is the much-embraced position of relativist historicism. It holds that philosophical thought is conditioned by the historical development of nonphilosophical factors, such that philosophical claims are always relative to the historical framework in which they are made. The proponents of this view have differed greatly in identifying which factors of convention have the privileged role of determining philosophical thought. However, whether they assign the role to current linguistic practice, economic organization, class interest, or cultural tradition, they all agree that since it limits what problems and approaches philosophy entertains, it is folly to presume the unconditioned autonomy that philosophy has traditionally claimed in its search for eternal truths. Instead, they argue, reason is governed by historical developments independent of philosophy, leaving philosophical argument endemically relative to its age and inherently corrigible.

As appealing as it may be, relativist historicism is plagued by the self-referential inconsistency that undermines every form of relativism. Despite their claims that rational argument is relative to historical conditions, and hence incapable of justifying any unconditioned universal truths, relativist historicists are advancing universally binding truths of their own. These consist in none other than their description of the factors whose historical development conditions reason, and the accompanying claim that these factors do determine philosophical thought, not just relative to our own historically conditioned views, but throughout history. No matter what is given primacy as the historically conditioning factor, it figures as a suprahistorical foundation of which the relativist historicist somehow has privileged knowledge. If relativist historicists were to apply their characterization of philosophy to their own position, they would have to admit that their theory about history and philosophy has no universal validity, but is merely a corrigible historical opinion, with no more weight than the opposing theories of this or any other age. If, conversely, they were to maintain the exclusive truth of their conception of the relation between history and philosophy, they would be contradicting their own claims concerning the historically relative character of philosophical discourse. Either way, the relativist historicist falls into self-contradiction.

The two most popular versions of relativist historicism, economic determinism and holism, exhibit most blatantly the dilemma involved. If, for instance, thought were conditioned by relations of production, how could one ever be sure that they permit access to valid knowledge of their own reality or of their conditioning role? Similarly, if, as holism maintains, thought were conditioned by standards of justification rooted in given practices, how could this predicament be known with any certainty? If certainty is denied, as the goal of a particular conceptual scheme, enshrined in its own specific practices, how can the holist claim any validity for his description of that or any other practice, or, most importantly, for his ultimate claim that all thought is context-dependent? Relativist historicists may well ignore their own self-referential inconsistency, but they can never surmount its fatal consequences.

The Superfluity of Absolutist Historicism

To escape this difficulty without denying the conditioning of reason by external historical factors, thinkers such as the young Marx and Lukacs have advanced an absolutist historicism drawing its inspiration from certain remarks of Hegel.[2] They have recognized that no theory about history and philosophy can enjoy exclusive truth unless philosophy can somehow arise in an unqualified, unbiased form. Only when this has already occurred can a conception of philosophy's historical character pretend to be more than an opinion. Hence, the avatars of absolutist historicism have claimed that history has given rise to institutions and practices of an absolute character that permit philosophy to attain the wisdom it may have always sought but could never obtain due to external conditions prevailing in the past.

This view ascribes to history an absolute development in two respects. On the one hand, it asserts that history comes to generate institutions that are rational, which is to say, conceptually determinate or universal. This makes possible for the first time a philosophical understanding of historical reality, for only when convention takes a universal form, as some have said has occurred in modernity,[3] can convention be transparent to reason. Naturally, if convention were not to become conceptually determinate, there could be no philosophical knowledge of convention, nor for that matter of its role conditioning philosophical reason.

On the other hand, absolutist historicism presumes that historical development not only produces a reality that is rational, and thus philosophically conceivable, but produces practices that no longer prevent philosophy from exercising its long-sought autonomy. For only if current convention leaves philosophy free to legitimate its arguments without any given restraints can reason provide truths whose justification is not jeopardized by a dependence upon unexamined factors. In this vein, the young Marx suggests (as Lukacs would later argue in *History and Class Consciousness*), that although all theory is predicated on class interest and is thereby ideological, history generates a universal class, the proletariat, whose interests are free of all particular bias, such that those who adopt the proletarian point of view are adopting an unbiased view of modernity from which reality can be conceived without any distortion.

In this sense, the history leading to the present could be regarded as the prehistory of a timelessly universal order, just as the past succession of philosophical theories could be regarded as the prehistory of the one eternal philosophy, whose previous practitioners are mere pretenders trying to pass off ideology, that is, theory grounded on extraphilosophical interests, for wisdom.

Although this view has the virtue of not vitiating the authority of its own pronouncements, it suffers from too much success. By affirming an absolute development of history that makes possible a philosophy unimpaired by historical convention, absolutist historicism effectively eliminates the historical character of reason. Prephilosophical thinking may be dependent upon historical factors that its own thinking can never evaluate nor justify. Knowledge of this very predicament, however, requires a cognition that does not share these limitations. Such is the cognition absolutist historicism is compelled to introduce. In laying claim to an absolute age, where the reality underlying discourse has developed so as to enable reason to grasp truth, absolutist historicism effectively sets philosophy in an eternal present, where the history that conditions discourse has come to a halt and thought jettisons its historical blinders. On these terms, all that is historically conditioned is the captive rhetoric of ideology, not the autonomous reasoning of philosophy that the absolutist historicists must themselves employ.

What their position reveals is that if philosophy can conceive its own relation to history without forsaking truth, it must view itself as a product of history whose argument is yet free from all dictate by the external historical conditions that may have made it possible. This means that the reason purportedly set free by historical development would not refer to any historical conditions in determining philosophy's problems and approach, nor would the validity of any of its claims depend upon any contribution by history. In other words, absolutist historicism ends up leaving philosophy proper entirely free of historical determination.[4]

The Nature of an Internal History of Philosophy

Taken together, the examples of relativist and absolutist historicisms indicate how no coherent argument can be given to show that philosophy is determined by an external history. At most, nature and convention may provide the natural, psychological, and linguistic prerequisites for philosophical discourse, but no factor external to reason can possibly be known to mandate what philosophy will accept or reject as true wisdom. Of course, this outcome does not automatically render philosophy an entirely ahistorical phenomena. It still leaves unresolved whether philosophy is determined by its own history and whether such determination could affect the validity of philosophical argument.

At first glance, the relation of philosophy to its internal history would seem to parallel the one between reason and external historical factors. Once again three options lie at hand, each involving the same problems encountered in the introduction of external history. First, philosophy might be just as juridically unconditioned by its own history as by the history of external institutions and practices. On the other hand, if philosophy is conditioned by its own history, there are these two alternatives: either wisdom is relative to the given conceptual schemes of the philosophical tradition, or this tradition reaches an absolute development, at which point the quest for wisdom sheds its self-biasing character and becomes actual wisdom.

Of crucial bearing on these options is what exactly the history of philosophy comprises. Is it the history of elaborations of the self-same philosophy, or is it rather the history of entirely different philosophical systems whose defining paradigms represent incommensurable frameworks?

That the history of philosophy could be but the saga of one—and indeed, of the one and only—philosophy sounds strange to anyone familiar with the mutually excluding arguments with which philosophers have waged their ceaseless wars. Nevertheless, there is something about this unrelenting combat that suggests an inescapable unity to philosophical thought. As Kant once asked, "Is it indeed possible for there to be more than a single philosophy?"[5] If, objectively speaking, there be but one self-same reason, how could more than one system of philosophy be founded on rational principles? The historical succession of different systems hardly rules out such a thought, for whenever a philosopher advances a new system, does he not, as Kant suggests, effectively declare that "there has been no other philosophy prior to his"?[6] After all, if any philosopher were to admit the existence of another philosophy, that is, another system of true wisdom, there would be "two different philosophies concerning the same thing, and that would be self-contradictory."[7]

Although the self-understanding of philosophers need not dictate the character of philosophical history, certainly the abiding unity of philosophy cannot be dismissed out of hand. If the history of philosophy were the genesis of one self-identical quest for truth, its history would have a prescriptive telos consisting in the complete development of the system of philosophy. Certainly, this normative goal would not entail that philosophical speculation would cease with its achievement, nor that thinkers could only conceive arguments in the order they would follow within that consummating system. It would mean that philosophical progress could be distinguished from either faulty elaborations or restatements of previously attained wisdom. Furthermore, if the nature of philosophical argument were such that no claims could count as wisdom unless the truth of their prerequisites were already established, genuine progress in the history of philosophy would duplicate the path of argument within the one system of philosophy.

One might ask to what extent the history of philosophy would be rational if this were the case. If thinkers need not be familiar with past philosophy, nor understand it if they are, nor be aware that they are simply duplicating it when they restate it, nor realize that they advance arguments already refuted by past efforts, nor follow any predetermined route in their reflection, any a priori knowledge of the history of speculation would seem impossible. The historical progress of philosophy, however, would be another matter. Instead of concerning whatever may have been thought, this progress would involve solely those theoretical achievements that contribute to the advance of the one philosophy proper. Its course would be rationally determinable precisely because it would trace over time the same succession of arguments that logically follow within the system of philosophy. Valid philosophical argument would thus always stand determined by previous philosophical progress in the following manner: either it would limit itself to retracing that progress and make no history, from a normative point of view, or it would make philosophical progress in its own right by appending its argument to that already achieved. In the latter case, its own addition could be made in ignorance or recognition of past accomplishments. Either way, the philosopher would have to work through and certify the arguments supporting his own novel contribution simply to present it in a justified form.

Of course, if the history of philosophy involves the elaboration of a unified system of wisdom, some thinkers will work out the initial arguments that rest on no others. For this reason, progress in the history of philosophy would proceed from an effort undetermined by any prior philosophical history. By contrast, subsequent contributions would rest on past achievements, either reproducing them or taking them as a given foundation on which to build. Nevertheless, this historical dependence would not condition philosophical argument, since it would involve nothing but the same order of conceptual precedence and succession by which the entire system of philosophy would unfold without reference to any antecedently given factor.

The situation is very different if the history of philosophy consists in the succession of disparate systems of philosophy. Conceivably this succession could be arbitrary or necessary.

If it were arbitrary, there would be no need for one system to precede or follow another. In that case, philosophizing would have no determinate relation to the history of philosophy, and there could be no rational history of philosophy. This would be true from either a descriptive or normative point of view. Even if one were to admit that one system had exclusive truth, which of course would have to be the system within which one is arguing about philosophy, this system would not provide any normative ordering for philosophical progress. Since all other systems, being incommensurate theories, would not be stages in the completion of the true system, their succession would have no normative significance whatsoever.

If, however, the succession of philosophical systems involved necessity, the situation would be quite different. Such necessity might be thought to lie in an allegedly paradigmatic situation for making history in philosophy. Such a situation might be one in which a thinker perceives the need for new arguments as a result of uncovering the shortcomings of past theory and then forwards a new theory to remedy these failings. On these terms, the history of philosophy might be thought to exhibit a necessary structure of determinate negation, where each new system negates or repudiates the errors of its predecessors, but carries their imprint within itself insofar as its novelty consists in an attempt to resolve the problems they have generated but failed to solve. Admittedly, such a situation might well reflect the experience of many a philosopher, and be readily documented in many a case. Yet is it really necessary to the development of philosophy, and even when it does occur, are the direction and validity of philosophical argument really conditioned in any determinate way by this predicament?

Naturally, the first system of philosophy could not be determined in this manner, nor, indeed, would any other subsequent theory whose author reasoned either in ignorance of or without reflection upon prior philosophies. Of course, it might be argued that philosophies developed without reference to any other systems would either have a certain necessary form, from which a philosophical tradition could be born according to an internally determined sequence, or else have an arbitrary character that nevertheless would necessarily determine whatever tradition might arise on its basis.

Either way, if the history of philosophical systems is to determine their argument, reference to previous systems would have to direct either the method or content of subsequent systems, and not just be an item of psychological or scholarly interest. Insofar as discrete systems of philosophy comprise mutually exclusive totalities of philosophical thought, rather than sections of one philosophical theory, the dependence of one system upon its predecessors signifies that philosophical argument would be founded upon something falling outside its reach. It would mean that philosophy operates from some given standpoint, conceptual scheme, or set of problems that it has not generated itself, but received from an antecedent body of thought incommensurate with its own. If this were not true, the internal history of philosophy would have no bearing on reason, and any philosopher could work out a new system bearing no imprint of prior philosophies.

Consequently, whether the history of philosophy determines the development of philosophical systems will depend on whether philosophical argument can be determined by any given standpoint or conceptual framework. This problem concerns not just subsequent systems, but the first philosophical system as well. Even though it has no prior philosophical history to mold its thought, it could still issue from the establishment of a philosophical viewpoint determined by a prephilosophical discourse. Hence, the problem at stake is whether philosophical discourse in general can be known to be bound by conceptual foundations. This problem is not answered by noting how it is certainly possible for a discourse on truth to be predicated on a given framework. What lies at stake is rather whether any argument can succeed if all philosophical discourse has that foundational structure.

Deconstruction Versus Rational Reconstruction of the History of Philosophy

If philosophy were conditioned by an internal history consisting in the succession of mutually exclusive philosophical systems, speculative reason would be inherently foundational, provided it did not arrive at an absolute threshold from which philosophy could argue without being biased by the theoretical heritage shaping all previous thought. Of course, if the internal history of philosophy did take an absolute turn, analogous to the one absolutist historicists ascribe to external history, valid philosophical knowledge would once again be ahistorical, in contrast to those earlier efforts of thought whose dependence on past theories rendered them prephilosophical impersonators of wisdom. If, however, such an absolute outcome were denied, philosophy would be deprived of all autonomous reason. Instead, it would stand reduced to a foundation-ridden endeavor whose quest for truth would always be frustrated by its attachment to given conceptual frameworks whose determining role could never be questioned without being presupposed.

On these terms, the only plausible approach to philosophy and its history would appear to be deconstruction. This would consist in an exercise in doxology, unmasking the antecedently given conceptual schemes underlying different systems of philosophy. Such deconstruction could provide no wisdom, but at best offer an edifying service promoting an opined self-awareness of our own assumptions. Deconstruction, however, cannot be coherently advanced as a replacement for philosophical investigation. Presenting it as the sole option for the study of philosophy is tantamount to claiming exclusive knowledge that philosophy is inherently foundational and hence a self-contradictory delusion requiring a sobering cure. As popular as that claim has become, particularly in the wake of Wittgenstein, it resurrects all the self-referential dilemmas afflicting relativist historicism. If all philosophy is burdened by assumptions determined by past philosophical tradition, how can the advocates of deconstruction consistently maintain that their approach has any more validity than that of any opposing view? If the deconstructionists were to admit that their conception of philosophy is itself relative to some given foundation, they would have to offer their description of the history of philosophy as a mere opinion with no privileged authority. If, however, they still affirmed the exclusive truth of their characterization of philosophy, they would be contradicting the relative character that they ascribe to all discourse.

The conclusion is unambiguous: if the history of philosophy is a history of discrete philosophical systems, these cannot be known to follow one another in any necessary order. Although most philosophers have indeed developed foundation-ridden theories, it makes no sense to argue that all philosophy must rest upon given conceptual schemes. That would be just as absurd as seeking to cure us of philosophical speculation by engaging in rational argument.

Hence, there can be no rational history of philosophy in any traditional meaning of the term. Whether philosophical history consists in contributions to the one abiding philosophy or in successions of different philosophical systems, the development of philosophical argument must be just as undetermined by the work of past thinkers as it must be free of external control. Any claim to the contrary is nothing less than nonsense.

Does this mean that philosophy must maintain silence regarding its own history? Not at all. The impossibility of arguing against a foundation-free, historically unconditioned philosophy does not leave the history of philosophy a matter solely for intellectual historians.

The conceptual dilemmas of historicism and universal deconstruction themselves indicate essential features of philosophical history. Since philosophy cannot and should not be bound by antecedent frameworks, philosophical argument does not depend upon any antecedent theorizing. Therefore, there can be no necessity to any temporal sequence of philosophical systems. If there is to be any rational ordering of successive philosophies, it can only be a conceptual one, completely independent of temporal considerations. Thus, to argue that it is impossible to be a Platonist today can only mean that conceptually speaking, current positions successfully repudiate Plato's views, not that it is impossible to philosophize in line with Plato's argument, either with knowledge or in ignorance of his theories.

This leaves open the philosophical task of a rational reconstruction of the history of philosophy. Unlike deconstruction, which unmasks the presuppositions underlying philosophical systems as testimony to the impotence of reason, rational reconstruction seeks what conceptual connection can be found in past philosophy in order to retrieve what is rational and incorporate it as a building block in conceiving truth. This, after all, is what all philosophers engage in when employing other theories as critical foils and supports for their own arguments. What this involves is tracing back the presuppositions on which past theories rest and then ordering them with regard to one another in view of how some account for the presuppositions of others while relying on the achievements of further theories for their own starting points. If any past theories can thereby be integrated into a unitary argument that somehow accounts for all its claims, they will be grasped in a rational ordering, revealing their conceptual dependence upon one another and certifying their own theoretical achievement. On these terms, the argument to which they contribute will neither depend upon nor necessarily follow their actual temporal succession. Although their history just might follow their rational order, this would be but a contingent development that no reasoning could foresee.

The same situation applies to the use philosophical argument makes of current usages, references to other theories, and introductions of other given contents. All provide material contributing to the expression of philosophical theory. However, that does not mean that they have any role in determining the validity of those arguments which employ them. If they were to be ascribed any juridical status, it would have no legitimacy, until the philosophy in question established their authority through its own argument. In this sense, we, as contemporary philosophers, stand on the shoulders of our predecessors only in so far as we are able to establish that their feet do not rest on arbitrary foundations. To do this, there is no need to deny that our speculation could not take place unless we inhabited a historical world providing us with language and particular intellectual traditions, as well as the natural prerequisites for rational life. Nevertheless, all these factors are conditions of consistent as well as inconsistent, valid as well as invalid theory. The moment they are assigned the status of principles of knowledge, determining what can and cannot be considered true, all the absurdities of foundationalism get reintroduced. There is little choice but to recognize that the existence of these factors leaves entirely undecided the course that philosophical inquiry will take.

Like Socrates, we must ultimately admit that philosophy's quest for wisdom can be guided by but two things: recognition of our own ignorance and an opined understanding that there is a difference in meaning between opinion and truth. There can be no other rational grounds for taking up philosophy, since any appeal to guiding reasons would presuppose prior knowledge, signifying that philosophizing had already begun. All that can coherently urge us forward are divine voices, feelings of wonder or some such name for an ignorant arbitrariness that leaves utterly undetermined what will follow.

No matter where we stand in history, the self-conscious ignorance from which philosophizing begins deprives us of all right to claim any given knowledge, including any knowledge of which questions to ask. Nevertheless, we can immediately engage in dialogue with past theory, just as Socrates listened and questioned the claims advanced by his interlocutors. Here we need not be burdened with deciding which questions to ask, for it is the assertions of past thinkers that provide us with direction. From the point of radical ignorance at which the quest for truth begins, all we can ask of these philosophers is to legitimate their claims. If we have yet to develop our own philosophy, and thus lack wisdom with which to judge their truth, we can do little more than observe whether past thinkers provide consistent or inconsistent arguments for the theses we have called into question. Either way, all our dialogue with the tradition can establish is its coherence or incoherence, not the truth or falsity of its claims. Thus, before we philosophize in our own right, determining what is true, previous thought can only offer us opinions whose philosophical worth remains to be established. Consequently, the philosophical tradition cannot impose itself upon our thought unless we arrive at the same ideas through our own independent argument. If such rational reconstruction fails to reappropriate prior theories, the history of philosophy remains an antiquarian study, of no bearing on philosophical argument. Today and tomorrow, only by reasoning in freedom from history can we determine whether the routes of the past are paths we must follow.

Notes

1. It is along these lines that Arthur C. Danto reduces history to a construct of narrative in his *Analytic Philosophy of History* (Cambridge: Cambridge University Press, 1965).
2. Hegel's famous comments on the relation of philosophy to its age in the preface of the *Philosophy of Right* have provided a touchstone for absolutist historicism.
3. Among the most prominent thinkers who have judged modernity to have a universal, rational character are Hegel, Marx, and Max Weber.
4. Leo Strauss has made an analogous argument in his critique of the various forms of historicism in chapter 1 of *History and Natural Right* (Chicago: University of Chicago Press, 1953).
5. Immanuel Kant, *The Metaphysical Elements of Justice*, trans. John Ladd (Indianapolis: Bobbs-Merrill, 1965), p. 5.
6. Ibid., p. 6.
7. Ibid.

Logic and History

Bowman Clarke

In the preface to his second edition of the *Critique of Pure Reason*, Immanuel Kant speaks of "the path of a science" and then writes,

> That logic has already, from the earliest times, proceeded upon this sure path is evidenced by the fact that since Aristotle it has not required to retrace a single step, unless indeed, we care to count as improvements the removal of certain needless subtleties or the clearer exposition of its recognized teaching, features which concern the elegance rather than the certainty of the science. It is remarkable also that to the present day this logic has not been able to advance a single step, and is thus to all appearance a closed and completed body of doctrine.[1]

Although one familiar with the history of logic may have an irresistible urge to smile at this statement, it is a rather important statement for Kant, as we shall see, and there are three important theses within it. First, logic has not had to retrace a single step since Aristotle. It may have had to get rid of "certain needless subtleties" or it may have had to clarify some of "its recognized teaching"; but these revisions do not concern "the certainty of the science." What Kant appears to be maintaining here is that no form of logical truth or valid rule of inference has had to be revised since Aristotle. Second, not only has logic not had to revise itself, it has not been able "to advance a single step" beyond Aristotle. What Kant appears to be maintaining here is that no form of logical truth or valid rule of inference has had to be added since Aristotle. In short, the logic of Aristotle is "a closed and completed body of doctrine." Let us refer to these two Kantian theses as the thesis of the nonhistorical character of logic.

In speaking of the nonhistorical character of logic, I do not mean that one cannot make historical assertions about logic, for to say, "Since Aristotle logic has not been required to retrace a single step," is to make a historical assertion about logic, an assertion which happens, as a matter of fact, to be false, even by Kant's own lights, as we shall see. Let us remove the historical inaccuracies from Kant's particular statement and state the thesis of the non-historical character of logic in this way: Once the form of a logical truth or a valid form of inference is discovered, or seen, by Aristotle or whomever, it is in no need of revision. These forms of logical truth and valid rules of inference constitute a set which is one logical system and which is in principle completeable. I say "in principle completeable," for the forms of logical truth and the valid rules of inference may be infinite in number, yet if a few could be discovered which would generate all others, then it would "in principle be completeable" and could be, to use Kant's terms, "a closed and completed body of doctrine." After all, even if it were Aristotle, as Kant suggested, who discovered such a set, it would be accidental to the body of doctrine, just as it is accidental to the Pythagorean Theorem that Pythagoras discovered it.

The third thesis contained in the quotation from Kant is that logic is a science with its own subject matter. This thesis may be contrasted with the position of the founder of logic himself, Aristotle. Logic, for Aristotle, was an organon, an instrument for organizing a body of knowledge, or a science. Aristotle never lists logic among the sciences (*Metaphysics* 1025b 25 and 1026a 18). Since it was a tool for organizing a science, it had no subject matter of its own. Ironically, there is one place in the *Rhetoric* where Aristotle does speak of "the science of logic," but he immediately goes on to say, "But the more we try to make either dialectic [i.e., logic] or rhetoric not what they are, practical faculties, but sciences, the more we shall inadvertently be destroying their true nature; for we shall be re-fashioning them and shall be passing into the region of sciences dealing with definite subjects rather than simply with words and forms of reasoning."[2] Kant does pay lip service to this Aristotlean position about the nature of logic when he speaks of logic as a "propaedeutic of the sciences." Kant writes, for example, "Logic . . . as a propaedeutic forms, as it were, only the vestibule of the sciences; . . . while logic is indeed presupposed in a critical estimate of them, yet for the actual acquiring of them we have to look to the sciences properly and objectively so called" (p. 18). I call this lip service to the traditional instrumental view of logic, for Kant does give logic itself a subject matter; namely, the understanding. He goes on to say, "That logic should have been thus successful [i.e., in its certainty as a science] is an advantage which it owes entirely to its limitations, whereby it is justified in abstracting . . . from all objects of knowledge and their differences, leaving the understanding nothing to deal with save itself and its form" (p. 18). What Kant appears to be saying here is that the success that logic has enjoyed in becoming a certain and complete science with a nonhistorical character is due to the fact that it abstracts from all objects of empirical knowledge and takes as its subject matter the understanding "itself and its form." This thesis is reinforced by later references to logic as "the science of the rules of the understanding itself" (p. 93), that which "treats of the understanding without regard to differences in the objects to which the understanding is directed" (p. 93), and that which "deals with nothing but the mere form of thought" (p. 94).

One can easily see why all three of these theses are interrelated and important to Kant. As every reader of Kant knows, the a priori and necessary categories of the understanding are gotten from his table of all possible kinds of logical judgments. They are the twelve necessary concepts involved or presupposed in making the twelve kinds of possible judgments. If logic were historical and evolved, then the very form of the understanding would have a history and evolve. The necessary categories would then lose their a priori and necessary status and become historical. Kant thus needs all three of the theses which are summarized in my opening quotation from the *Critique of Pure Reason*. It was suggested earlier that one who was familiar with the history of logic, particularly logic's post-Kantian history, would have an irresistible urge to smile at what Kant says here. I say this because there does appear to be abundant evidence that logic does change and grow. Let us look at some of this evidence; ironically enough, the *Critique of Pure Reason* is rather pivotal in this apparent evolution of logic.

When Kant constructs the table of all possible kinds of logical judgments from which he derives his a priori categories of the understanding, he adds to the traditional list of universal and particular judgments of quantity a third possible kind of judgment, the singular judgment. In justifying his addition to the list, he writes, "Logicians are justified in saying that, in the employment of judgments in syllogisms, singular judgments can be treated like those that are universal," but then he justifies his triadic distinction by telling us that the singular judgment "is . . . essentially different from the universal" (p. 108). The history behind Kant's proposed revision here is an interesting one. Aristotle's view of a science was that it did not treat of singular individuals; consequently, there was no need for singular propositions in logic. The medieval view of science is somewhat different. After all, theology was a science, and theology does treat of singular individuals. Jesus of Nazareth was a singular individual. Propositions concerning singular individuals take on an importance for science. In syllogistic forms, there was a general tendency to treat singular propositions as universal propositions, although some logicians treated them as particular propositions. Neither alternative, however, proved to be fully satisfactory. Prior to Kant these difficulties were pointed out by Peter Ramus in the sixteenth century, and in the seventeenth century by that logical genius whose insights frequently outstripped his ability to handle them, Leibniz.[3] Kant's treatment of the singular judgment as distinct from and in addition to the universal and particular judgments is without question an expansion of the Aristotelean logic as such.

Another illustration of Kant's suggested improvement, or expansion, of Aristotelean logic can be found in his three judgments of relation. Here again we find three forms of judgment: categorical, hypothetical, and disjunctive. Now all the propositions in an Aristotelean syllogism are of the first kind—categorical. There are no hypothetical or disjunctive propositions in the Aristotelean syllogistic logic. There were, however, appendices in the logic textbooks treating the traditional Aristotelean logic, and these appendices were devoted to a treatment of hypothetical propositions and their valid rules of inference, such as *modus ponens, modus tollens* and the hypothetical syllogism, and of the weak and strong forms of disjunctive propositions and their valid rules of inference, the disjunctive syllogisms. These appendices had their root in an entirely different, and at times quite antagonistic, tradition—the Stoic logical tradition.

Now for Kant there can be only one logic, for there can be only one form of the understanding, not two. By expanding the table of judgments to include not only categorical judgments, but also hypothetical and disjunctive judgments, Kant is suggesting an incorporation of the two traditions into one logic. This was an insight first vaguely glimpsed by Leibniz and more systematically seen by George Boole in the nineteenth century, but only fully systematized by Frege in his *Begriffsschrift* in 1879. This systematic incorporation of the two logical traditions into one logical system was historically so important it led Quine to write, "Logic is an old subject, and since 1879 it has been a great one."[4]

This whole historical development from Aristotle and the Stoics to Frege is one illustration of the way in which logic has developed historically. This particular development of logic could perhaps with some justification be termed a "clearer exposition of its recognized teaching, features which concern the elegance rather than the certainty of the science," to use Kant's terminology. This could also, perhaps, include the modal judgments which Kant incorporated in his table of judgments and later were systematized by C. I. Lewis. Unfortunately, there are alternative modal logics; but even more disturbing, there are alternative logics to the logic systematized by Frege in 1879. It is these developments, developments of alternative logical systems, which most seriously call into question all three of Kant's logical theses.

I have taken a logical system to be a consistent set of forms of logical truth and valid rules of inference. A logical system could be more precisely characterized, but I think this is sufficient for our present purposes. An alternative logical system would, then, be another such set which is apparently inconsistent with the first. In a two-valued logical system, for example, 'p or not-p' is a form of logical truth; in an intuitionist logical system it is not. Now apparently 'p or not-p' cannot both be and not be a form of logical truth; consequently an intuitionist logical system is an alternative to a two-valued logical system. In the classical two-valued logic, the old standby, *modus ponens*, is a valid rule of inference; in a relevance logic it is not, for p must have some relevance to q as well. Here we have alternative logical systems. Again, in classical quantification theory, existential generalization is a valid rule of inference; in a free logic it is not. Here again we have an alternative logical system.

One of the ironies of the *Critique of Pure Reason* is that despite the quotation with which we began this discussion, Kant himself in the work suggests two of these alternative logics to the Aristotelean-Stoic-Fregean tradition. One, in fact, is more closely related to the *Critique* than mere suggestion. Kant's own view of mathematics in the first *Critique* led to certain mathematical statements being neither true nor false. As a consequence, a two-valued logic with 'p or not-p' as a form of logical truth could not be used to systematize a constructivist mathematics. The intuitionist logic was constructed as a tool for systematizing a Kantian mathematics. Likewise, if one takes Kant's theology seriously, one might interpret him there as suggesting a free logic, another alternative to the Aristotelean-Stoic-Fregean tradition. In a free logic one can make true statements about an individual, yet cannot infer from them the existence of such an individual; that is, existential generalization is not a valid form of inference. There is little question that in the *Critique of Pure Reason* the judgment, 'The *ens realissimum* is omniscient,' is taken to be a true judgment (p. 490). From this true judgment, however, it does not follow that 'There exists something which is omniscient' is a true judgment. There are other conditions required for existence. In short, in the case of the *ens realissimum*, as well as perhaps of an individual soul and of the cosmos, one can make true statements about it and yet not infer the existence of any such individual—a clear case in which existential generalization fails.

The reason why alternative logical systems pose such a problem for Kant is obvious. One wishes to know which of the alternative logical systems is "the science of the rules of the understanding" or which "deals with . . . the mere form of thought." The understanding cannot be chameleonlike and change its very nature as it is presented with different objects; after all, its nature is obtained, Kant told us, by abstracting from the different kinds of objects to which it directs itself. Alternative logics threaten Kant's theory of the understanding in much the same way that non-Euclidean geometries threaten his theory of the pure forms of sensuous intuition.

Despite Kant's own difficulties posed by alternative logical systems, even the philosophic neophyte wants to know which among the alternative logics is the correct one. Susan Haack, in her book *Philosophy of Logics,* offers us a rather useful way of categorizing the possible alternative responses to the question, Which is the correct logic? She suggests that there are three possible responses: (1) There is only one correct logic, which she calls monism; (2) there are many correct logics, referred to as pluralism; or (3) there is no correct logic, for the term 'correct' is not applicable to a logical system; this she calls instrumentalism.[5]

If Kant were around today and read Haack's book, I am sure he would have been a monist, for as I suggested above, in his view the nature of the understanding cannot be chameleonlike nor is it divided. I am also sure, however, that Kant never faced such a question. There is a published series of his lectures on logic, but there is no indication in it that he was even aware of possible alternative logical systems.[6] I rather think he merely assumed there was only one logic in much the same way as he assumed there was only one geometry. Unfortunately we cannot make the same assumption. When we look up the adjective 'correct' in an English dictionary we will usually find the entry to be something like, "conforming with or adhering to a conventional standard." Now conventions are rather important to lexicographers; they make their living on such. For a philosopher who takes logic as seriously as a Kant, though, "conforming with or adhering to a conventional standard" hardly conveys what he means by the one correct system of logic, and for several reasons. For one thing, conventions are highly cultural things, and even in one culture they tend to be in a state of flux. If the very form of the understanding itself is based on convention, then the very form of the understanding becomes culturally conditioned. The nonhistorical character of logic and the a priori nature of the understanding are lost. Also, it is very difficult to find one clear and consistent set of conventions, even logical ones, to use as a standard. Quine, if he has taught us anything, has taught us that conventions are rather shaky reeds to use in the construction of any a priori edifice.[7] And third, few philosophers (including our contemporary ones) and virtually no logicians are content with our conventions; they keep wanting to modify them. We found Kant, for example, calling Aristotelean logic a "closed and completed body of doctrine," yet wanting to add to it singular judgments and even incorporate in it the Stoic logical tradition. In his list of the three judgments of quality, he also distinguishes between two forms of negation, a distinct innovation as far as any convention is concerned.

If one is interested in justifying one logical system among the alternative ones, as the correct system, then one must seek some other standard than convention. That standard is usually found in some form of rational intuition. The correct logical system is that one which conforms with or adheres to our rational intuitions. Our rational intuitions might be somewhat more systematic, but unfortunately they do not come off much better than our conventions. If the history of philosophy has taught us anything, it should have taught us that philosophers' rational intuitions vary about as much as our conventions, and in much the same way. After all, Descartes had not even published his *Meditations,* in which he maintained he had a clear and distinct intuition of God and that God existed, when Hobbes maintained that he had no such intuition at all, causing Descartes to break off the discussion in apparent utter frustration.[8] This has been the pattern in philosophy every time someone resorts to some form of rational intuition. What appears self-evident to one philosopher does not seem so to another, and there is no recourse. In the light of this, as Peirce suggested, what we need is a faculty to tell us which of our apparent intuitions are the correct ones; and such a faculty appears not to be forthcoming.[9] In fact, in his discussion of what he calls the a priori method, Peirce goes so far as to suggest that our rational intuitions have much in common with matters of taste, or even worse, with fashion (5.383). Given the history of philosophy, I for one would be hard pressed attempting to refute Peirce here.

The difficulties in finding a standard by which to judge one logical system as correct and the others as incorrect has led to pluralism—the contention that there is more than one correct alternative logical system. In order to make this position viable, however, the pluralist must maintain that the alternative logical systems are only apparently incompatible. This is usually done by proposing that such notions as "the form of a logical truth" and "a valid rule of inference" are system-dependent. We can say without contradiction, then, that 'p or not-p' is a form of logical truth in a two-valued system and that 'p or not-p' is not a form of logical truth in an intuitionist system. We can equally say without contradiction that *modus ponens* is a valid rule of inference in a two-valued system and not a valid rule of inference in a relevance logic. This leaves us free, then, to say that it is possible for both systems to be correct, for their incompatibility is only apparent. This appears to me to be the case, for a logical system is a set of rules governing a formal language, and the set of rules do define and interpret the logical signs in the language. A different set of rules gives a different interpretation of the signs. Thus an 'or' and a 'not' have a different interpretation in a two-valued system from what they do in an intuitionist system.

Before, however, we can judge two alternative systems to be both correct, they both must conform with or adhere to some standard, and in this case, different standards. The pluralist usually seeks the standards in our conventions crystallized in our ordinary language. The question of the correctness of a logical system now boils down to this: does the system explicate some sense of 'a form of logical truth' and 'a valid inference' in the conventions of our ordinary discourse? Whereas we saw the monist tending to flee from the heterogeneous and culturally conditioned nature of our conventions and seek refuge in some form of rational intuition, the pluralist on the other hand embraces our conventions with open arms. Pluralism is a very hospitable position. In fact Haack, who is a confessed pluralist, appears proud of her hospitality.[10] If we listen to logicians, however, we find about as much disagreement over just what our conventions are as we do over what our intuitions are. What we actually find happening, is that alternative logics are quite frequently developed and proposed on the basis that some already-existing conventional system does not give an adequate explication of "our conventions."

Modal logic itself grew out of precisely this kind of disagreement. C. I. Lewis felt that the so-called paradoxes of material implication in the conventional two-valued statement logic did not give an adequate expression to our conventions.[11] Despite the fact that he confused the statement connective, 'if . . . then,' with the logical relation of implication, this is the reason which he gave. Likewise, relevance logics are developed on the basis that the two-valued rules of inference do not adequately explicate our conventional notions of validity; these logicians maintain that relevance is an essential part of our conventional notion of validity. Anderson and Belnap, for example, write, "The fancy that relevance is irrelevant to validity strikes us as ludicrous, and we therefore make an attempt to explicate the notion of relevance of A to B."[12] Does this mean that according to our conventions it is ludicrous to call *modus ponens* a valid rule of inference? It has been called one since the Stoics and it is taught as one to every student in introductory symbolic logic. If that is not a convention, what is a convention? To allow multiple "correct" logical systems, each supposedly explicating some convention, does not resolve the problem, for there is as much disagreement over what our conventions are as over what our intuitions are; and disputes over conventions are no more easily settled than disputes over intuitions. I recall hearing a paper by a logician of some prominence in which he was presenting a new logical system. He began by justifying the new system on the basis of "our linguistic conventions." He then switched to "our intuitions," and ended up with, "Well, according to my intuitions, anyway." I shall leave it to you to speculate on why the retreat, and why in this order.

What has historically brought about this plethora of alternative logical systems is the important discovery, first glimpsed by Leibniz and more clearly seen by George Boole, that a logical system has a mathematical model. As a result all one has to do is to alter some condition of the model and one has produced an alternative logical system, much as the alternative geometries were produced by altering Euclid's postulate concerning parallel lines. A large number of alternative modal logics were produced in this manner, as were alternative tense logics, and many-valued logics. It does not take an Einstein, however, to find some convention that the new logical system can be said to explicate or systematize. It only takes a little ingenuity. This is not to say that logicians produce logical systems and then look around for some convention for it to explicate. Usually it is the dissatisfaction with some previous system's explication of our conventions that leads them to alter it. It is, however, the historical conjunction of these two facts—the mathematical ease with which new systems can be introduced and the lack of agreement over our conventions—that has produced this plethora of alternative logical systems which characterizes the present logical scene. It is, so to speak, an entirely different ball game from the one Aristotle played.

Given the wide disagreements over just what our intuitions and conventions are, is it not time to admit that the evaluative terms 'correct' and 'incorrect' are of little value when applied to logical systems? Of what use is the term 'correct' when you have such a rubbery standard as "our intuitions" or "our conventions?" I personally think that the time has come to ask, What can a particular logical system do? rather than, Is a particular logical system correct? If we focus on the former question then we are going back to the founder of logic, Aristotle, and viewing a logical system as an instrument or a tool for doing something. For Aristotle, logic was an instrument for organizing a body of knowledge. Now one may, if one wishes, think of a logical system as an instrument for systematizing some linguistic convention or other. In either of the cases, however, the more appropriate evaluative term is not 'correct,' but 'better for.' A screwdriver is a better instrument for screwing down a screw than a hammer. A two-valued logical system is a better instrument for organizing classical mathematics than an intuitionist system; but an instuitionist logic is a better instrument for organizing a constructivist mathematics than a two-valued one. Personally, I consider classical mathematics to be more important than constructivist mathematics, but this is a judgment about bodies of knowledge, not about logical systems. We may even say that a particular conditional logic is better for systematizing some particular use of conventional statements in our language, but if there is a dispute, then it will be over what our linguistic conventions are with regard to the use of conditionals, not over logical systems. However we conceive of the general task of logic, either with Aristotle or with many contemporary logicians, we need to focus on tasks and what particular logical systems can do, before we begin to make evaluative judgments about alternative logical systems. It is pointless to say that a screwdriver is better than a hammer unless we focus on some assigned task. I myself would rather see logicians focus on the general kind of task that Aristotle assigned to logic than the general kind of task many contemporary logicians seem to assign it, but this is a disagreement over the relative importance of the two general kinds of task. I feel organizing knowledge is more important than systematizing our linguistic conventions.

It may appear that I am turning the logician into a kind of sales representative with a showcase containing many different tools. Even though I prefer to see the logician as a designer of very precise and very useful tools, I do not object to the analogy with a sales representative. The logician is both designer and seller of these tools. What I do not want, however, is the logician to sell me a particular logical system as the "correct tool to buy because it conforms to our intuitions or adheres to our conventions." In doing so, she becomes like the car salesman who tells me this is the "correct" car to buy because it shows good taste or it is fashionable. I want to know what the logical system can do.

Haack has criticized the instrumentalist view of logic which I am here advocating. She tells us she has "persistent doubts whether an instrumentalist can have anything sensible to say about how one is to choose between logical systems." The reason she gives is this: "The instrumentalist normally concedes that, at least for certain purposes, one logical system may be judged better than another, perhaps as more convenient, more fruitful, more appropriate, yielding the desired inferences. . . . But no matter how convenient or fruitful it might be if one could infer 'A and B' from 'A,' this would, so it seems to me, be *no* reason to prefer a system which represented that inference as valid."[13] The obvious objection to the rule of inference Haack offers is that since B may be any statement of the system, true or false, then from a true statement, A, we can always infer a false statement; we can even infer 'A and not-A' from A. I do not consider her problem here so much one of evaluating alternative logical systems, as a problem of what is going to count as a logical system in the first place. I do not think anyone would call such a system as she has suggested a logical system. How we are going to use the term 'logic' is a matter of convention. Suppose, however, someone did call Haack's system a logical system; it would be like calling a smoked oyster a screwdriver. If enough people followed someone in doing so, then the screwdriver sales representative would just have to add smoked oysters to his collection of tools— stranger things than that have happened. There would be little harm done beyond the initial confusion. The same goes for the logician-salesman. If enough people wanted to call Haack's suggested system a logical system, then the logician–sales representative would add it to her instruments; but she is still under obligation to tell us what it will do. It would certainly be useless for organizing a body of knowledge and, so far as I know, for systematizing any linguistic convention. In all likelihood it would merely remain in the logician's showcase as a curiosity.

This discussion began with a presentation of three theses from Kant on logic and history and I used a brief sketch of the history of the development of logic to call all three theses into question. There simply is no one logical system with the nonhistorical character Kant wanted and which can serve as the science of the form of the understanding itself. Does this mean, however, that an evaluation of a logic is historically conditioned and culturally relative, or even individually relative, as my anonymous logician suggested when he resorted to, "Well, according to my intuitions, anyway"? If we accept the instrumentalist view of logic, I think not. Certainly, if anything is historically conditioned and culturally relative, our tasks, our needs, and our purposes are. This was reflected in my comments concerning the change from the Aristotelean lack of a need for singular propositions to the medieval need for them, also the change from the lack of a need for a third value between truth and falsity and the constructivist's need for it. Aristotle, and the medievalist, perhaps, had no need for a screwdriver either. What is not historically conditioned nor culturally relative is the judgment that logical system A is better than logical system B for task C.

Whether or not Aristotle and the medievalist had screws to screw down or not was historically conditioned and culturally relative. That a screwdriver is a better instrument for screwing down screws than a hammer is neither historically conditioned nor culturally relative. This, of course, will not satisfy the person who has the feeling that there must be some one correct logical system which transcends culture and history and upon which we can erect some a priori and certain structure. Until, however, we can find some clear and universally agreed-upon standard, the question, Which is the correct logical system? if not meaningless, is certainly an unfruitful one.

Notes

1. Immanuel Kant, *The Critique of Pure Reason*, trans. Norman Kemp Smith (London: Macmillan, 1963), p. 17. Subsequent citations are in the text.
2. 1359b 10–15. The quotations from Aristotle are from *The Basic Works of Aristotle*, ed. Richard McKeon (New York: Random House, 1941).
3. See Gottfried Whilhem Leibniz, *Die philosophischen Schriften*, ed. C. J. Gerhardt (Berlin: G. Olms, 1960–61), 7:211.
4. W. V. O. Quine, *Methods of Logic* (New York: Holt, Rinehart, and Winston, 1950), p. vii.
5. Susan Haack, *Philosophy of Logics* (Cambridge: Cambridge University Press, 1978), p. 221.
6. Immanuel Kant, *Logic*, trans. Robert S. Hartman and Wolfgang Schwarz (New York: Library of Liberal Arts, 1974). It is interesting to note that here Kant essentially restates his thesis: "Present day logic has developed out of Aristotle's *Analytic*. . . . Logic, by the way, has not gained much in content since Aristotle's time and it cannot, due to its nature. But it may well gain in exactness, definiteness and distinctness. . . . Aristotle had omitted no moment of the understanding; we are herein only more exact, methodical, and orderly" (p. 23). In the light of the discussion of the intuitionist logic it is worth noting that in the *Logic* Kant accepts the principle of excluded middle (p. 58). Also, his view of logic and the understanding given above is repeated: "Logic is therefore a self-cognition of the understanding and of reason, not, however, as to their faculty in respect of objects, but solely as to form." (p. 16)
7. See W. V. O. Quine, "Two Dogmas of Empiricism," *Philosophical Review* 60 (1951): 20–43.
8. I have in mind here Hobbes's objections to Descartes' *Meditations* and his replys.

9. C. S. Peirce, *Collected Papers*, ed. Charles Hartshorne and Paul Weiss (Cambridge: Harvard University Press, 1934, 1935), 5.214. Subsequent references are in the text.
10. Haack, pp. 231, 3.
11. See C. I. Lewis, *A Survey of Symbolic Logic* (Berkeley and Los Angeles: University of California Press, 1918).
12. A. R. Anderson and N. D. Belnap, Jr., *Entailment*, vol. 1 (Princeton: Princeton University Press, 1975), p. 18.
13. Haack, p. 227. The ellipses and italics are hers.

Philosophical Problems and Historical Solutions

Nancy Streuver

I wish to consider the issue of the value of history, construed in its strictest and simplest sense: the ethical value of historical inquiry. It is certainly the case that we have moved in point of view from an attitude of easy acceptance to one of troubled ambivalence in our use of the *topos* "the lessons of the past." In the good old classical days, Cicero proclaimed history as *magistra vitae*—teacher of life—and *lux veritatis*—light of truth—proclaimed indeed that the past offered authentic insights which may still constrain present decisions.[1] Contemporary unease is precisely depicted in the summary offered by Jane Kramer, in her account of the strange and restless reactions of prominent Frenchmen to the forthcoming trial of Klaus Barbie, the notorious German agent in World War II; Kramer suggested that the source of their fear lay in the shared premise that "history is too dangerous to be left to its own surprises and its own truths."[2]

There is, of course, a popular dimension to the rejection of history: we observe Know-Nothingism in Henry Ford's "History is Bunk" as well as in the late sixties and early seventies battle cry, "History is Irrelevant." But I prefer to focus on the academic dimension: the ongoing debate over the worth and place of historical investigation within the community of serious inquirers. I choose to see this as an irresolute and unresolved confrontation of the philosophically inclined and the historically inclined. If every recent attempt by the historians to generate a philosophical account of their trade seems essentially flawed and ultimately unconvincing, every attempt of the philosophers to define historical values seems essentially ill-motivated, distrustful.

From the point of view of the historian, contemporary philosophers speaking of history speak in metaphors of condescension, relegation. This is nothing new; there is no thrill of surprise when we hear J. L. Mackie contrast the "intrinsic interest" of philosophical problems with the contingent nature of historical research results.[3] And when Michael Oakeshott, in his recent collection *On History and Other Essays*, stipulates that history must deal only with the "past which has not survived," he typifies the strategy which tries to define a historical project of such purity, and such inanity, as to make the choice of a historical career a fatuous one.[4] For Oakeshott wants the historian to reject the task of describing the past as surviving in and therefore useful to the present. The thought of practicality, the consideration of use, destroys objectivity. True history is by definition vacuous, intrinsically impractical.

Today, then, the relation of the discipline of philosophizing and the discipline of historical investigation is—collegial pieties apart—an essentially contentious one. I shall argue, however, the uses of controversy. In the first place, a description of the points of contest between the protagonists generates an account which specifies that the philosophical perspective is the origin of the idea that the subversion of history is edifying, and in the second place, a description of the civil, or political, or ethical value of well-motivated historical inquiry generates a case for history as edifying, and substantiates the old claim that we can learn from the past.

I shall begin by considering the history of philosophy (which is a wholly owned subsidiary of the philosophical profession) as diagnostic of the philosophical problem with history. I shall turn to the work of Richard Rorty: first, because he asserts the importance of the history of philosophy as the domain in which the important issues at stake in the philosophical discussion must be confronted; and second, because he himself has embarked on a wholesale critique of philosophy. Rorty has recently presented a paper on the four historiographical genres, three of them ill motivated, one well motivated.[5] The first project of historical reconstruction is trivial because it deals primarily with the contexts of formation of ideas; it attempts an account of philosophical genres which may or may not have any analytic rigor. The second project of rational reconstruction, on the other hand, may have entirely too much rigor; its usual tactic is to restate the problems of former periods as continuous with and formative of modern problems; it is intractably anachronistic, ahistorical. The third genre, *Geistesgeschichte*, is a metahistorical or metaphilosophical attempt to set all problems and texts in a single array, where each text is assigned its canonic status and intellectual importance. The fourth genre is not history of philosophy but intellectual history; it is produced by historians, not philosophers, and Rorty approvingly assigns it the lowly but useful status of handmaiden. Since it deals with institutions, not ideas, it does not extend beyond trivial intellectual concerns; yet, in Rorty's phrase, it keeps the philosopher's history "honest," because it describes not only environmental factors but the actual resonances, the specific effects or lack of effects, of the philosophers' work.

The dominant mode of philosopher's history is rational reconstruction. To the historian, this is not simply antihistory, it is bad history. In his study of philosophical writing, John Richetti has recently suggested that the modern philosopher, engaged in the history of the discipline, is engaged in a process of translation which is at the same time a process of reduction. The philosophical writing of the past is transferred into the dry prose of contemporary philosophical discourse—the "language of unparalleled difficulty and stiff professionalism of the learned journal and the advanced seminar."[6] The texts of Plato or Montaigne or Augustine are rendered down into articles which could be submitted to *Mind*, or the *Journal of Philosophy*, or the *Monist*. Thus, in a perfect synchronization of means and end, translation secures the rejection of the past through discursive effacement.

Richetti goes on to list some contextual factors which bear upon this double initiative of rejection of the past and the development of professional prose; philosophy is beset by "academic specialization, anxious mimicry of the physical sciences, the emergence of mathematical logic, the decline of literary and historical education."[7] For Rorty, "the anxious mimicry of the natural sciences" is a fundamental motive underlying the Whiggish premises which vitiate philosopher's history. "Whiggery," of course, is a familiar epithet to historians: originally applied to the smug maneuvers of British institutional historians who tended to wish to read all of history as leading up to the foundation of the Mother of Parliaments, it is a general tactic of reading the past either as successful anticipation of the present or as failed countermovement. It is, of course, a metaphor of condescension; wishing to confirm the progress of the present, it is forced to condemn the unprogressive stupidity of the past; past philosophers, alas, are not living now. Further, the rejection of the past is a necessary corollary of engagement in progressive science, of a commitment to a methodology which accumulates true propositions. Strong methods require the dynamic obsolescence of the past.

But, I shall now claim that the distrust of past achievement attentuates present argument; Whiggery is a context of philosophical jiggery-pokery. For the distrust of past philosophical actions elides into a distaste for "event" in general, in a pervasive difficulty in coping with actions, and in integrating accounts of events into philosophical discourse.

As a historian, I have tried to come to terms with my inability to speak idiomatic philosophese; but a lingering pique prompts me to mention that my favorite citation from a philosopher about philosophical language is J. L. Austin's lament about the "constant and obsessive repetition of the same small range of jejune examples" in philosophical discourse.[8] Indeed, philosophical use of example indicates to me a deep, pervasive, and insufficiently self-conscious unease in confronting, in particular, the domain of social or civil act, the very domain the historian must order in a particular way. Bernard Williams has claimed that in analytical philosophy, the linguistic preoccupation with the distinction between fact and value has led to a concentration on only the most general features of moral language.[9] Within philosophical arguments, the need for examples which falsify these indigestible generalizations leads to a search for counterexamples of the most outré nature. Thus Bernard Williams's own book on moral issues, The Problems of the Self, is in many ways a very wise book, but it is stuffed, literally stuffed, with bizarre examples: there are split personalities, amoebalike fissions of the body, nuclear fusions of minds, brain transfusions—a monstrous zoo seems to be the proper arena of discovery.

Exemplary of this philosophical difficulty in confronting social reality, in dealing with the historical tissue of events and process, is

John Rawls's *Theory of Justice.* According to Milton Fisk's "History and Reason in Rawls' Moral Theory" Rawls, like other political philosophers who aim at an "objective" explanation of politics and ethics, faces a problem: how much account should be taken of historical facts, the phenomena of social reality? Their response, Fisk submits, confects a dilemma, since they give themselves only two options: first, leaving too much out, and second, including too much in.[10] Rawls neatly impales himself on both horns of this dilemma, according to Fisk. Only through confection of a fictional humanity—the "people of the original position" (POPs to R. M. Hare), representing a state of mind which needs radical isolation from reality, needs a "veil of ignorance"—can Rawls evoke the objective principles for real society, for "people of ordinary life" (POLs to Hare).[11] But Rawls includes too much in, as well. Hare calls the text a picture or parable, a fantasy, and certainly there is a strong flavor of science fiction in the *Theory of Justice.*[12] Rawls's description of a minimal humanity is full of elaborate and cosy detail; just as science fiction domesticates the extraterrestrial by attributing familiar human motives and techniques, so Rawls creates a Utopian community, described to its last minor premise, a community which resembles a group of tenured academics at a private liberal institution. As Hare puts it, the POPs are "replicas of Rawls with a veil of ignorance clapped over his head."[13] The detail is all of a period; Rawls does not produce a timeless recipe but a very time-bound description of nineteenth- and twentieth-century liberal democratic forms, beliefs, and values, and the bearing of Rawls's theory is the bearing of a critique of that society on that society.

Fisk's main argument, however, is that Rawls has an inadequate sense of political reality; Fisk claims, and we shall return to this point, that all political and ethical speculation must begin with the irreducible fact that "humans are members of groups."[14] But Rawls's irreducible fact is the isolate individual; Rawls's effort may be seen as simply the latest move in a Cartesian strategy that dominates modern philosophy still. In this moment, Richetti claims, "the modern philosopher is a man alone, a sort of voluntary Robinson Crusoe or self-appointed philosophical Adam whose thought tends to represent itself as a new beginning."[15] Rawls, then, is representative of a modern tendency toward solitary and self-cancelling discourse, creating texts which ask that the reader's private mental history be matched with that of the author. For a Cartesian Whig, cancelling history is a part of cancelling sociability in a discourse that claims radical transparency.

While Rawls, claiming objectivism, may resist history, he locates himself neatly in the history of philosophy. Consider Hare's charge that Rawls is not an objectivist at all, but that ultimate in hermitry, an intuitionist. Rawls's evidence is basically introspective, private; his text is full of appeals to himself, and Hare claims that he has found in two pages thirty expressions of reliance on intuition: "I assume that there is a broad measure of agreement that," "it seems reasonable to suppose," "is arrived at in a rational way," "which we can affirm upon reflection," "we are confident," "we think," etc., etc.[16] Rawls, we see, is given to moving as quickly as possible to "consensus"; when he claims "we all agree," he attributes *his* intuitions to everyone else.

But Rawls is moving as far as possible from accosting public problems and social process, and he may be guilty of the morally dangerous fault Hannah Arendt called "vulgar aloofness."[17] In Rawls's theory one can only move from isolate individuals to a congeries of isolate individuals; from atomist premises he derives atomist conclusions; it is, in short, not a social, or political, or ethical theory at all.

We seem, then, to be confronted with a paradox. The construction of an ethical philosophy as "practical," a practice capable of meaningful improvement and therefore significant use, at the same time requires a reconstruction of social reality as social fiction. The more practical, the more surreal. The truly accomplished (as opposed to amateur) philosopher cannot function in a domain of social fact and ethical event.

The failures I have tried to stipulate are failures in "social realism," a vital disconnection of philosophy from the tissue of event and civil praxis. A discussion of these philosophical problems, I claim, throws light on the possibility of edification by the past, learning lessons from the past, because philosophical and surreal formulations have contaminated historical inquiry. We are not edified by history because our tainted discourse disallows it. Further, I have been trying to suggest that the history of philosophy with its Whiggery is the tail that wags the philosophical dog. No Whigs, no philosophers. History of philosophy does not simply diagnose dysfunction for us, it creates it. It is not a peripheral activity, but a central source of irritation radiating disabling thoughts. This, of course, is simply another way of saying that the anxious self-concern of the philosophical profession has attenuated its identity. The denial of one's own philosophical past was the first, vital step in their choice of incivility as procedure.

But Rorty tells us we must be concerned not so much with where philosophy places itself, but where careful historical analysis will place what he refers to as "capital-P" Philosophy texts in a continuum of philosophical writing. Unconvinced by Philosophy's destruction of the past, Rorty claims that the real necessity is to read Philosophy into the past. "The real issue is about the place of Philosophy in western philosophy, the place within the intellectual history of the West of the particular series of texts which save the 'deep' Philosophical problems the Realist wants to preserve."[18] Rorty's Philosophers are Realists, but the locus of difficulty for the Realists is "reality." Both Rawls and Oakeshott insist that practical or civil affairs are best dealt with by political philosophers who get down to "deep" essences, and dispense with contingencies. But in a truly maddening maneuver we see this Philosophy condemning the historian of philosophy to spend his life investigating phenomena his premises define as obsolescent and uninteresting, while condemning the historian to antiquarianism in order to keep the present 'pure' for deep research.

Rorty's basic critique of modern philosophy, then, is that it lacks the pragmatic turn. Both K.-O. Apel and Rorty stipulate as the most vital and fruitful innovation in philosophy since Kant the development of pragmatism.[19] Realism is unreal, impractical. But Rorty's "practical" post-Philosophy contaminates, too. When Rorty claims that we must develop a "new intellectual tradition" he seems to turn to history to save Philosophy from itself, but this is not the case. For Rorty, the proper attitude toward the past of the new "Writer" who supplants the Philosopher as hegemonous intellectual inquirer is one of "amused condescension."[20] A post-Philosophic culture would be one where "trying to get out from under the mistakes of the past" is a dominant investigative motive; indeed, he says with satisfaction, such a culture "would be one in which men and women felt themselves alone."[21] Rorty, then, is as progressive and as condescending to a regressive past as the scientistic philosopher, although Rorty's progress is in amusement value, rather than in the accumulation of true propositions.

But since I have suggested that these philosophical problems may have historical solutions, we must now move from a consideration of the philosophical difficulties with social "facts"—with political and ethical "reality" and thus with past reality as meaningful and enlightening—to a consideration of historical premises and procedures as therapy. I choose to move back in history as well, away from the trendy theories of today, back to the eccentric figure of R. G. Collingwood. To be sure, it is, in a way, an indictment of the present state of the theory of history that Collingwood's flawed essay, *The Idea of History*, is still in the discussion as the starting point for contemporary arguments on the merits and demerits of formulating a philosophy of history. But behind *The Idea of History* lies a much more generous project which Collingwood defined in his *Autobiography*.[22] In the 1920s and '30s Collingwood saw the relation of history and philosophy as the rivalry of two undernourished and ill-motivated disciplines. Collingwood was reacting on the one hand to a general crisis—the barbarism of World War I, which the historians neither anticipated nor explained—and, on the other hand, to a local crisis: the vapidity and dysfunction of the philosophical faculty at Oxford, of which Collingwood himself was a distinguished member.

Therefore, Collingwood, since he was convinced that history and philosophy were not doing well separately, proposed a strategy of rapprochement between philosophy and history, a rapprochement which would be, he claimed, at the same time a rapprochement between theory and practice.[23] Collingwood specifically raised the issue of edification by history: World War I seemed to tell him that we either learn to learn from the past, or we are doomed. But the Oxford philosophical faculty was having none of it; Collingwood describes the local academic crisis primarily as an outgrowth of the difficulties of the philosophers in coming to terms with history. Thus, in Collingwood's view, history must save philosophy from itself.

Starting from the hypothesis that philosophical prejudices undermined the historical enterprise, Collingwood decided that it was necessary to develop more hospitable premises and procedures which would allow history, history of philosophy, and philosophy itself a more useful development. To a certain extent, the most interesting contemporary critiques of philosophy and the history of philosophy simply restate the Collingwoodian project. Most importantly, the premises of Collingwood are restated as the premises of "social realism." "Social realism" is not bad Stalinist painting; rather, it is the economical thesis that the reality that is both topic and context of an investigative action is social action. The only evidence we have for this thesis is linguistic and semiotic evidence of exchange, of communicative activity; it seems simply prudence to stipulate, then, that the use of evidence reconstructs community acts and social processes. Further, it is a secondary, derived, and difficult task to extrapolate from or look behind this evidence to reconstruct private states of mind; it is a favorite task of the romantic biographer, but it is a very uneconomical maneuver indeed.

Thus, social realism substitutes for Rawls's assumption that the elementary given of political theory is the atomistic individual, the postulate that the primary subject of well-motivated inquiry is society and the processes of community formation. (Rorty's premise of the ubiquity of language should lead him to this postulate, but it does not.) Further, Collingwood's rapprochment of philosophy and history can be stated as the inextricability of three strands of inquiry: history, politics, and ethics are investigative aspects of a single project; the social domain is a single domain.[24]

The interlacing of political and historical concerns has been, on the whole, a nonproblematic issue for historians; most history has been political history. The intertwining of history and ethics is more confusing, for philosophical discussions of this issue, as we have seen, dispute unity and attempt to sever the historical dimension from the ethical, or to keep it at one remove, as a nonessential realm of illustrative accident. Social realism must, then, further stipulate the inextricability of "fact" and "value"; on the one hand, the model for history cannot be social science, "value-free" inquiry, and on the other hand, the definition of value is necessarily specific, historical. Inquiry that destroys specificity imposes ideologies: that is to say, initiatives of transcendental colonization.[25] We should be aware of resistance to transcendental claims within the philosophical discipline; recall that Williams insists that "no human characteristic which is relevant to degrees of human esteem can escape being an empirical characteristic, subject to empirical conditions, psychological history, and individual variation, whether it be sensitivity, persistence, imaginativeness, intelligence, good sense; or sympathetic feeling; or strength of will."[26]

Further, the specificity is a temporal specificity, and again we must take account of philosophical elaborations of this point. Hare, for example, develops a jurisprudential model of ethical decision-making: "Though principles are in the end built upon decisions of principle, the building is the work of many generations and the man who has to start from the beginning is to be pitied; he will not be likely, unless he is a genius, to achieve many conclusions of importance, any more than the average boy, turned loose without instruction upon a desert island, or even in a laboratory, would be likely to make any of the major scientific discoveries."[27] Once one accepts the historical specificity, the temporality of evidence, it becomes obvious that there is no easy place to draw the line between past and present dimensions of community; wild disparities eventually will fade into distressingly entangled similarities. Thus temporality founds a strong interconnection of premise and procedure; while maintaining the necessary hypothesis that there can be radical disjunctions between periods and cultures, that certain past cultures may be unreadable by present codes, one must also maintain the hypothesis that there is no obvious and complete warrant for rejecting a particular past community as irrelevant to present ones, and that one's procedure must take account of the axiom that linguistic meaning is generated by systemic relationships, and that therefore past cultures, no matter how radically disjoined, are accessible to systematic analysis.[28]

Then, the premise that all evidence is discursive, is qualified by the corollary that all the texts of communication are dialogic in nature; the most monologic meditative treatise responds to earlier texts and shapes new responses.[29] Again, historical procedures follow readily from historical premises; the account which employs this evidence must be an account of reality as dialogic, an account which argues arguments. There is no need, then, for gross methodological revisions in the historical enterprise. The majority of contemporary historians are social and economic historians; that is to say, they have both impeccable social-realist premises (the object of their research is social structure and process) and a tidy sense of evidence (they deal in social communication and economic exchange). "Normal" history, therefore, needs to change neither its topics nor its research habits. And the new focus in intellectual history on larger discursive practices and communicative events is simply a synchronization of intellectual history with social-intellectual history, which has known all along that it is concerned with interactive practice and exchange structures.

Further, the dialogic premise allows us not only to save new history, as the account of exchange, but to save classical history as well. For it is certainly the case that Thucydides, as egregious classical historiographer, chose to represent dialogue in his history of the Peloponnesian War; the antithetical speeches of Athenians and Spartans were to epitomize, if not what the protagonists actually did say, what they *should* have said in defense of opposing policies. The classical habit of confecting speeches is an investigative procedure for the description of dialogic forces.[30]

To be sure, the tidiness of the methodological solution, where history is the representation of the structures and processes of exchange and communication, may be the source of dysfunction as well. Economics turns into a dismal science when the innocent neatness of economic history tempts it into premature conclusions. But in pursuit of Collingwood's rapprochement, the inquirer assumes reciprocity; if history brings the premises and procedures of social realism to philosophy, philosophical procedures can be used to undo the reification of historical constructs; if the philosopher needs to learn how to construe "facts" as "events," the philosopher can train the historian how to prevent an account of market growth from becoming a tract on the Free Market. The historian learns through analytic practice to eschew overweening extrapolations from research results, and to discriminate ideologizing maneuvers. And, with specific reference to the ethical dimensions of civil practice, the philosophic procedures may clarify and critique the logical rules of particular moral arguments for ethical consistency, as well as disambiguate the historian's use of moral categories to generalize moral experience. Historians also learn to avoid ascription of intentionality to social strategies they have carefully described as the product of unconscious constraints; on the other hand, they learn to locate rationalization, even in the midst of the play of socioeconomic forces.

Then, to assume social reality as dialogic places particular constraints on our notion of history as edifying. A focus on dialogue subverts a preoccupation with the definition of a single consensual truth—subverts, indeed, the production of world-view, *Zeitgeist*, paradigm as the end or culminating achievement of an intellectual history of a period. Just so, the past can not edify in a direct, didactic mode. History does not edify by producing unarguable moralism; rather, it is a kind of continuous moral work—a disciplined assembly and reproduction of the materials of civil debate, an assembly which is assumed to qualify and extend our appreciation of the potential for civil debate. Moral lessons are not constituted by proverbs and saws, but by precise comprehension of strategic conflict. Thus, it is possible to define Machiavelli's political historical texts as moral work. Machiavelli's *Prince* and *Discourses on Livy* leave the debate in, they permit subversion, and therefore tell us more about the moral tone and temper of the early sixteenth century than a consensual account. Consensus is only momentary; it is a delicate, ephemeral balance, and as such, historically insignificant. But then, we might proceed to define Rawls's theory as inadequate moral work. We have confronted Rawls's difficulty with reality; both his POPs and his POLs inhabit worlds which are surreal, drained of contingency, described by static formulae. His accounts of these societies are constituted by endless chains of contrary-to-fact conditionals; he speaks in a continuous subjunctive mode. But Rawls's work is also crude work; he employs the ancient and inefficient tactic of ingesting facts by use of the argument from example; the *exemplum*, of course, is an illustration of a moralism, a story that supports a proverb.

It is painful to watch. For in what I regard as a choice piece of history, K.-H. Stierle describes an important Renaissance innovation in historiography as the transformation of the *exemplum* into the "histoire."[31] Where the medieval or classical *exemplum* was construed as a narrative, fictional or factual, which confirmed an ethical or religious imperative, Boccaccio's stories "problematize." That is to say, the event or action is made to raise questions, not provide answers. Thus in a Boccaccesque story about adultery, it is not that 'adultery' as term loses its ethical valence, but adultery in the incident is connected with generosity as virtue in a quirky but provocative rationale. The stories make the reader think more complicated thoughts, they adumbrate two sides to the question. Where Rawls attempts monologic closure, history uses dialogue to open dialogue. The premises and procedures of well-motivated historical inquiry thus may furnish a simple distinction: not the past, but investigating the past is edifying. From this follows the very economical decision not to apply moral criteria to historical actions, not to stipulate morality as present or absent in historical actors, but rather to apply moral criteria to the acts of investigating historical events. "Justice as fairness," Rawls's central moral definition, should motivate equity in investigative discourse. Thus, "fairness" as criterion would exclude the philosophers' reductive tactics. When Richetti describes the tactics of modern philosophic historians in translating Plato into journalese, he deplores the counterproductive strategies as blatantly unfair. And certainly a motive of Quentin Skinner's championing of historical reconstruction, as opposed to rational reconstruction, is the avoidance of reductive inequity.

On the whole, I tend to think it better to make philosophy the handmaiden of history, than to make history the handmaiden of philosophy. I think this was Collingwood's goal as well. In truth, in the plot of mutual dependence, I am constrained to say that philosophy has far more to gain by becoming historical, than history has to gain from becoming philosophically kosher.

Now, after all this discussion of interdisciplinarity, I would like to consider the issue of the specificity of history, because I want to be able to claim that history is especially edifying. The most over-utilised definition of history in premodernity is certainly Cicero's praise of history in the *De oratore*, which I have referred to earlier;

history, he claims, is "testis temporum, lux veritatis, magistra vitae, nuntia vetustatis," but also "vita memoriae".[32] Of this list of
epithets the phrase *vita memoriae* is at once the least recognised
and, potentially, the most fruitful. For I shall now suggest that the
peculiar task of historical investigation as opposed to other kinds
of investigation has to do with memory, and that history is not
simply commemorative, but it constitutes memory. And now bring
to mind Williams's very sophisticated and very detailed exploration of moral theory in *Problems of the Self.* Here he assumes a
strong, if not completely resolved connection of memory with
moral identity; he hesitates at one point in his argument as to
whether memory constitutes identity, or, as Butler would have it,
memory presupposes identity. But thus we arrive at our unpreten-
tious definition of history as edifying: if history constitutes memory, memory constitutes, or reinforces, moral identity. Memory,
which is "the possession of a particular past," according to
Williams, forms the grid through which we perceive civil choice.[33]

There is, of course, a major classical text which offers a very rich
description of memory of benefit as one of the chief elements of
social identity. For Seneca, the failure of imperial politics forced a
shift in focus away from public policy toward informal and intimate social ties. This is, in the *De beneficiis,* a focus on "benefit"
as social bond. "What we need," he claims, "is a discussion of benefits and the rules for a practice that constitutes the chief bond of
society."[34] Benefits, of course, are construed by Seneca as not simply *res,* "gift," but *fides,* "trust," *gratia,* "influence," *consilium,*
"advice," and *praeceptum,* "instruction," as well.[35] But most importantly, Seneca underlines the reciprocity of benefit and gratitude in the well-ordered society; society functions on its memory;
therefore, Seneca enjoins "those who work to heal the human soul,
to maintain faith in the dealings of men, and to engrave upon their
minds the memory of services, let them speak with earnestness
and plead with all their power."[36]

Like Seneca, I mean to assign more than a custodial or janitorial
function to the investigation that generates memory. The constitution of memory is a much thicker project than the simple additive
function Skinner attributes to history; Skinner, recall, began a paper on Machiavelli by claiming it as a "possible means of enlarging

our present understanding of the concepts we employ in social and political argument."[37] Seneca talked about our intimate entanglements with memory, while Skinner advocates "skimming": we take the juicy bits from the past and slot them into our current argument. For Skinner, an examination of unfamiliar theories works much as the philosophers' production of counterexamples works: as an elucidation of familiar theory.

Therefore, where Oakeshott insists that pure history must be impractical, the historian may argue that intellectual history, and even history of philosophy, is most practical, in the sense that intellectual history recalls whole problem-solving practices and describes interactive competences. Let us, for example, contrast the prim presentation by Rawls of his vital moral strategy—which is, of course, the old birthday party trick of "You cut; I choose the slice of cake"—with a historian's account of Florentine politics in the Renaissance. Rawls needs to hypothesize a "veil of ignorance" for the generation of his principle; not knowing what role they will play in ordinary life constrains the people of the original position to impartiality as virtue; the birthday guests are constrained by ignorance. But when the birthday party device appears in the Florentine mechanism of voting for office-holders by lot, and, moreover, voting by lot for very short terms of office that cannot be repeated within a certain period—here is a constraint of memory, psychologically viable. The Florentine citizens elected as officials were constrained by ignorance of who would constitute the next set of officials, but the constraint was motivated by memories of the abuse of public power for private benefit in the past. The Medici, of course, manipulated this republican system in the fifteenth century, but they were forced to manipulate carefully; the memory was still green of the efficacy of the strategy at the end of the early Medicean period of power. What is memorable about Florentine history is not the solutions to political problems but the specific processes, the sense of a propriety of decision and choice which emphasizes not Rawls's ignorance, but collective memory. Where "blindness" is the qualification of insight for Rawls, what is intriguing to the historian is his conviction that the Florentines learned from the past, and evolved Rawls's "you cut; I choose" principle to anticipate and counter future malfunction. History, in underlining the efficacy of memory, is underlining the efficacy of history.

Rawls's insight impinges as a moralism; but when we specified history as a kind of moral work, we rejected it as a treasure house of moralisms. Because the historian views social reality as dialogic, he reconstitutes the memory of past debates. Past solutions, of course, are more liable to distortion by the colonizing tactics of reconstruction than the unresolved confrontations and failed debates of the past. And a focus on the arguable, not the unarguable, requires an analysis of debate as well- or ill-motivated, on precisely Hare's important topic of critique of the logical rules of moral argument. In one sense, of course, moralisms are ahistorical because they are truisms: above debate, and beyond history. Just so does Fanny Price rebuke her scoundrel-suitor Henry Crawford in *Mansfield Park:* "We have all a better guide in ourselves, if we would attend to it, than any other person can be."[38] Usage stipulates that equity is a virtue and inequity not, that fairness is better than unfairness, and justice, prudence, temperance, and courage are desirable; but it is also the case that casuistry would lose its meaning without the continued presence of controversy on issues such as whether cruelty is better than kindness *at times.* The brilliance of Jane Austen's reproduction of moral debate lies in its mockery of moralism; the usefulness of history lies in its reconstitution of our memory of specific controversy, bitter quarrel, endless debate. The history of the use of casuistry is interesting, the history of employed moralisms is not.[39]

To insist on history as constituting a shared memory of our confections of moral identity is a restatement of Collingwood's project of a rapprochement of history and philosophy, theory and practice. An intriguing example of successful integration is the project of Alasdair MacIntyre: *After Virtue* could be described as a historicization of ethical theory.[40] MacIntyre, you will remember, developed an opposition between classical ethical theory, which is a theory of virtue, and modern inquiry, which does not have a concept of virtue and therefore does not constitute a proper ethical theory. But classical virtue is very richly specified by MacIntyre as embedded in historical practice. Classical virtue had to invest a narrative unity of life and thus constitute a plausible ethical version of a life;

it had to be efficacious within a life practice—medicine, law, physics—and it had to specify its place in a tradition, the historical continuum of its own society. Ethical competence, then, is tested in historical practice, recollected and projected in lives and periods.

We may usefully compare MacIntyre's historicized ethics with Hare's piece of history moralisée. In Hare's jurisprudential model of ethical decision-making, the utility and moral tone of jurisprudence depends upon the accountability and responsibility of generations of jurists, a linear succession of judges who hold themselves accountable to past scholarship as well as future need.[41] Equity, as a criterion of scholarly discourse, increases the value of memorable constraint, of jurisprudential types of decision. The model constrains us to acknowledge the importance of memory, constrains us to a noncondescending attitude toward the populations of the past—constrains us, simply, to positive as well as negative considerations of past manifestations of moral competence.

To be sure, when history embraces memory as duty, it must divide itself from certain philosophical initiatives at the same time. Consider Rorty's still doggedly philosophical approach. It seems the leopard cannot change his spots. While Rorty holds to the admirable premise of the ubiquity of language, and thus to some primitive sense of sociability, he envisages an investigation which is a parody of philosophical thinness and unsociability. His "culture-critic" is "to play vocabularies and cultures off against each other"; the enjoined acts of comparison and contrast of culture will produce new and better ways of talking and acting. But the sniff of classroom practice conveyed by the phrase 'compare and contrast' signals inconsequence—the better ways will, according to Rorty, "only *seem* better."[42] Hare's jurisprudential model is to be juxtaposed to Rorty's oxymoronic imperative that we must develop a "new Tradition";[43] his post-Philosophical world is a Utopia populated by virtuoso but snotty writers, all succeeding in "getting out from under the mistakes of the past," all looking with "amused condescension" on their forbears.[44]

If we can return now to Kramer's statement that history is too dangerous to be left to its own truths, I think it becomes clear that historical inquiry is not mere descriptivism. The descriptions constrain. In a most brutal and elementary sense, historical memory has its negative, prohibiting, punitive aspects. It is the specificity of the recollection of history which is dangerous, which causes anxiety in Kramer's Frenchmen, in President Nixon contemplating his tapes. It is those calls upon our memory which threaten. Any emphasis on memory is subversive of the manipulations of the moment; the poll, for example, tries to assert the instantaneous importance of the result, relying on its self-transcending capacity. The political function of the poll is not to provide evidence for judgment, but to cancel memory. Perhaps we could develop a phenomenology of memory. Soviet military policy, we are told, is hedged about by its memories of World War II; the Soviet allows its memories too much influence, where poll-ridden America allows long-range memory too little influence.

Kramer's prominent Frenchmen, in short, suffer from the burden of memories which they wish to dismiss. They warn us, therefore, that the serious researcher must have at least as strong a commitment to the constitution of memory as the general public has to its repression.

For even negative thoughts about the past are ethically viable; Williams's expression "creative regrets" points to the uses of a bad past.[45] The historian must not adopt the radical frivolity of Rorty's culture-critic. Rather, he must proceed on the assumption that the communication of the investigative community can be folded into and affect the general communication community. And finally, to admit that history does not edify directly, does not garner moralism from its events, is the same as admitting that the end of history is not the constitution of wisdom. Yet to say that history is "the life of memory" is to claim that history has the peculiar civil obligation, the moral task of the constitution of shared memory; whether this memory is allowed to contribute to wise civil decisions or not may have something to do with historiographical excellence, or may have a lot to do with anti-intellectualist and ideological trends in the receiving public. In either case, history is ineluctably civil, and political, and ethical: "practical," in sum. Oakeshott's notion of history as a purely antiquarian revel, a revel of old ladies and gentlemen in tennis shoes, perhaps, is another Philosopher's dream. The capital P-Philosophers all dream of essences, of course, because to wake is to deal with the messy contingency of the transactions of the social realm—a realm where, if one wakes, one needs to remember yesterday, not the dream.

Notes

1. Cicero, *De oratore*, trans. E. W. Sutton, H. Rackham (Cambridge: Harvard University Press, 1959), 2: 9, 36. The first version of this paper was read at Hobart and William Smith Colleges during my tenure as Mel Hill Visiting Professor, 1983–84.
2. Jane Kramer, "Letter from Europe," *New Yorker*, 16 May 1983, p. 54.
3. J. L. Mackie, *Problems from Locke* (Oxford: Clarendon Press, 1976).
4. Michael Oakeshott, *On History and Other Essays* (New York: Oxford University Press, 1983).
5. Richard Rorty, "The Historiography of Philosophy: Four Genres," in *Philosophy in History*, ed. R. Rorty, J. B. Schneewind, and Q. Skinner (Cambridge: Cambridge University Press, 1984).
6. John J. Richetti, *Philosophical Writing: Locke, Berkeley, Hume* (Cambridge: Harvard University Press, 1983), p. 16.
7. Ibid., p. 9.
8. J. L. Austin, *Sense and Sensibilia* (New York: Oxford University Press, 1962), p. 3.
9. Bernard Williams, *Problems of the Self* (Cambridge: Cambridge University Press, 1973), p. 208.
10. Milton Fisk, "History and Reason in Rawls' Moral Theory," in *Reading Rawls: Critical Studies of a Theory of Justice*, ed. Norman Daniels (New York: Basic Books, n.d.), p. 53.
11. Ibid., p. 75: "The Locke-Kant-Rawls concept of human nature . . . [is] a falsifying abstraction." R. M. Hare, "Rawls' *Theory of Justice*," in *Reading Rawls*, pp. 81–107.
12. Hare, "Rawls' *Theory of Justice*," pp. 86, 97.
13. Ibid., p. 105.
14. Fisk, "History and Reason," p. 60.
15. Richetti, *Philosophical Writing*, p. 7.
16. Hare, "Rawls' *Theory of Justice*," p. 84.
17. Hannah Arendt, *The Life of the Mind: Thinking*, cited in Richetti, *Philosophical Writing*, pp. 26–27.
18. Richard Rorty, *Consequences of Pragmatism* (Minneapolis: University of Minnesota Press, 1983), xxix.
19. K.-O. Apel's account, *Transformation der Philosophie*, trans. G. Adey and D. Frisby as *Towards a Transformation of Philosophy* (London, Harcourt Brace Jovanovich, 1980), is both more generous and more enterprising than Rorty's.
20. Rorty, *Consequences of Pragmatism*, p. xxx.
21. Ibid., pp. 208, xlii.

22. R. G. Collingwood, *An Autobiography*, intro. by S. Toulmin (New York: Oxford University Press, 1978).

23. Ibid., p. 147.

24. Ibid., pp. 148–49: "My notion was that one and the same action, which as action pure and simple was a 'moral' action, was also a 'political' action as action relative to a rule, and at the same time an 'economic' action as means to an end. . . . There were, I held, no merely moral actions, no merely political actions, and no merely economic actions. Every action was moral, political, and economic."

25. Paolo Valesio, in the chapter "Rhetoric, Ideology, and Dialectic," in *Novantiqua: Rhetorics as Contemporary Theory* (Bloomington, Indiana University Press, 1978), pp. 61 ff., contrasts transcendental ideologizing with useful, dialectical investigation that prescribes specificity, defies hypostatization.

26. Williams, *Problems of the Self*, p. 226.

27. R. M. Hare, *Language of Morals* (Oxford: Clarendon Press, 1952), p. 76.

28. This double premise is formulated brilliantly by Pierre Kuentz, "Les 'oublis' de la nouvelle rhetorique," in *Materialités discursives* (Lille: Presse Universitaire, 1981), pp. 35–43.

29. L. Apostel, "Communication et action," in *Le Langage en contexte: Etudes philosophiques et linguistiques de pragmatique*, Linguisticae investigationes, no. 3 (Amsterdam: Benjamins, 1980), pp. 193–315, esp. 260–61.

30. See J. de Romilly, *Histoire et Raison chez Thucydide* (Paris: Les Belles Lettres, 1956); esp. ch. 3, "Les Discours antithetiques," pp. 180 ff.

31. K. H. Stierle, "Histoire comme Exemple, Exemple comme Histoire," *Poetique* 10 (1972): 176–98.

32. Cicero, *De oratore*, trans. E. W. Sutton and H. Rackham, (Cambridge: Harvard University Press, 1959), 2: ix, 36.

33. Williams, *Problems of the Self*, pp. 3–4.

34. Seneca, *De beneficiis*, in *Moral Essays*, trans. J. W. Basore (Cambridge: Harvard University Press, 1975): "De beneficiis dicendum est et ordinanda res, quae maxime humanum societatem alligat," 1.4.2.

35. Ibid., 1.2.4.

36. At qui ingenia sanare et fidem in rebus humanis retinere, memoriam officiorum ingerere animis volunt, serio loquantur et magnis viris agant." Ibid., 1.4.6.

37. Quentin Skinner, "The Idea of Negative Liberty: Philosophical and Historical Perspectives," in *Philosophy in History* forthcoming.

38. Jane Austen, *Mansfield Park*, (London: J. M. Dent & Sons, 1934), p. 361.

39. See Stanley Cavell, *The Claim of Reason* (New York: Oxford University Press, 1979), p. 307; "No rule or principle could function in a moral context the way regulatory or defining rules function in games. It is as essential to the form of life called morality that rules so conceived be absent as it is essential to the form of life we call a game that they be present." Cited in Rorty, *Consequences of Pragmatism*, pp. 185–86.

40. Alasdair MacIntyre, *After Virtue: A Study in Moral Theory* (Notre Dame: Notre Dame University Press, 1981); see especially chs. 14 and 15, "The Nature of the

Virtues," and "The Virtues, or the Unity of a Human Life, and the Concept of a Tradition," pp. 169–209.

41. Hare, *Language of Morals*, p. 76.
42. Rorty, *Consequences of Pragmatism*, pp. xxvii, xl.
43. Ibid., p. xxx.
44. Ibid., pp. 208, xxx.
45. Williams, *Problems of the Self*, p. 175.

PART 2 On History and Its Uses

The Place of History in Nietzsche's Thought

Ofelia Schutte

In his opening remarks to the *Meditation on History,* Nietzsche reflects on the beasts of the field:

> Consider the herd grazing before you. These animals do not know what yesterday and today are but leap about, eat, rest, digest, and eat again, . . . only briefly concerned with their pleasure and displeasure; enthralled by the moment and for that reason neither melancholy nor bored. It is hard for a man to see this, for he is proud of being human and not an animal and yet regards its happiness with envy because he wants nothing other than to live like the animal, neither bored nor in pain, yet wants it in vain because he does not want it like the animal. Man may well ask the animal: why do you not speak to me of your happiness but only look at me? The animal does not want to answer and say: because I always immediately forget what I wanted to say—but then it already forgot this answer and remained silent: so that man could only wonder.[1]

These words speak of the inevitability of addressing the meaning of memory, and therefore of history, in human life. Nietzsche argues that what distinguishes humanity from the animals is precisely the sense of wonder that makes human beings attentive to the remembrance of the past, even if at times they may prefer not to bear the burden of their history. Out of an imagined face-to-face encounter between human being and animal, between historical and unhistorical consciousness, Nietzsche weaves the theme of his *Meditation,* namely, what would an absence of history mean in a human life—or stated more objectively, what is the advantage or disadvantage of history for life?

The Historical Sense in Nietzsche's Epistemology

Let our first question be, According to Nietzsche, what can a historical perspective contribute to philosophical knowledge? If this question is approached from a Nietzschean perspective, our first task is to distinguish between authentic and inauthentic knowledge. The question may be rephrased as, What is an authentic as opposed to an inauthentic use of history, for the philosopher? This reformulation of the question places Nietzsche's analysis of history within a complex set of theoretical assumptions, particularly his own views on ontology and anthropology, which are the parameters setting the context and boundaries of his analysis.

In dealing with Nietzsche's epistemology, some prefatory observations are appropriate. Unlike most philosophers, Nietzsche does not favor the use of a scientific, rational perspective as the ultimate authority on human knowledge. In this he differs most significantly from Hegel, his great predecessor in German philosophy; interpretations that tend to liken Nietzsche's thought to Hegel's miss this point.[2] As many contemporary critics have suggested, reality for Nietzsche can be likened to a text whose interpretation bears no absolute meaning and, in any event, has no absolute closure.[3] As I have argued elsewhere, rationality as such, in abstraction from life, does not constitute a test of truth for Nietzsche.[4] Throughout his works Nietzsche pursues what one may call an integral theory of interpretation from the standpoint of the interpreter and an intertextual theory of interpretation from the standpoint of what is interpreted. In these terms, authentic philosophers would evaluate the meaning and role of historical knowledge through a combination of their human faculties and not through the exclusive use of reason. Similarly, they would consider any version of history produced within a given culture intertextually—that is, as one of many texts that could be written at a given time—in relationship to the written and oral traditions of a given period.

Whether Nietzsche is ultimately correct in holding these views is not the object of my analysis. Rather, its aim is to develop Nietzsche's thoughts in a coherent manner. Briefly stated, the polemic between Nietzsche and Hegel rests on one unresolvable conflict, namely, that for Nietzsche, reality (as known by the human mind) cannot be reduced to facts, while for Hegel, it cannot be reduced to fiction. What the Hegelian philosopher calls world history (historical reality as known and determined by reason), Nietzsche calls interpretation, illusion. This basic criticism of Hegel, as well as Nietzsche's other thoughts on history, underwent several transformations throughout the course of his writings.

The development of Nietzsche's theory may be divided into three stages:

Stage 1, the period of the *Untimely Meditations*, including the *Meditation on History;*

Stage 2, the period of *Human, All Too Human* and *Daybreak;*

Stage 3, the period of *Zarathustra* and beyond, including the studies on the will to power and the genealogy of morals.

Stage 1: The Meditation on History

Part 2 of Nietzsche's *Untimely Meditations*, entitled *On the Advantage and Disadvantage of History for Life*, was first published in 1874. A sequel to part 1, *David Strauss, the Confessor and Writer* (1873), it was followed by two other essays, *Schopenhauer as Educator* (1874) and *Richard Wagner in Bayreuth* (1876). At this stage in his life Nietzsche was strongly influenced by the philosophy of Schopenhauer. The meditation on history presents a silent tribute to Schopenhauer at the same time that it openly challenges Hegelian thought. The key move made by the young Nietzsche was to change the terms of the Hegelian question, What is the relationship between history and philosophy? to a Schopenhaurian question, namely, What can a knowledge of history contribute to the meaning of life? To understand Nietzsche's maneuvering of these two questions and, in particular, the embellishment of Schopenhauer achieved in the course of repudiating Hegel, it is important to review Schopenhauer's departure from the rationalistic optimism of the time.

In *The World as Will and Representation* (1819), Schopenhauer argued that the will-to-live is ineradicably mixed with cruelty, given that the desire to survive makes each living organism kill or destroy other life forms in order to guarantee its own life.[5] He concluded that nothing that lives is innocent. Existence is tainted with metaphysical guilt, and so, in a sense, whatever is alive rightfully deserves to perish. Because everything perishes or deserves to perish, this theory questions whether there is anything truly valuable in life. To this Schopenhauer had responded that the works of artistic genius and of exceptionally great men had a high, even if ultimately transitory, value.

Influenced by Schopenhauer's metaphysics, the young Nietzsche of *The Birth of Tragedy* claimed that only as an aesthetic phenomenon could existence be justified.[6] But this left open the question of *human* existence—could it be justified? Nietzsche's answer was to apply to human specimens the same criterion giving value to art. In the *Meditation on History,* he therefore argued that humanity could be justified in its highest specimens, in its works of genius and of great personages, that is, in everything that is exceptional when seen from the far-distant standpoint of eternity.

The view that all of existence suffers from metaphysical guilt is profoundly nihilistic. Nietzsche later came to repudiate this position, arguing for an alternative metaphysical perspective which he characterized metaphorically as "the innocence of becoming."[7] What he did not give up, however, is the view about human nature, itself also largely nihilistic, which claims that human existence as such is justifiable only through the work or artistic production of great and exceptional human beings.[8] Assuming one is not an exceptional person, then, what comfort could one derive from life? Here Nietzsche found a useful application for the study of history. His reasoning, which is not entirely explicit, is that if one is not to sink into despair for failing, as an individual, to attain an exalted status, one needs to believe in models of humanity which one may strive to imitate in one's life. In addition, one must practice the virtue of modesty in reminding oneself that perhaps, in spite of all of one's striving, one may never reach these heights reserved for exceptional persons. The themes of the third and fourth meditations ("Schopenhauer as Educator" and "Richard Wagner in Bayreuth") show that Schopenhauer exemplified such a man to Nietzsche and, to a great extent, so did Wagner. Within this context of human beings who felt insecure about their human, all-too-human worth and who needed great figures as models of inspiration so as not to sink into existential despair about their own vulnerable and questionable humanity, we may place Nietzsche's most important definition, in the early stage of his career, of the place of history in human knowledge. Thus he argued that the study of history is valuable as an opportunity for self-enrichment because it provides one with a positive view of one's heritage and, more importantly, it provides *models of great human beings* whose exceptional life and works one could imitate (*UMH*, pp. 14–17).

Within this theoretical plane it is easy to recognize the role assigned by Nietzsche to (a) monumental, (b) antiquarian, and (c) critical history, the three types of historical knowledge which in the *Meditation* he claimed to be advantageous for life (*UMH*, pp. 14–22). Monumental history provides the present-day man who is "active and striving" with models of inspiration from the past whom he can imitate to fulfill the value of his own humanity. Antiquarian history provides another type of service, that of making such a man proud of his origins by giving him stability regarding his roots and by nurturing an attitude of admiration and reverence for his past and that of his people. Lest we stay too captivated by the past, lest the past become a cage out of which present-day persons could not step without risking self-destruction, Nietzsche adds one last category of the type of history that can be useful to life. This is critical history, which he describes in Schopenhauerian terms by stating that while it involves negating the past—sometimes even a total negation, as might take place in a revolution— such a negation is justified because everything that enters life at any point also deserves to perish.

So far, Nietzsche's indebtedness to Schopenhauer's ethical nihilism has been emphasized. There are other, more positive aspects of Nietzsche's debt that deserve to be mentioned. Chief among them is Nietzsche's decision to situate the value of history for life as part of a continuum within a range of aesthetically valuable experiences. This point may be explained psychologically, as follows. Taking as a point of departure the individual's state of awareness in time, perception may be understood with respect to three different reference points: the present moment, eternity, and temporality (that is, the passing of time). With respect to the present moment, Nietzsche considers the importance of developing the capacity for awareness of present immediacy, as may be practiced by attending to present experience, without the mediation of categories such as past and future. To refer to this state of mind Nietzsche used the category of 'the unhistorical' (*UMH*, pp. 10–14, 62–64). To the state of mind that imagines what any experience would mean in the light of eternity, Nietzsche applied the category of 'the suprahistorical.' As one might guess, to the state or perspective that gives meaning to a range of experiences in light of the passing of time, Nietzsche applied the category of 'the historical.' These are all aesthetic categories in the *Meditation*, insofar as none of them depend on the discursive use of reason, and all of them depend upon some kind of refinement or sublimation of faculties other than reason per se, such as perception, imagination, and memory. The value of history here is tied to the proper (that is, aesthetic) exercise of memory. Memory is understood as a dimension or aspect of a cognitive process related to perception and imagination, rather than as a faculty acting in subordination to reason. Schopenhauer's emphasis on the suspension of willing and on the contemplative state of awareness achieved in aesthetic experience thus provided the young Nietzsche with an alternative metaphysical ground upon which to locate his assessment of the value of history. Particularly significant here is the contrast between this approach and the exclusively rational ground of values promoted by Hegel and, generally, by traditional philosophy.

From this anthropological perspective, history for Nietzsche is primarily a development of the human memory, or a specific development of the human capacity to remember certain things. History appears in the interplay between memory and forgetfulness, the latter being a state we human beings have in common with animals. (This attribution of forgetfulness to animals is conjectural, but forms part of the structural groundwork of Nietzsche's *Meditation*, as seen by his initial remarks on the disparity between human and animal attitudes toward immediacy.) To dwell in this realm of forgetfulness that Nietzsche links to immediate experience, or to what he labels 'the unhistorical,' is to experience life without the mediation of the historical sense. In Nietzsche's schema the structure of history as a narrative text results from the interplay of perception, imagination, and memory, while it is this interplay of faculties that determines to what extent history may be said to serve life. Nietzsche's application of this method to the analysis of history has been characterized above as the liberation of the historical sense from an exclusive dependence on reason as its sole legitimating faculty.

If memory is a properly human capacity, then history is a properly human activity, for history is the organized, systematic use of memory, which a people uses to enhance its own life. Like Hegel, but for very different reasons, Nietzsche distinguishes between history as an academic discipline or a scientific pursuit and history as the living body of beliefs held by a people about its past.[9] In neither sense is history a matter of pure knowledge to Nietzsche; but obviously in both cases history counts as an interpretation of life in the service of specific interests. Thus Nietzsche begins to tread a path different from that of both Schopenhauer and Hegel. He differs from Schopenhauer by accepting knowledge as determined by interests, in contrast to Schopenhauer's ideal of the self as a pure subject of knowledge, devoid of will. And he differs from Hegel by supporting the legitimacy of extrarational interests at the foundation of history and life. I have spoken sufficiently of Nietzsche's relationship to Schopenhauer. Let me briefly turn now to Nietzsche's challenge of the Hegelian conception of history, based on the claim that the interests served by the Hegelian interpretation are too narrow to do justice to the thriving multiplicity of contexts which may be collectively referred to as life.

Hegel on Reason and History

Claiming that reason "is its own sole precondition, and its end is the absolute and ultimate end of everything," and, moreover, that reason "is itself the agent which implements and realizes this end," Hegel argued in the 1830 draft of his introduction to the *Lectures on the Philosophy of World History* that the one and only premise of his philosophy of history is "the idea that reason governs the world, and that world history is therefore a rational process.[10] As he explains it: "That world history is governed by an absolute design, that it is a rational process—whose rationality is not that of a particular subject, but a divine and absolute reason—

this is a proposition whose truth we must assume; its proof lies in the study of world history itself, which is the image and enactment of reason" (p. 28). As those who are familiar with Hegel's work are aware, these views led him to believe that the design of reason in history had culminated in European culture as a whole and in the specific political supremacy of the German nation, in particular. Believing that he spoke from the standpoint of absolute reason, Hegel criticized everything and anything that did not meet his expectations of what is reasonable. For example, of the government of the United States of America Hegel observed that it had not yet reached its rational perfection, since it had not yet discovered the need for a monarchy (p. 169). Of the inhabitants of America at the time of the European discovery of the New World, Hegel declared that native Americans were weak and imperfect specimens of humanity. Of the entire flora and fauna of the Americas, he held the same view, namely, that all of it was inferior to plants and animals found in Europe. "Even the animals show the same inferiority as the human beings," declared Hegel, representing what he took to be the voice of absolute reason in history. "We are even assured that the animals [in America] are not as nourishing as the food which the Old World provides." Hegel dismissed the evidence of high developments of cultural life in Mexico and Peru, saying that all of this reflected only a natural culture "which had to perish as soon as the spirit [that is, the European conquerors] approached it" (p. 163).

This is not the place to criticize Hegel for a series of prejudices that were widely held in his time, and which he thus mistook for the universal voice of reason. The point Nietzsche was to make about all of this is that if one does not begin with a faith in Absolute Reason and its agency in history (as Hegel did), then one is less likely to fall into the error of believing that one's interpretation of history, or history as one knows it, constitutes a record of what counts as rational for the Absolute. Morally speaking, the virtue Nietzsche recommended to the Hegelians of his time was modesty. Epistemologically, he criticized precisely those structural aspects or limitations of Hegelian reasoning which led Hegel and his followers to believe they were speaking for the universal and the absolute. Moreover, the view that world history somehow culminates in one's own age is something that Nietzsche perceived as a narrow and idiosyncratic understanding of reality. As such, it was something that thwarted the development of human life. As he eloquently puts it in the *Meditation,* by excessively emphasizing the opposition between civilization and barbarism, or between reason and nature, an age incurs the danger of considering itself more just than any other age (*UMH*, p. 25). It considers itself older, wiser, a higher manifestation of reason. Such an age, Nietzsche believed, is ultimately more prone to promote cynicism and egoism. It lapses into deterioration and weakness, believing that it possesses the last word on the knowledge of world history. Nietzsche charged that an age that believes it has seen everything obstructs its own future, especially that of its youth, who are trapped in a cultural universe devoid of the desire for new challenges (*UMH*, pp. 38, 47–49, 58–64).

In place of the Hegelian historical sense and its product of reasoning, "world history," Nietzsche proposed a tripartite perspective for understanding human affairs in relationship to the passing of time. I have already alluded to these three layers of understanding, which he called the unhistorical, historical, and suprahistorical perspectives. In the *Meditation on History* he argued that these three perspectives, or rather, a combination of the three, provided an integral vision of human reality of which humanity would be deprived if it followed the historical sense in an excessive way.

To conclude this analysis of Nietzsche's *Meditation,* we note that his essay constitutes an argument for an antireductionistic model of knowledge as well as for an antireductionistic conception of history. Its aim is not to destroy the historical sense but to give it a place, that is, to situate it in the context of other human activities. The ultimate context determining the ground of all values is what one might call the light of eternity, symbolized at this stage in Nietzsche's career by the suprahistorical perspective inherent in art, religion, and philosophy. Philosophy, in this sense, is both separate from and different in kind from history as an epistemological activity, since philosophy is defined by Nietzsche as the search for an eternal wisdom, while history is concerned with temporal knowledge—namely, knowledge of the past. Art, religion, and authentic philosophy are thus expressions of the suprahistorical perspective through which alone humanity can fulfill its highest aims.

Stage 2: Human, All Too Human and Daybreak

Nietzsche's first departure from the views outlined above is to change his assessment of the relationship between history and philosophy. The specific change is in favor of history, in favor of integrating historical and philosophical knowledge in a way he had not envisioned in the *Meditations*. There is a clear contrast between the position argued in the *Meditations* and statements from Nietzsche's next productive period. In his *Meditation on Schopenhauer* (1874), for example, Nietzsche had argued that "the learned history of the past has never been the business of a true philosopher, neither in India nor in Greece, and if a professor of philosophy involves himself in such work he must at best be content to have it said of him: he is a fine classical scholar, antiquarian, linguist, historian—but never: he is a philosopher."[11] On the other hand, in the opening statements of *Human, All Too Human* (1878), we read that "a lack of historical sense is the congenital defect of all philosophers.[12] Here it would be appropriate to mention that Nietzsche is also throwing some arrows at Hegelian philosophers, apparently for their lack of historical sense. In particular, he condemns the view that treats the human being of the last four thousand years (as he puts it) as if he or she were eternal: "But everything has evolved: there are no *eternal facts*, nor are there any absolute truths. Thus *historical philosophizing* is necessary henceforth, and the virtue of modesty as well" (pp. 14–15).

At the same time that Nietzsche argues for the necessity of a historical perspective in understanding human evolution, he criticizes those who all too quickly circumscribe the whole of world history to the last four thousand years. Repeating a point he had made earlier in the *Meditations*, he warns that "present day man" (who is a product of Prussia and all that this implies) cannot be taken as a universal. In arguing for the historical sense, Nietzsche's intent is to expand human consciousness to the reality of spans of millennia, as opposed to focusing attention on a unilinear record of development covering a few thousand years. Nietzsche's reassessment of the historical sense would thus embrace what is generally considered prehistory as well as much that falls outside history. Another way of stating this would be to say that history should pay special attention to the findings of the rest of the sciences, particularly the biological and social sciences—among the latter, cultural anthropology.

A second and important change to be noted in Nietzsche's revised assessment of the relationship between history and philosophy is his explicit demand for the need to maintain a critical perspective vis-à-vis history. Nietzsche reminds his contemporaries that history is not a pure science. Even in its scientific character, history is an interpretation of reality. When this is not noticed, especially by experts and scholars who control the field, the consequences range from the spreading of ignorance and prejudice to a special arrogance about the status of one's knowledge of the past. Nietzsche called attention to abuses of historical knowledge, which he attributed to the failure on the part of educators and scholars to be sufficiently self-critical. In *Daybreak* (1881) he warns:

> Nothing grows clearer to me year by year than that the nature of the Greeks and of antiquity, however simple and universally familiar it may seem to be before us, is very hard to understand, indeed is hardly accessible at all, and that the facility with which the ancients are spoken of is either a piece of frivolity or . . . thoughtlessness. We are deceived by a similarity of words and concepts, but behind them there always lies concealed a situation which *has to be* foreign, incomprehensible or painful to modern sensibility.[13]

Later on in the same work, referring to "so-called world history," he notes that "all historians speak of things which have never existed except in imagination" (p. 156). In other words, as he had already observed in the *Meditation*, history is always rooted in an attempt to use the past in such a way as to interpret the present and influence the future. Moreover, as his warning about our common misunderstanding of past and foreign cultures has shown, to hold a nonperspectival or an uncritical view of history is tantamount to the promotion of ignorance. Thus in the second phase of his work Nietzsche suggests that an authentic alliance between history and philosophy is possible as long as each exercises a disciplined practice of self-criticism with respect to its method and scope. We witness here a process typical of Nietzsche's own development as a philosopher, that is, his demand for self-criticism in human knowledge. This brings us to his mature works, particularly *Thus Spoke Zarathustra* (1883–85), *Beyond Good and Evil* (1886), and *On the Genealogy of Morals* (1887). One of the virtues of the historical sense, as Nietzsche puts it in *Beyond Good and Evil*, is to learn from its own limitations that it must make room for other approaches to knowledge.[14]

Stage 3: Zarathustra *and Beyond*

Due to limitations of space, it is not possible here to review in detail the place Nietzsche assigns to history in his mature and late works.[15] One may note, however, that apparently as a result of having been struck by the idea of the eternal recurrence, Nietzsche's attention shifts away from the role of history as a branch of knowledge, focusing sharply instead on the potential role of human beings in history as agents of historical transformation. With the dawning of the will-to-power theory in *Thus Spoke Zarathustra*, Nietzsche's orientation effectively turns into that of an activist, in addition to a critic of cultural values. This turn to activism is well disguised. Many are the passages in *Thus Spoke Zarathustra* where the teacher of the *Übermensch* and the eternal recurrence falls into a deep despair, resulting in prolonged periods of inaction. Yet the prevailing theme of this work is that of the return of life to life, the constant activity of the will to power, which ultimately moves all of history.[16]

Nietzsche's turn toward a conceptual activism is also well disguised in the genealogical method of interpretation, best developed by him in *On the Genealogy of Morals* (1887). Here he appears to be offering a philosophical alternative to a purely historical interpretation of the origin of values. The question, "Where does X originate?" used repeatedly by Nietzsche to analyze the meaning of guilt, belief in truth, virtue, and so on, is an interpretive device enabling him to distract the psychological attention of his readers from one set of values to another. The genealogical method functions as the theoretical component of a practical desire on Nietzsche's part to effect a transvaluation of all values, as he himself suggests toward the end of this essay.[17] Such a transvaluation, if followed in all of its implications, would amount to no less than a cultural revolution within the prevailing Western European culture.

With regard to these changes attributed to Nietzsche's late thought, someone might point out that what appear to be new elements in his late period essentially amount to a few reelaborations of important elements already found in his early works. For example, the desire for a radically different cultural environment than that of modernity, one in which the artist, genius, or educator could thrive in the practice of his work, is a theme informing the whole of *The Birth of Tragedy* as well as the *Untimely Meditations*. The inspiration leading to *Thus Spoke Zarathustra*—the thought of the eternal recurrence, which Nietzsche said he received "6000 feet beyond man and time"[18]—could simply be one more attempt to locate his perspective in a suprahistorical context, as had been his earlier attempts to claim a status superior to that of his contemporaries based on his intimate acquaintance with Wagner's art and Schopenhauer's philosophy. Indeed, there is such a line of continuity in Nietzsche's work. One might note that while there was a brief interval, during the time of *Human, All Too Human* and *Daybreak*, when Nietzsche achieved the closest reconciliation between philosophy and history, in fact this phase was short lived. It ended with a moment in which history, demanding its own self-criticism, simply made room for a yet more passionate drive on the part of Nietzsche to root his philosophy in a suprahistorical or eternal context.

These observations are valid, especially insofar as they serve to shed light on the patterns of continuity to be found throughout Nietzsche's works. Yet the notion of a will-to-power-in-history overcoming itself completely into a state of transcendence beyond history and then, out of the power gathered there, initiating a reentry into history that would altogether transform the shape of the future world, is a new idea of Nietzsche's Zarathustra. It differs from Nietzsche's search for an instinctual foundation of art in *The Birth of Tragedy* (where he is also looking for a source of value outside of history) by positing the radical separation of the will to power from history as opposed to the continuity, stressed in his first work, between the human artistic instincts and historical achievement. Moreover, the Zarathustra-idea is one whose structure constitutes a parody of the Christian doctrine of the Incarnation, where the motion of the divine will is from eternity into history and back to eternity rather than from history to the suprahistorical, and from there back to history and time, as Zarathustra's case exemplifies.

To come to terms with the place of history in Nietzsche's late thought we therefore need a new category as the focus of our analysis. I will label such a category "the will to power in history." The aim of this will to power (if it has an aim) is, as I have mentioned, to effect a transvaluation of all values or a cultural revolution. For Nietzsche, this cultural revolution would have consisted of a rejection of slave values in favor of creative, autonomous values—words that sound simple when put on a page but whose implications are as deeply enlightening as they are problematic.[19]

The procedure through which Nietzsche envisioned the steps of this revolution involved, first, a separation of the will to power from history and, second, its triumphal reentry into historical space. The first step may be characterized as an exodus of the will to power from its current historical base. In his own case this implied a separation of the philosopher from the historical activity applicable to life in nineteenth-century Germany. The notion of exodus helps to explain the journey and destiny of Nietzsche's Zarathustra, that is, his flight to the mountains, his attempts to elevate present-day humanity to these heights, his failure in this attempt, and his eventual refuge in solitude. What this will to power wishes to leave behind in historical space are the democratic or so-called plebeian movements of modernity, most of whose faults Nietzsche saw all too clearly and therefore abhorred. His exodus was toward the mountains, symbols of eternity and of the suprahistorical in Nietzsche's figurative writing. Zarathustra's speeches are intended as parables of spiritual elevation. They are meant to inspire in Nietzsche's readers a sense of destiny more powerful than the force of history itself. Yet the second movement of this will to power which takes partial leave from history is to return to history with such a force gained from the period of separation as to radically transform the future of human beings. The will to power of which Nietzsche speaks emerges on the horizon of the present moment as the creator of its historical future. In this way the relationship between the philosopher and history is no longer confined to the analysis of the past and to an enlightened understanding of the present, but now extends into the task of forging a specific type of future, a future whose political structure would in all likelihood conform as much as possible to the level of creativity inherent in this will.

The reentry into history of this elevated will to power is accompanied by a message of resistance against all structures of the old slave morality. The power involved in this act of reentry is characterized by Zarathustra as a flash of lightning that breaks open the future of humanity for possibilities other than those known under the current domain of the slave consciousness.[20] Nietzsche believed that anyone who had truly understood the message of his Zarathustra would be able to "cut the history of humanity in half," as he puts it in *Ecce Homo*.[21] He envisioned a psychological and cultural revolution brought about by the rejection of slave values—the rejection of a life of systematic underdevelopment for human beings—and, on the positive side, by the affirmation of a different world in which human life would be one of creative development marked by the courage to face existential challenges and to take the appropriate existential actions and risks.

Contradictions

In bringing to a conclusion this analysis of the place of history in Nietzsche's thought, a brief mention must be made of some contradictions contained between the perspective I have attributed to him and the status of his work, which at times negates this perspective. Two issues are at stake: (1) what it means to reject or transcend a slave consciousness, and (2) what it means to give up a belief in the Absolute. I have followed Nietzsche's claims in arguing against both the slave consciousness and the Absolute. Yet there remain some unresolvable contradictions regarding these is-sues unless one were to delete or modify specific portions of Nietz-sche's arguments.

The conflict between, on the one hand, Nietzsche's rejection of a slave morality, and, on the other, his own endorsement of values which took slavery and other forms of domination for granted, can-not be ignored. I have addressed the nature and implications of this problem elsewhere.[22] Here it is relevant to mention that such a problem arises for Nietzsche because he leads his readers to believe that the symptoms of slave morality (such as envy, *ressentiment*, reactive thinking, measuring oneself vis-à-vis the achievements of the other) are transcended in his theories of the will to power and the transvaluation of all values. Yet a philosopher's theoretical em-phasis on liberating philosophy as well as the new history from the domain of slave values does not guarantee that such a liberation actually is achieved in his or her own work. This was the case with Nietzsche. He did not appear to be aware that the master morality he advocated as an alternative to slave morality is as much a part of the slave consciousness as the *ressentiment* he criticized in the latter. For this reason, as I have argued elsewhere, if one wishes to be rid of slave morality, one has to move entirely beyond the mas-ter/slave dichotomy—a perspective that Nietzsche reaches only in some of the more metaphorical or poetical expressions of the *Über-mensch* and will-to-power ideas. Insofar as Nietzsche chose to make concrete statements about the higher politics (*grosse Politik*) that ought to rule the world, he did not transcend the ideology of domination which an important part of his philosophical project sought to oppose. He therefore stopped short of the full implica-tions of the message carried by Zarathustra, when he sought to open new horizons for human creativity through the metaphor of the death of God.

Secondly, another conflict or contradiction appears in relation to Nietzsche's rejection of reason as an absolute, especially as this affects the distinction between authentic and inauthentic knowl-edge implied by it. In the context of the emphasis given earlier to the perspectival, intertextual method of interpretation employed by Nietzsche, the question arises as to the status of those views which he sometimes claimed were the official text of destiny. The force of destiny to which Nietzsche appealed is not identical to the power of Absolute Reason. In his view, destiny is an extrarational force, marked by a high dose of irrationality. Yet the identification of a particular philosophical perspective with such a force, irrational as it may be, is structurally analogous to Hegel's identification of a particular philosophical perspective with the universal, absolute voice of reason. In each case the philosopher closes himself off from historical vulnerability as well as criticism by believing that if he grounds his perspective on an extrahuman standard, such a standard will be an absolute one which will remain valid for all time, at the very least as the principle that always generates valid temporal truths. Nietzsche, himself a critic of the Absolute, fails to remain consistent in his critique of absolute values to the extent that he reintroduces privileged theories under the claim that these represent a triumphant movement in the forces of destiny governing the universe. Such metaphysical reifications of philosophical theories, whether they are rationalist or irrationalist, and whether espoused by Hegel or by Nietzsche, have little place within a philosophy that practices self-criticism and that adopts an attitude of modesty before history, as Nietzsche himself advocated during the more critical periods of his thought.

Despite these contradictions, however, Nietzsche's philosophical work stands out for its perceptive contribution to the analysis of what the presence of history—the fact that human beings are historically rooted—adds to human life. He pondered the best and the worst that would happen to humanity if it were to live unhistorically, without a sense of memory or the capacity to understand the present in terms of the past. Not convinced that history would prove to define the end of all knowledge, Nietzsche gave history a limited yet valuable place in the philosopher's quest for knowledge, especially insofar as the knowledge of history would prove to be of service to life. For a people, too, Nietzsche held that history was an invaluable tool for the comprehension of its own past. But, as I have shown, there is also another side to Nietzsche, a side that was not content with the cultural world of which he was a historical inhabitant. For this reason he sought every means within his theoretical grasp to argue for a transformation of his historical environment. Failing to achieve immediate success in his lifetime, he contemplated the hope that these changes would be brought about by future generations. It is up to his readers to take up his challenge.

Notes

1. Friedrich Nietzsche, *On the Advantage and Disadvantage of History for Life* (1874), part 2 of *Untimely Meditations*, trans. Peter Preuss (Indianapolis: Hackett Publishing Company, 1980), p. 8. Hereafter cited as *UMH*. For the most complete German edition of Nietzsche's published works as well as the *Nachlass*, see Giorgio Colli and Mazzino Montinari, eds., *Nietzsche Werke: Kritische Gesamtausgabe*, 20 vols. (Berlin and New York: Walter de Gruyter, 1967–82).

2. One of the most influential readings of this kind has been Walter Kaufmann's. See his *Nietzsche: Philosopher, Psychologist, Antichrist*, 4th ed. (Princeton: Princeton University Press, 1974). One may note the high proportion of space devoted to Hegelian concepts in Kaufmann's interpretation of Nietzsche.

3. See, among others: Bernd Magnus, *Nietzsche's Existential Imperative* (Bloomington: Indiana University Press, 1978); Gilles Deleuze, *Nietzsche and Philosophy* (New York: Columbia University Press, 1983); David Allison, ed., *The New Nietzsche: Contemporary Styles of Interpretation* (New York: Delta Books, 1977); Jacques Derrida, *Spurs: Nietzsche's Styles*, trans. Barbara Harlow (Chicago: University of Chicago Press, 1979). Cf. David Hoy, *The Hermeneutic Circle: Literature, History, and Philosophical Hermeneutics* (Berkeley and Los Angeles: University of California Press, 1978).

4. Ofelia Schutte, *Beyond Nihilism: Nietzsche Without Masks* (Chicago: University of Chicago Press, 1984), pp. 21–28.

5. Arthur Schopenhauer, *The World as Will and Representation*, trans. E. F. J. Payne (New York: Dover Publications, 1969), 1:146–48.

6. Friedrich Nietzsche, *The Birth of Tragedy* (1872), trans. Walter Kaufmann, in *The Birth of Tragedy* and *The Case of Wagner* (New York: Vintage Books, 1967), pp. 52, 141.

7. Friedrich Nietzsche, *Twilight of the Idols* (1889), trans. R. J. Hollingdale, in *Twilight of the Idols* and *The Antichrist* (New York: Penguin Books, 1968), p. 54.

8. Nietzsche's arguments for a higher culture and a master morality implicitly carry this theme.

9. *UMH*, pp. 14, 23, and 58–64. Cf. G. W. F. Hegel, *Lectures on the Philosophy of World History*, trans. from the German edition of J. Hoffmeister by H. B. Nisbet (Cambridge: Cambridge University Press, 1975), pp. 29–31. Hegel argued that professional historians were not sufficiently rational, while Nietzsche regarded them as excessively scientific.

10. Hegel, *Lectures*, p. 27. This reference is to Hegel's manuscript. Subsequent references are to the student notes comprising portions of the text. Defenders of

Hegel claim that he has been misunderstood in his argument that reason rules world history. See Duncan Forbes's introduction to the *Lectures*, pp. xii–xv.

11. Friedrich Nietzsche, *Schopenhauer as Educator*, in *Untimely Meditations*, trans. R. J. Hollingdale (Cambridge: Cambridge University Press, 1983), p. 186.

12. Friedrich Nietzsche, *Human, All Too Human*, trans. Marion Faber (Lincoln: University of Nebraska Press, 1984), p. 14.

13. Friedrich Nietzsche, *Daybreak*, trans. R. J. Hollingdale (Cambridge: Cambridge University Press, 1982), p. 116.

14. Friedrich Nietzsche, *Beyond Good and Evil* (1886), trans. Walter Kaufmann (New York: Vintage Books, 1966), p. 152.

15. Such an analysis would entail a discussion of several complex questions, among them: the role given to history in relation to the ideas of the will to power, the *Übermensch*, and the eternal recurrence; Nietzsche's use of history in his analysis of the higher culture; the relationship between the historical sense and the genealogical method; and the role of memory in human evolution and in the transition to the *Übermensch*.

16. Friedrich Nietzsche, *Thus Spoke Zarathustra* (1883–85), trans. Walter Kaufmann (New York: Viking Press, 1954), pp. 113–16, 215–21, and 224–28.

17. Friedrich Nietzsche, *On the Genealogy of Morals*, trans. Walter Kaufmann and R. J. Hollingdale, in *On the Genealogy of Morals* and *Ecce Homo* (New York: Vintage Books, 1967), 3:159–60.

18. Nietzsche, *Ecce Homo*, p. 294.

19. I am referring here not only to Nietzsche's rhetorical call for the death of God and the end of slave morality but to the specific characteristics of his theoretical analysis of these issues.

20. Nietzsche, *Zarathustra*, p. 14.

21. Nietzsche, *Ecce Homo*, section 8.

22. Schutte, *Beyond Nihilism*, pp. 105–93.

Bertrand Russell on History: The Theory and Practice of a Moral Science

Kirk Willis

Of twentieth-century British intellectuals, Bertrand Russell was by any measure the most celebrated and influential. For a full seventy years, from the 1890s through the 1960s, Russell was, in the words of the philosopher Ronald Jager, "a commanding presence both in the Anglo-Saxon philosophical world and on the larger intellectual scene of Europe, as a public figure, storm centre, foe of orthodoxy, [and] friend of mankind."[1] His influence and notoriety derived from the astonishing range of his writings, the remarkable scope of his activities, and the contentious nature of his opinions, as well as, more prosaically, the extraordinary length of his life. Philosophical subjects from mathematical logic to aesthetics, popular issues from educational reform to the role of science in society, and public crusades from female suffrage to nuclear disarmament, all commanded his intellectual attention, literary energy, and emotional sympathy. For Russell himself, such diverse interests and disparate commitments, although often jostling together uncomfortably, nonetheless comprised an intellectual and emotional whole; he was at one and the same time a bloodless reasoner, an impassioned moralist, and a defiant crusader. For students of Russell, this same complexity poses a perplexing and challenging problem: how to lace together both his varied interests and the several strands of his personality. Indeed, this is a central question for Russell scholarship: how to join Russell the technical thinker with Russell the popular propagandist and social activist.

There is one area of Russell's work, heretofore almost entirely neglected, which offers an opportunity to make such connections: his writings on history and the philosophy of history.[2] As will be seen, Russell quite consciously viewed his historical writings as an essential part of his social reformism. Through them he sought to refashion the intellectual presuppositions, alter the moral consciences, enlighten the social sensibilities, and modify the political behavior of his readers. Russell believed, in short, that historical study, done properly, was an intellectually demanding, personally inspiriting, culturally redemptive, socially useful, and politically beneficial moral science. Moreover, in the course of these writings, as well as in specific essays on the nature of history, he advanced a philosophy of history that was explicitly intended both to justify this ambition and to recommend it to other historians.

In the pursuit of these aims Russell wrote a great deal of history —far more, indeed, than is usually realized. He published two books of unalloyed history: *The Policy of the Entente 1904–14* (1915), a study of the diplomatic maneuverings of the Great Powers in the decade before the First World War, and *Freedom and Organisation 1814–1914* (1934), a survey of the intellectual, economic, and political history of Western Europe and the United States in the century after Waterloo. Chapters of political and intellectual history appeared in his *German Social Democracy* (1896) and *The Problem of China* (1922); essays on intellectual history were contained in *In Praise of Idleness* (1935) and *Unpopular Essays* (1950); and passages of family and political history were included in *The Amberley Papers*, two volumes of the letters and diaries of his parents, which he coedited and published in 1937.[3] Russell also wrote a classic work on the history of philosophy: the celebrated *History of Western Philosophy* (1945). Finally, he published three essays on the philosophy of history: "On History," written in 1904; "How to Read and Understand History," which appeared in 1943; and "History as an Art," which was printed in 1954. Russell's historical writings, then, were extensive and serious-minded. No mere dilettantism, they addressed—and offered informed solutions to— many of the major philosophical problems in historical study.

History, as an academic subject, an intellectual pastime, and a living force, was important to Bertrand Russell from his earliest childhood. Born into one of the oldest, proudest, and most distinguished families of the Whig aristocracy, Russell became vividly aware at a very young age of his family's past and through this of his nation's history. The Russells, as he was taught by tutors and members of his household, had been one of the first families of the realm since the reign of Henry Tudor. They had, as well, been at the very heart of the Whig kindred since the late seventeenth century, when Russells had led the fight for the Petition of Right, directed parliamentary armies against Charles I, played prominent roles in the Exclusion Controversy and Rye House Plot, and even commanded the ship which, driven by the "Protestant wind," brought William of Orange to England in 1688. Fiercely proud of this heritage and resolutely determined to see it perpetuated, the Russells patiently bequeathed it to each generation. The young Bertrand Russell (b. 1872) was therefore inculcated with the staples of mid-nineteenth-century aristocratic Whiggism. Not only did he listen to romantic stories of the exploits of his sixteenth- and seventeenth-century forebears and vainglorious tales of the triumphs of seventeenth-century Russells over the forces of Charles I and James II, but he cut his historical teeth on the standard popular Whig histories of the mid- to late nineteenth century. As he later recalled, the instruction he received was "unadulterated indoctrination with as little attempt at impartiality as under any totalitarian régime. Everything was treated from a Whig point of view, and I was told, only half in joke, that history means 'hiss-Tory'."[4]

This early indoctrination in the major tenets of the Whig interpretation of history inculcated in Russell several attitudes toward history which he would never completely abandon. Perhaps most strikingly, he embraced the conviction that history, taken as the sum of human experience, was moving toward ever greater enlightenment and virtue: politics had advanced from tyranny to democracy; morals had improved from barbarism to civility; ideas had progressed from superstition to science. The mechanism of this change, moreover, was not abstract historical "forces," but the combined labor of individual men and women, whether statesmen, moralists, or thinkers. Finally, the schooling in history that Russell received as a young man stressed by example and in theory that historians ought in some measure to reflect, if not to mold, these realities; they ought, that is, to explain the course of progress, to promote the means of continued change, and to focus on the human instruments of social advancement. These were the legacies of Russell's early education in history, and they permanently influenced both his own historical writings and his mature philosophy of history.

Fifty years separated Russell's various essays on the philosophy of history, a half-century—between 1904 and 1954—during which historiographical fashions changed dramatically. Russell's own philosophy of history, however, was scarcely altered by such changes in style. To be sure, in his later essays emphases changed slightly, tones were more muted, and stakes were raised, but the main lines of approach and argumentation remained remarkably consistent with those he set down in 1904. Indeed, the force of Russell's philosophy of history can be viewed as a sustained polemic against these changes (specifically the spread of "scientific," Marxian, and social and economic history, and the condemnation of traditional Whig history), innovations of which Russell was well aware through his own extensive historical research, omnivorous recreational reading, prolific book reviewing, and frequent conversations with friends and acquaintances who were themselves historians, such as G. M. Trevelyan, Sidney and Beatrice Webb, G. D. H. Cole, R. H. Tawney, and J. L. and Barbara Hammond.

Russell's first formal work on the philosophy of history was "On History," a lyrically written and emotionally charged essay which set out all the themes of his mature philosophy of history. The provenance of the essay, published in the *Independent Review* of July 1904, was a request by G. M. Trevelyan, one of the editors of the *Independent* and a friend of Russell's from their undergraduate years at Cambridge.[5] In appealing to Russell for an article on the nature of history, Trevelyan had a definite polemical purpose in mind: to enroll his old friend's literary abilities, intellectual powers, and academic reputation in his own struggle against the growing consensus among professional historians in Britain that history could be made "scientific" through exhaustive archival research, meticulous analysis of sources, and dispassionate presentation of facts. To Trevelyan's mind this was a pernicious doctrine, given its quintessential formulation in J. B. Bury's controversial inaugural lecture as Regius Professor of Modern History at Cambridge in January 1903, which had to be combatted vigorously both within the university community and without.[6] He therefore not only turned his own formidable literary talents to the task, but sought to recruit capable allies as well. "On History" therefore appeared at a time of lively intellectual debate over the nature of history and the future course of historical scholarship in Britain, and it was intended—by both its author and its editor—to make a powerful contribution to that discussion.

"Of all the studies by which men acquire citizenship of the intellectual commonwealth," Russell opened his essay, "no single one is so indispensable as the study of the past." "To know how the world developed to the point at which our individual memory begins," he explained, "how the religions, the institutions, the nations among which we live, became what they are; to be acquainted with the great of other times, with customs and beliefs differing widely from our own—these things are indispensable to any consciousness of our position, and to any emancipation from the accidental circumstances of our education" (p. 76). For Russell, then, historical study not only offers intellectual knowledge but, through comparison and sympathy, promotes social understanding and individual self-awareness, which in their turn lead to compassion and tolerance. History is an essential and, above all else, a *useful* subject of study, one of value "not only to the professed student of archives and documents," but to all thinking men and women who desire to understand their circumstances and to better them (p. 76).

True to the polemical purpose of the essay, Russell began his description of the utility of historical study by insisting upon a negative: the usefulness of history does not derive from any scientific "laws" of human behavior or social change that its practitioners may claim to reveal. To be sure, history does provide approximate parallels and rough analogies helpful to understanding contemporary politics—"that history has great utility in this respect, it is impossible to deny"—but it is necessary "very carefully to limit and define the kind of guidance to be expected from [those parallels and analogies]." Such circumspection is required, Russell cautioned, because of a point of elementary logic consistently overlooked by practicing historians: any notion of "the 'teachings of history' . . . pre-supposes the discovery of causal laws, usually of a very sweeping kind." And the difficulty here, Russell elaborated, is that " 'teachings' of this sort . . . are always theoretically unsound" (p. 78). History is not an inductive science productive of universal laws of human behavior; nor, Russell maintained, can it ever be made such. It is debarred from scientific status because it lacks the two essential traits of all truly scientific subjects: the capacity to test its hypotheses and replicate its results, and the ability to predict future events. To quality as a legitimate historical law, Russell argued, a hypothesis must be shown both to "fit the facts" of past circumstances and to be applicable to any and all future concatenations of similar facts. It must also be demonstrably superior to all alternative hypotheses. In historical study, however, true comparisons and guarantees of universality are not possible. Controlled experiments on the model of physical or biological science cannot be performed; nor can conditions ever be precisely duplicated and findings exactly reproduced. Such trials founder on one unavoidable and irremovable obstacle: the sheer complexity of historical experience. "No broad and simple uniformities are possible," Russell maintained, because "in history, so many circumstances of a small and accidental nature are relevant" (p. 77). History does not repeat itself in every detail, and in scientific enquiry the details are everything. The complexity of the past also makes it impossible to test rival hypotheses with the necessary precision. To conduct a genuinely scientific trial, "it is necessary that two or more hypotheses should have been invented, each accounting for a large number of the facts, and that then a crucial fact should be discovered which discriminates between the rivals." "But," he observed, "it will hardly be maintained that history has reached, or is soon likely to reach, a point where such standards are applicable to its facts" (p. 77). Putative scientific "laws" of history are just not open to repeated experimental verification, and without this capacity they are epistemologically illegitimate and intellectually fraudulent. "Such generalizations as have been suggested" by ambitious historians ignorant of the true nature and methods of science are therefore so indefensible and "so plainly unwarranted as to be not even worthy of refutation." The only authentic "lessons" which history has to offer, Russell concluded, are "minor maxims, whose truth, when they are once propounded, can be seen without the help of the events which suggested them."[7]

Not only is the study of history unable to overcome insurmountable theoretical barriers necessary for scientific status; it also faces an impassable practical obstruction: the bias of the individual historian. Some historians, Russell asserted (taking a swipe at Trevelyan's Oxbridge enemies), believed that through the complete "self-effacement of the historian before the document" they could avoid the "intrusion" of their own personalities, allow the facts "to speak for themselves," and achieve thereby a perfect "objectivity" which they regarded as synonymous with "scientific" (p. 76). In practice, Russell argued, this is an impossible ambition, as well as an improper equation of "scientific" with "objective." It is an unattainable goal because it misrepresents the nature of actual historical study. Working historians, even the most scrupulous among them, do not simply reproduce or report historical facts; they do not, that is, merely reprint documents or offer all-inclusive chronicles. Instead, Russell observed, historians order their evidence, and in so doing give prominence to certain facts, reject others, and treat still others with indifference.

But according to what principles is this ordering done, Russell asked? Certainly not on purely "objective" grounds with "truth" as the sole criterion for selection. There is, after all, nothing to choose between facts "objectively"—"all facts are equally true" (p. 77). But they are not equally significant, and when historians order their facts they do so according to some "standard of value" of their own—a standard which they bring to and impose upon their evidence. And what is this, Russell asked, if not to intrude their personalities on their material and to demonstrate at worst a prejudice and at best a point of view? In either case, it is to have some guiding principle of historical explanation other than the dispassionate presentation of unadorned "truth."[8] Bias, Russell concluded, is therefore an unavoidable part of all historical endeavor, and those historians who claim otherwise—who purport to offer a disinterested, "scientific" approach to, as well as demonstrable laws of, history—are guilty of elementary theoretical and practical misconceptions.

History is necessarily subjective and imperfect; it is not, however, any the less valuable because of those qualities.

Indeed, the usefulness of historical study is considerable. Besides suggesting certain "minor maxims" of political wisdom, historical study provides four major benefits. First, it "enlarges the imagination." Knowledge of the accomplishments and heroism of past generations, Russell claimed, "suggests possibilities of action and feeling which would not have occurred to an uninstructed mind" and "makes visible and living the growth and greatness of nations," thus "enabling us to extend our hopes beyond the span of our own lives." History "relates the present to the past, and thereby the future to the present" and "is capable of giving to statesmanship, and to our daily thoughts, a breadth and scope unattainable by those whose view is limited to the present."[9]

Secondly, an appreciation of history is inspirational; it "fills our thoughts with splendid examples, and with the desire for greater ends than unaided reflection would have discovered." By celebrating the achievements and praising the characters of great men and women, history encourages us to imitation: "The great are not solitary; out of the night come the voices of those who have gone before, clear and courageous; and so through the ages they march, a mighty procession, proud, undaunted, unconquerable." And it is the ambition "to join in this glorious company, to swell the immortal paean of those whom fate could not subdue" that history imparts. And to those who in imagination or in deed succeed in so joining, "to them is given what is better than happiness: to know the fellowship of the great, to live in the inspiration of lofty thoughts, and to illumine in every perplexity by the fire of nobility and truth" (pp. 80–81).

At the same time, and this is Russell's third point, the study of history tempers the arrogance and self-righteousness that all too often accompany such grandiose ambitions. It teaches tolerance, counsels moderation, and provides perspective on our individual conceits by exposing the "curious thinness" of our aspirations in comparison with the achievements of the past. It also offers larger goals than the mere "dominion of Mammon" and finer ends than "Action, Success, [and] Change" (pp. 79–80).

Finally, the study of history is "a defeat of Time." By calling "pictures before our minds, pictures of high endeavours and brave hopes, living still through his care, in spite of failure and death," the historian makes us aware that we are members of the immortal collective "Man." This knowledge, in turn, enables us to "transcend" the "blindness and brevity" of our transient concerns and offers a new meaning to our lives as "all human experience is transformed, and whatever is sordid or personal is purged away" (pp. 80–81). We do not, to be sure, know what that meaning—the ultimate purpose of the life of Man—may be. All we know (and this we should take solace in) is that "we, too, in all our deeds, bear our part in a process of which we cannot guess the development: even the obscurest are actors in a drama of which we know only that it is great. Whether any purpose that we value will be achieved, we cannot tell; but the drama itself, in any case, is full of Titanic grandeur" (p. 81). The knowledge that we play a role, however minor it may be, in such a "Titanic" drama is, according to Russell, both psychologically salutary and socially inspiriting; it inspires us to live an active life, sustains us despite our limitations, and consoles us in our failures. Indeed, "gradually, by the contemplation of great lives, a mystic communion becomes possible, filling the soul like music from an invisible choir."[10]

"On History" delighted its editor and satisfied its author. Trevelyan rejoiced that the essay was "about the best thing we have a chance of publishing in our Review," and remarked with his customary modesty that "your 'History' makes me feel ashamed of the essay I am attempting on the same subject."[11] For his part, Russell also felt comfortable with the essay. He had exposed the pretensions of those who sought to elevate history into a science, and he had made an eloquent case that history, although a "purely descriptive" study, was nonetheless productive of much practical wisdom and moral counsel (p. 77). Indeed, perhaps the most striking feature of the essay is Russell's absolute certainty on this score. His statements about the general benefits of historical study and, specifically, about its compelling power to change our behavior for the better are not conditional but categorical: admiration of the deeds of past great men and women must inspire us to similar achievements; awareness of our shared experience and common heritage must prompt us to behave with tolerance and empathy toward others; knowledge of the sweep of the historical past necessarily provides us with a healthy perspective on our own lives as well as with a profound sense of worth. In every case, an appreciation of history will necessarily enter into "our daily thoughts" and give us political judgment, personal inspiration, and social awareness. That historical study would improve us, Russell, in 1904, had no doubts whatsoever.

By the time he came to write his two other essays on the philosophy of history—"How to Read and Understand History" (1943) and "History as an Art" (1954)—forty years later, Russell's belief in the benefits to be gained from historical study remained strong, although no longer completely unquestioned. In both these essays he reaffirmed his conviction that an appreciation of history is "an essential part of the furniture of the educated mind" as well as a means to human enlightenment and a precondition for social reform.[12] Indeed, he repeated in detail the litany of benefits produced by historical study that he had earlier advanced in "On History." In "History as an Art" he declared that history gives "a new dimension [to] the individual life, a sense of being a drop in a great river rather than a tightly bound separate entity."[13] History offers comparison with other individuals and past civilizations and thereby provides perspective on our individual lives and those of our community, nation, and race; this perspective, in turn, brings "sanity to our intoxicated" species (p. 191). History argues against the damnable "cock-sure certainty" of the young, the ambitious, and the fanatic that is "the source of much that is worst in our present world" and teaches, by contrast, the invaluable lessons that "tragedy comes of hubris" and that "so much that was thought wisdom turned out to be folly" (pp. 182, 191). Finally, since "heroic lives are inspired by heroic ambitions," history inspires us through the examples of past great men and women to strive after achievements of our own: "individuals can achieve great things, and the teacher of history ought to make this clear to his pupils. For without hope nothing of importance is accomplished."[14] And in the task of locating the boundary between proper ambition and excessive hubris, what subject is more useful than history?

But if Russell remained certain in the 1940s and 1950s that history was still an immensely useful and beneficial field of knowledge, he had also come to realize that there was a dark side to historical study. A half-century of military destruction, economic chaos, social dislocation, and political upheaval had tempered his earlier confidence that historical understanding necessarily leads to improved human behavior. In particular, experience of the misuse of history by propagandists, apologists, and demagogues had shaken Russell's faith in the categorical beneficence of history.[15] Indeed, even by the end of the Great War he had come to believe that history was only conditionally beneficial; historical study, that is, could have real value only if it were properly done. Improperly done, it had the capacity to do great harm, an eventuality he had not raised in his earlier work. Not surprisingly, therefore, Russell devoted the bulk of his later essays to an explanation of precisely how history should be written to ensure that its value would be wholly positive.

Russell offered five rough-and-ready guidelines to proper historical writing. In the first place, he suggested, history must be lucidly and compellingly written; only if it is comprehensible and written "with lively fancy" will it be read. Second, history ought to be written "in the grand manner" of Gibbon, Macaulay, and the Whig historians he had enjoyed as a boy. Russell recognized that such a style of "epic grandeur" was out of fashion, but he insisted that it must be brought back into vogue, since only when events are described and themes developed in the context of a large sweep of the past can the essential perspective be drawn and the vital emphasis on the life of "Man" be made plain. Third, historical writings should have a definite point of view. "This requires first and foremost that the historian should have feelings about the events that he is relating and the characters that he is portraying," Russell explained. It also means that historians should not shy from making those feelings plain to the reader; historians ought to offer their own opinions about the events and individuals being discussed, ought to condemn or praise the actions of their subjects, and ought to draw morals from their stories. This does not mean, Russell elaborated, that historians should wilfully distort their facts; it does recognize, however, that history is necessarily a subjective, bias-ridden discipline and that historians ought therefore to confess their prejudices, explain their reasons for holding those views, and then allow readers to judge for themselves how persuasive the account may be.[16]

Fourth, proper historical writing should be resolutely presentist and didactic in its focus and purpose. Although historical facts have an undoubted intrinsic interest and importance, Russell argued, a single-minded concentration on them transforms history into sterile, self-indulgent antiquarianism; history for its own sake should be buried in recondite scholarly journals, but the great bulk of historical writing ought to be addressed to the lay reader. Historians ought always to be alive to the many uses which even the most distant or ancient societies possess for contemporary readers; as he had explained earlier, history can be made to enter "our daily thoughts" through many avenues, and proper historical writing ought to follow one of those paths. A celebration of the courage of Lincoln or the genius of Galileo or a denunciation of the rapacity of Genghis Khan or the cruelty of Torquemada can therefore be presentist if it inspires us to imitation on the one hand and revulsion on the other; a discussion of the fall of Rome can be presentist if it emphasizes that no values or institutions are immortal; an account of the death of Socrates can be presentist if it raises the issues of individual conscience versus the tyranny of the state. Finally, historical writing ought to stress the role of individuals in history. Not only does this approach provide examples for emulation, but, by focusing on individuals like ourselves in situations which we recognize and may well face, it makes a whole range of moral issues and ethical choices much clearer.[17]

In "History as an Art" Russell acknowledged that the modern historiographical emphases on collectivities—whether class or nation—and on common men and women as opposed to exceptional individuals are doubtless useful correctives to much previous historical writing. But, he warned, they must not be taken too far:

What, though important, is not true, but most perniciously false, is the suggestion, which easily grows up when history is studied *only* in this way, that individuals do not count and that those who have been regarded as heroes are only embodiments of social forces, whose work would have been done by someone else if it had not been done by them, and that, broadly speaking, no individual can do better than let himself be borne along by the current of his time. What is worst about this view is that, if it is held, it tends to become true. Heroic lives are inspired by heroic ambitions, and the young man who thinks that there is nothing important to be done is pretty sure to do nothing important. (p. 187)

What is required in historical writing, Russell concluded, is an approach which takes into account both the common and the extraordinary man. To focus on only one or the other is to produce either a sense of impotence or a cult of the hero.

Russell's own extensive historical writings were remarkably faithful to the principles of his philosophy of history; there was, indeed, scarcely any division between the theoretical precepts of Russell the abstract philosopher of history and the practical methods of Russell the working historian. His historical books and essays both embodied all his prescriptions for good historical writing and strove to engender in his audience the many benefits of true historical understanding. In his historical writings, moreover, Russell fought shy of offering any "lessons" or "laws" of history and remained unremittingly skeptical toward, and in some instances positively hostile to, works that purported to reveal comprehensive, "scientific" laws of historical change.

Clarity of style and liveliness of argument were Russell's first precepts of good historical writing, and his books and essays of history all contain a full measure of his customary verve, humor, erudition, contentiousness, and self-assurance. They are unfailingly lucid, irrepressibly dogmatic, and irresistibly witty—full of lyrical passages, provocative judgments, and humorous asides. Indeed, nearly every page is marked by the easy elegance of style, the casually worn learning, and the high-minded moralism so characteristic of all of Russell's popular writings. Even the more technical *History of Western Philosophy* is, in the judgment of Isaiah Berlin, "written in clear and elegant and vigorous prose, with that peculiar combination of moral conviction and inexhaustible intellectual fertility which in some measure characterises all, even the most ephemeral, of Russell's writings."[18] It is, therefore, scarcely surprising that Russell's historical writings gained the wide readership he desired; the *History of Western Philosophy* was a best seller and became an instant classic, while *Freedom and Organisation, German Social Democracy, The Problem of China,* and *In Praise of Idleness* were also highly popular and ran through many editions, reprintings, and translations.

Russell's historical writings also aspired after the "grand manner." The *History of Western Philosophy* was by far the most successful in this regard; its ambition—to cover the main developments in Western thought from the pre-Socratics to the logical positivists—and its length—840 pages—are nothing if not grand. Similarly, *The Problem of China* and *Freedom and Organisation,* although they did not approach this scale, are by no means narrow monographs; *China* ranges, albeit with unnerving briskness, from ancient times to the 1920s and *Freedom and Organisation* surveys the course and consequences of industrialism on the politics, foreign policy, economic conditions, and social life of the United States, Britain, and Europe from 1815 to 1914.

Russell's writings of history were also proudly partisan. Often written in the first person, they were resolutely polemical, highly moralistic, and unafraid of passing judgment on the policies of statesmen, the maneuverings of diplomats, the arguments of intellectuals, the strategies of generals, and the aspirations of businessmen long dead. Indeed, Russell's wit, sense of irony, and capacity for moral indignation were all allowed full play. "Politically, the Prince Regent stood for all that was most reactionary; privately, for all that was most despicable" is a characteristic statement, as is the judgment that the Liverpool ministry was "one of the worst and most cruel governments with which England has ever been cursed" and the assertion that "the decadence of Spain in the late 16th and the 17th Centuries" was due "almost entirely to stupidity and fanaticism." Metternich is described as a man full of "pompous priggery," Kaiser William II as "uncompromisingly hostile to every advance in civilisation or freedom," Nicholas II as the embodiment of "cruelty, perfidy, and feeble arrogance," Palmerston as a "blustering old ruffian," and Bismarck as a "clever rogue" who "sought to remould the world in his own image" and "unfortunately . . . was largely successful." The "shameful abominations" of working-class life in early nineteenth-century Britain are condemned as a product of "our lunatic period"; the foreign policy of the Asquith ministry is denounced as "criminal," "predatory and brutal," and as guilty of "an amazing unscupulousness"; carpetbagging politicians in the American South during Reconstruction are castigated as "a gang of shameless miscreants"; and the courtiers of medieval Japan dismissed as "degenerate and feeble," "stereotyped and unprogressive."[19] Russell, that is, made no attempt to hide his prejudices or to aspire after a fraudulent, because impossible, objectivity. Rather, he put into enthusiastic practice his theoretical admonition that historians ought not to shrink from explicitly and zealously condemning the errors and immorality of past men and policies—always with the proviso, of course, that such criticism not be gratuitous but based on demonstrable evidence and rigorous argumentation.

Each of Russell's historical writings not only had a self-proclaimed polemical purpose, but was also resolutely presentist in intent. *The Policy of the Entente*, Russell declared in its introduction, aimed at refuting the contemporary (1915) conviction in Britain that Germany was solely responsible for the coming of the First World War and at explaining, as he titled his final chapter, "What Our Policy Ought to Have Been."[20] The book, indeed, was as much a polemic in favor of decolonization, disarmament, open diplomacy, and the creation of an "International League of Great Powers" as it was a history of the serpentine diplomacy of the Great Powers in the decade before 1914. *The Problem of China*, by comparison, had as its purpose the destruction of the prevalent—if dangerous, ill-founded, and arrogant—sense of superiority of the West toward China and Japan.[21] And the aim of *Freedom and Organisation*, to offer a final example, was the presentation of Russell's conviction that the economic, political, and imperial history of nineteenth- and early twentieth-century Europe teaches that only the establishment of a world government based on socialist principles and the enforcement of a universal disarmament can preserve civilization in this century.[22] In fact, all of Russell's historical writings were true to their individual declarations of purpose; all were full of asides to contemporary events and replete with references to current issues. Eloquent and impassioned admonitions against past military proliferation, imperial expansion, diplomatic alliance-making, unregulated economic development, and the restriction of civil and religious liberties appeared in his works, and the reader was left in no doubt about the existence of what Russell judged to be parallels to contemporary conditions.

Finally, Russell's books and essays of history stressed the role of individuals. This emphasis, although most evident and natural in his later works on the history of philosophy, was in fact a feature of his historical writing and philosophy of history from the very start; not only was it defended in theory in "On History," but it appeared in practice even earlier in *German Social Democracy* (whose first two chapters, for instance, are devoted to biographical sketches of Marx and Lassalle). His writings were full of personality sketches and character studies—ranging from the superficial to the perceptive, the devotional to the malicious, and the impish to the cruel— and nowhere were Russell's wit and capacity for indignation more in evidence. Indeed, Sidney Hook's sagacious observation on the nature of *Freedom and Organisation* applied to all of Russell's history: "*Freedom versus Organization* [its American title] is full of delightful vignettes of historical characters written with charm and subtlety, spiced with a little malice."[23] In every case Russell, again true to his precepts for good historical writing, made plain his prejudices, held individuals up as either inspirational models of proper behavior or contemptuous examples of immoral conduct, demonstrated their crucial roles in the larger "Life of Man," and used vivid accounts of their careers and personalities as a means of enlivening his writing and thereby making his work more readable and popular.

This concentration on individuals also served another purpose: it provided Russell with plentiful ammunition in his constant struggle against allegedly "scientific" philosophies of history, and allowed him to develop (albeit in implicit and vague terms) his own positive theory of historical change. In the first place, those thinkers who purport to offer general principles or universal laws of historical change—and who are therefore, to Russell's mind, purveyors of "scientific" history—mistakenly confuse the basic standards of clarity and rigor common to all scholars with the exclusive techniques of scientists, impertinently offer bogus causal laws of historical development, illegitimately predict the future course of civilization, and inevitably fail to satisfy the basic criteria of the true scientific method. In truth, no matter what their protestations to the contrary, they are neither scientists nor lawgivers. And in the second place, such historians, by advancing what they claim to be irrefutable laws of historical change and by stressing the necessary determinism of their theories, almost always produce any one of a number of damaging effects in their readers and adherents. The determinism which such laws must logically imply, Russell insisted, promotes either a fatalistic complacency, a fanatic sense of being "on the side of history," or an enervating sense of impotence in the face of forces too overwhelming to resist. In every case the consequences are socially, politically, psychologically, and intellectually injurious. As Russell never tired of insisting: "Heroic lives are inspired by heroic ambitions," while the loss of this conviction all too often becomes a self-fulfilling prophecy, since "without hope nothing of importance is accomplished." Indeed, such doctrines threaten to "reduce all human effort to complete futility."[24]

Russell's explicit analyses of such bogus, "scientific" philosophies of history—specifically those of Marx, Hegel, Spengler, and Toynbee—were, unfortunately, breezily perfunctory at best and irresponsibly slapdash at worst. Indeed, he preferred to dismiss rather than to refute them. Marx, a thinker for whom Russell had considerable respect and for whose theoretical work in economics he showed genuine admiration, received short shrift as a philosopher of history. In the first place, Russell asserted, Marx's philosophy of history is guilty of the same mistakes of elementary logic which all such grandiose schemes of universal history commit— errors which he had exposed in "On History" and repeated in his later essays; nor, and again in common with other alleged "scientific" philosophies, could Marx's doctrines successfully predict future developments. In the second place, Marx's philosophy of history is based on an economic theory which is deeply flawed; "indeed, it has been rejected by all orthodox economists, and every step, down to the establishment of surplus-value, contains at least one fallacy."[25] Thirdly, Russell insisted, Marx's dialectical materialism is epistemologically and metaphysically untrue; it is based on a set of assumptions which the work of late nineteenth- and twentieth-century philosophers has convincingly demonstrated to be mistaken.[26] And finally and most damningly, Marx's philosophy of history is unacceptable because it "ignores intelligence as a cause"; that is, it ignores the role of exceptional individuals in altering the course of history.[27] Hegel, a man for whom the mature Russell had virtually no respect, he chose to ridicule rather than treat seriously. As he wrote in a characteristic passage:

> Hegel's theory of history is not a whit less fantastic. According to him, there is something called 'The Idea,' which is always struggling to become the *Absolute* Idea. The Idea embodies itself first in one nation, then in another. It began in China, but finding it couldn't get very far there, it migrated to India. Then it tried the Greeks, and then the Romans. It was very pleased with Alexander and Caesar—it is noteworthy that it always prefers military men to intellectuals. But after Caesar it began to think there was nothing more to be done with the Romans, so after hesitating for four centuries or so it decided on the Germans, whom it has loved ever since, and still loved in the time of Hegel. However, their dominance is not to be eternal. The Idea always travels westward, and after leaving Germany it will migrate to America, where it will inspire a great war between the United States and Latin America. After that, if it continues to travel westward, I suppose it will reach Japan, but Hegel does not say so. When it has travelled round the world, the Absolute Idea will be realized, and mankind will be happy ever after. The Absolute Idea corresponds to the Second Coming.[28]

Spengler and Toynbee he dismissed with the back of his hand and a stinging quip: "Most societies have perished by assassination, and not by old age."[29] In sum, Russell concluded, "men who make up philosophies of history may be dismissed as inventors of mythologies."[30] The most that can be said about historical change, Russell concluded, is that history appears to possess dispositions or inclinations; for example, "The greatest creative ages are those where opinion is free. . . . Ultimately, however, skepticism breaks down moral tabus, society becomes impossibly anarchic, freedom is succeeded by tyranny, and a new tight tradition is gradually built up." But these inclinations are not, and must not be seen as, necessary and irresistible forces of historical change.[31] Such tendencies and loose patterns make the past intelligible and the future malleable, but they are neither "scientific" nor predetermined. History, then, offers us wisdom, not axioms; likelihoods, not certainties.[32]

Russell's historical writings, as well as his essays on the philosophy of history, were therefore in complete harmony with his social and political libertarianism, with his desire to devote so much of his intellectual energy to the writing of history, and with his career as a tireless public campaigner on behalf of a number of unpopular causes. He wanted to free men and women of exceptional talent from governmental control, public harassment, and conventional opinion, in the conviction that these men and women, if given opportunities, could (potentially) alter the course of history. His writing of history had as its aim the direct and immediate inspiration and enlightenment of his readers; already powerful and talented men and women ought to begin to act nobly, potentially great men and women ought to be inspired to pursue greatness, and ordinary men and women ought to acquire if not ambition then at least wisdom about moral, political, economic, and social issues of the day. And his public career had, not as its goal, but rather as its intellectual precondition, the conviction that an individual could in fact make a difference, could in fact redirect the policies of his government and remold the values of his society. Issues concerning the philosophy of history were not, therefore, merely abstract problems for Bertrand Russell; rather, they went to the very heart of his political philosophy, social activism, and moral purpose.

Notes

1. Ronald Jager, *The Development of Bertrand Russell's Philosophy* (London: George Allen and Unwin, 1972), p. 25.
2. Only one study of Russell's historical writings has yet appeared: Sidney Hook, "Bertrand Russell's Philosophy of History," in *The Philosophy of Bertrand Russell*, ed. Paul Arthur Schilpp (Chicago: Open Court, 1944), pp. 645–78. Hook's

essay was written, however, before most of Russell's historical writings and essays on the philosophy of history were published.

3. Russell's historical essays include "An Outline of Intellectual Rubbish," "Ideas That Have Helped Mankind," and "Ideas That Have Harmed Mankind" in his *Unpopular Essays* (London: George Allen and Unwin 1950), pp. 95–212, and "The Ancestry of Fascism" in his *In Praise of Idleness and Other Essays* (London: George Allen and Unwin, 1935), pp. 82–108.

4. Bertrand Russell, *Fact and Fiction* (London: George Allen and Unwin, 1961), p. 35.

5. For an excellent discussion of the genesis of "On History" see the editorial headnote in Bertrand Russell, *The Collected Papers of Bertrand Russell*, vol. 12, *Contemplation and Action 1902–14*, ed. Richard A. Rempel, Andrew Brink, and Margaret Moran (London: George Allen and Unwin, 1985), pp. 73–75. All subsequent references to "On History" will be to this now-standard edition.

6. Trevelyan's views received their classic formulation in his essay "The Latest View of History," *Independent Review* 1 (1903–4): 395–414.

7. Russell, "On History," pp. 77 and 79. Russell did not, however, offer any examples of such "minor maxims" and instead contented himself with this vague statement: "These will only apply where the end is given, and are therefore of a technical nature. They can never tell the statesman what end to pursue, but only, within certain limits, how some of the more definite ends, such as wealth, or victory in war, are to be attained" (p. 79).

8. As Russell pointed out, the "truth is not the sole aim in recording the past" (p. 77).

9. Russell, "On History," p. 79. Russell repeated the point forty years later: "History has perhaps its greatest value in enlarging the world of our imagination, making us, in thought and feeling, citizens of a larger universe than that of our daily preoccupations. In this way it contributes not only to knowledge, but to wisdom." Bertrand Russell, "Reply to Criticisms," in *Philosophy of Russell*, p. 741.

10. Russell, "On History," p. 80. As in his contemporary essay "The Free Man's Worship," Russell thus offered a view of human life and its purpose almost existential in its confused combination of defiance and renunciation, and he ended his essay with an elegiac statement of the harsh nature of human life and the consolations to be found in the study of history: "Year by year, comrades die, hopes prove vain, ideals fade; the enchanted land of youth grows more remote, the road of life more wearisome; the burden of the world increases, until the labour and the pain become almost too heavy to be borne; joy fades from the weary nations of the earth, and the tyranny of the future saps men's vital force; all that we love is waning, waning from the dying world. But the past, ever devouring the transient offspring of the present, lives by the universal death; steadily, irresistibly, it adds new trophies to its silent temple, which all the ages build; every great deed, every splendid life, every achievement and every heroic failure, is there enshrined. On the banks of the river of Time, the sad procession of human generations is marching slowly to the grave; in the quiet country of

the Past, the march is ended, the tired wanderers rest, and all their weeping is hushed" ("On History," p. 82).

11. Quoted in editorial headnote in "On History," pp. 74–75.
12. Bertrand Russell, "History as an Art," in his *Portraits From Memory and Other Essays* (London: George Allen and Unwin, 1956), p. 181.
13. Ibid., p. 182. "Our bodily life is confined to a small portion of time and space," he elaborated in "How to Read and Understand History," "but our mental life need not be thus limited. What astronomy does to enlarge the spatial habitat of the mind, history does to increase its temporal domain. Our private lives are often exasperating, and sometimes almost intolerably painful. To see them in perspective, as an infinitesimal fragment in the life of mankind, makes it less difficult to endure personal evils which cannot be evaded." Bertrand Russell, "How to Read and Understand History" in his *Understanding History and Other Essays* (New York: Philosophical Library, 1957), p. 54.
14. Russell, "History as an Art," p. 187, and "How to Read and Understand History," p. 14.
15. The misuse of history as the basis of all sorts of "pernicious myths" was condemned by Russell in both his later essays on history as well as in "The Ancestry of Fascism," in *In Praise of Idleness*, pp. 82–108.
16. Russell, "History as an Art," pp. 183–84. As he explained, "It is of course imperative that the historian should not distort facts, but it is not imperative that he should not take sides in the clashes and conflicts that fill his pages. . . . If this causes an historian to be one-sided, the only remedy is to find another historian with an opposite bias" (p. 183).
17. Russell, "How to Read and Understand History," pp. 22–27, 40–41.
18. Isaiah Berlin, review of *A History of Western Philosophy* in *Mind* 66 (1947): 151.
19. Bertrand Russell, *Freedom and Organisation 1814–1914* (London: George Allen and Unwin, 1934), pp. 14 and 19; "How to Read and Understand History," p. 29; *Freedom and Organisation*, p. 16; *German Social Democracy* (London: Longmans, Green and Co., 1896), p. 162; *Freedom and Organisation*, pp. 497, 156, 430, 433, 85, 121; *Policy of the Entente* (reprinted in his *Justice in War-Time* [Chicago: Open Court, 1916]), pp. 201–9; "How to Read and Understand History," p. 49; *Problem of China* (London: George Allen and Unwin, 1922), p. 89.
20. "If we remain to the end wrapped in self-righteousness, impervious to facts which are not wholly creditable to us, we shall," Russell warned, "in the years after the war, merely repeat the errors of the past, and find ourselves, in the end, involved in other wars as terrible and destructive as the one which we are now waging" (*Policy of the Entente*, p. 123).
21. "We must cease to regard ourselves as missionaries of a superior civilization, or, worse still, as men who have a right to exploit, oppress, and swindle the Chinese because they are an 'inferior' race." Otherwise, Russell warned, this "provincialism, which impregnates all our culture, is liable to have disastrous consequences politically, as well as for the civilization of mankind" (*Problem of China*, pp. 5, 23).

22. "It is not by pacifist sentiment, but by world-wide economic organization, that civilized mankind can be saved from collective suicide" (*Freedom and Organisation*, p. 510).

23. Hook, "Russell's Philosophy of History," p. 664.

24. Russell, "How to Read and Understand History," pp. 14, 17.

25. Russell, *German Social Democracy*, p. 17. For a fuller discussion of Russell's early critique of Marx and its place in late nineteenth-century English writings on Marx see my "Introduction and Critical Reception of Marxist Thought in Britain 1850–1900," *Historical Journal* 20 (1977): 417–59.

26. Russell, *History of Western Philosophy* (New York: Simon and Schuster, 1945), pp. 782–90.

27. As he elaborated, "I do not wish to suggest that intelligence is something that arises spontaneously, in some mystical uncaused manner. Obviously it has its causes, and obviously these causes are in part to be sought in the social environment. But in part the causes are biological and individual. . . . Men of supreme ability are just as definitely congenitally different from the average as are the feeble-minded. And without supreme ability fundamental advances in methods of production cannot take place" ("How to Read and Understand History," pp. 35–36).

28. Ibid., pp. 15–16. In another typical denunciation Russell commented, "Everything proceeds by thesis, antithesis and synthesis, and what moves it is the self-development of the Idea, and the Idea is what Hegel happened to believe. The whole course of the universe is making it just as Hegel thought it was." In Huntington Cairns, Allen Tate, and Mark Van Doren, eds., *Invitation to Learning* (New York: Random House, 1941), p. 411.

29. Russell, "History as an Art," p. 180. On the more serious side, Russell observed that both Spengler and Toynbee attempted to generalize from far too few examples: "The instances of past civilizations are too few to warrant an induction" ("How to Read and Understand History," p. 17).

30. Russell, "How to Read and Understand History," p. 17. The kindest word Russell could offer about philosophies of history was this: "For such vast laws, I should say, there is not, and never can be, any adequate evidence; they are reflections of our own moods upon the cosmos" ("Reply to Criticisms," p. 734).

31. Russell, "How to Read and Understand History," p. 52. He put the point slightly differently in *A History of Western Philosophy*: "Every community is exposed to two opposite dangers: ossification through too much discipline and reverence for tradition, on the one hand; on the other hand, dissolution, or subjection to foreign conquest, through the growth of an individualism and personal independence that makes co-operation impossible. In general, important civilizations start with a rigid and superstitious system, gradually relaxed, and leading, at a certain stage, to a period of brilliant genius, while the good of the old tradition remains and the evil inherent in its dissolution has not yet developed. But as the evil unfolds, it leads to anarchy, thence, inevitably, to a new tyranny, producing a new synthesis secured by a new system of dogma" (p. xxiii).

32. Russell, "Reply to Criticisms," p. 741.

Two New Histories:

An Exploratory Comparison

Ernst Breisach

Edward Eggleston's presidential address, read to the members of the American Historical Association in December 1900, was entitled "The New History." The phrase has not fallen out of use since. In 1912 James Harvey Robinson took it as the title of his well-known work and in 1976 Lawrence Stone subsumed under it a now broad and multifaceted historiographical enterprise.[1] While a common label does not assure an identity of substance, it is nevertheless proper to ask whether the American New History of the early 1900s does share concepts, goals, and problems with the primary initiator of the present New History, the *Annales* group. Be it ever so slender, a bridge between the two schools, whose triumphs occurred decades apart and whose cultural settings differed radically, would be of considerable interest. Let us see whether such a bridge exists.

In 1911, one year before Robinson's *New History* appeared, a young Frenchman, Lucien Febvre, published his doctoral thesis, *Philip II et la Franche Comté*. This work, strong on geography and psychology, began a career in which Febvre was to link history with geography, psychology, and the social sciences, an aim he shared with Robinson. That intellectual kinship between the two archetypical historians was no accident, but stemmed from their participation in a broad revolt against the historiographies then current in their countries. These historiographies were positivist endeavors, based on features of Ranke's and Comte's thought. They worshiped critically established "facts," expected patterns of history to emerge from the cumulative facts, and generally concentrated on events and personalities of political history, whose trail of evidence could be found in the archives. Although it all seemed to be a technical quarrel among historians over methods of investigation or the subject matter of history, the controversy really revolved around the nature of historical reality. It was no mere *Methodenstreit*, but a philosophical debate that had been triggered by the collapse of the nineteenth-century interpretations of history, which were mostly philosophies of history in the grand manner.

Accordingly, both groups began with assaults on the prevailing concepts of historical reality. Their common *bête noire* was traditional history, with its political emphasis, the product of "scientific" historians in the United States and the historical complex built on the rules and principles of Charles-V. Langlois and Charles Seignobos in France. Traditional history, focusing on political phenomena that were often selected for their dramatic quality rather than their importance, could not yield a useful past for the new age. It was "little concerned . . . with economic and social problems; slightly disdainful towards the achievements of civilization, religion, and also of literature and the arts, the great witnesses of all worthwhile history."[2] Robinson derided traditional history as being "unedifying in scope," episodic, melodramatic, static, and with no sense for genesis and long-range developments. The *Annalistes*, too, never tired of condemning, even ridiculing, *l'histoire événementielle* (or *l'histoire historisante*). Braudel likened events to the dramatic but short-lived bursts of light emitted by fireflies that illuminated only a tiny area. And, in general terms, the two groups of scholars even agreed on the antidote: to extend history's scope so as to encompass all of life, all its aspects, all its time, and all of mankind. Both groups sought an expanded history that would relinquish its preoccupation with the dramatic, the unique individual, and the actions of elites, and would highlight instead the common life, the routine, and the behavior of the masses.

Yet culture and the passage of time made the agreed-upon inclusion into history of the broad masses, the people, a different matter in France from that in the United States. Early on, Turner had admonished that history must not remain a collection of the "brilliant annals of the few" but must recognize that the "focal point of modern interest is the fourth estate, the great mass of the people." Early, too, Eggleston had predicted in his presidential address that "a hundred years hence, there will be, do not doubt it, gifted writers of the history of the people. . . . We shall have the history of culture, the real history of men and women."[3] But the New History, sturdily planted in a vigorous, still self-confident American culture, never wished to escape from that matrix into a social history based on the "people" as a universal abstraction. At its center were the American people of the American Progressive Era, striving for their full emancipation in the future while demanding a recognition of their real role in the past. For American New Historians the new historiography became the theoretical counterpart to the actual, imminent emancipation of the common people. That correspondence accommodated the desire to use history as a tool for social reform.

But what type of social history would best combine the requirements of theory (science) and praxis (reform)? The American New Historians differed among themselves in their answers. Was one simply to describe the dress, occupations, amusements, manners, and literary canons of the times while noting morals and the growth of the humane spirit, in John Bach McMaster's manner? Such cultural surveys suited a country of great ethnic complexity, with no rigid class antagonisms, with a national culture constantly being shaped, and with a strong faith in progress. For his part, Robinson, when he wanted to emphasize the collective as the proper object of history, stressed the study of institutions—"those broad habits of people"—born long ago, matured over generations, and in need of genetic analysis. And Beard stressed social dynamics in his conflict-oriented view of American society's progress. But all of the new American social history was based on a perception of history as shaped by individual human agents, whose actions were sufficiently voluntary so as to deny social phenomena a role and status separate from individuals. Society remained the sum of human interactions and could be both studied and shaped accordingly. That stipulation and history's intended role in social reform separated the American New Historians sharply from Lucien Febvre and the later *Annalistes*.

Lucien Febvre and his later colleague, Marc Bloch, working in an intellectual climate marked by Durkheim's sociology of "social facts," lacked the strong nominalist voluntarism of the American New Historians. For Durkheim, social phenomena were not created by individual actions. Rather, these actions were functions of the "social facts." Hence, although Febvre in his early work on the *Franche Comté* described its bourgeoisie in true life colors, the concern with the individual as the "atom" of society and history was foreign to him and other *Annalistes*. Febvre embedded the individual firmly in a network of forces, resolving the traditional "individual versus collective" opposition by dismantling the predominant position of the individual in the interest of a science of history. To structure the realm he relied on group psychology, not differential psychology (Febvre's term for psychology centered in the individual). As early as the 1920s Febvre discerned structures in the collective consciousness of great power and long duration, which he eventually captured in the concept of *mentalité*, a collective psychological structure that delimits the range of possible manifestations for sensibilities, motives, and thoughts at a given point in time. Yet Febvre's comrade-in-arms, Marc Bloch, still identified the "social" in a rigorously Durkheimian manner as a category of life per se. It transcends the individual not as a *mentalité* but as a category of existence itself.

Years later, betraying an increasing nominalism, Braudel could say: "By social realities I mean all the major forms of collective life, economies, institutions, social structures, in short and above all, civilizations."[4] Such a definition—operational, free-spirited, experimental, and eschewing any implication that there was anything "real" in the concept of the social, be it *mentalité* or "social fact"—appealed to the loose theoretical spirit of the post-1945 *Annalistes*. But conversely it abandoned whatever explanatory power resided in the realist approach of Durkheimian sociology or *mentalité* in favor of prevailingly descriptive presentations. This shift opened the door for structuralist explanations of the social with their temptation to reject diachronic interpretations of human phenomena in favor of synchronic ones, even though Braudel protested that his was a historian's structuralism that "does not tend towards the mathematical abstraction of relations expressed as functions, but instead towards the very sources of life in its most concrete, everyday, indestructible and anonymously human expression."[5]

Thus, while the American New Historians had stressed the need for a history focusing on the life of the people in the interest of progressive reform of American society (although with implications for all nations), the *Annalistes* discussed social history with hardly a sign of pragmatic involvement. The passionate Febvre deplored past views of the masses as merely having done the "donkey work" of history. But on the whole the *Annalistes* strove to grasp the concept of the social in an abstract manner, as a tool of analysis or a temporary location for synthesis.

The vastly different courses taken by the American and French scholars in social history can be accounted for to a high degree by different intellectual contexts. In that connection, however, special attention must be given to the divergent attitudes toward the concept of progress: its affirmation by the American New Historians and its rejection by the *Annalistes*. For the latter, who denied a universal aim of all of history, social history did not explore the contribution of the French people in particular toward a putative human progress but attempted to establish a science of human society in the abstract.

But history, as all New Historians agreed, must not only be encompassing but also "scientific." Modernity demanded that as the price for history's inclusion in the new "science of man." The American New Historians harbored no doubts about history's relevance and, with it, survival as a distinct discipline. They saw the world as just becoming historically minded, with timeless verities falling under the onslaught of pragmatism and evolutionism. Yet, a few decades later, Febvre worried about his period's contempt for history and hoped that the *Annaliste*-type New History could make the discipline rise phoenixlike from the depths of doubt and uncertainty. He even tried, unsuccessfully, to change the term 'history' itself, which he perceived to be hazy and laden with unwanted connotations inherited from the past.

American New Historians felt they were safely within the range of "scientific" history, convinced that their stress on the collective not only celebrated the people but also allowed for a "scientific" social history. At first, in the early 1900s, they even shared the expectation of the prevalent positivist school of historiography, namely, that once the subject matter had been properly redefined, the patient collection and chronologically exact, causal arrangement of well-documented facts could yield an objective history with general conclusions, perhaps even laws. But the New Historians went their own way as they discovered the complexity of historical interpretation, first, through the issue of perspectivism and second, by virtue of their progressivist philosophy of history.

Already in 1904, Robinson conceded that there were limits to the hope for a self-interpreting history because, despite all efforts, "history is and must always remain, from the standpoint of the scientific observer, a highly inexact and fragmentary science." This is so not only because it deals with unpredictable human beings and their "devious ways and wandering desires, which can never all be brought within the compass of clearly defined laws," but also "because it must forever rest upon scattered and unreliable data, the truth of which we too often have no means of testing."[6] The young Carl L. Becker had a more sophisticated view of that area of irremedial uncertainty; he soon grasped the necessity of interpretation and what it implied for objectivity and certainty. For other New Historians, their faith in progress prevented the uncertainty factor from assuming any menacing scope. The knowledge of where history "was going," gleaned by Robinson from reason's evolution and by Beard from industrialism's push toward fuller democracy, was a firmer guarantor for the certainty of historical knowledge than any scholarly objectivity could ever be. Later, in the 1930s, Beard would see in the "scientific" historian's attachment to objectivity a misguided emulation of German ideals, which reflected "the inhibitions placed upon German historians by their bureaucratic status and by their rivalry for advancement."[7] With the exception of Becker, the American New Historians were not fond of long arguments in the epistemological mode about the scientific character of history. Eager to place history into the realm of action, they relied on the progressivist philosophy of history, rather than on epistemological considerations, for certainty about the past.

The *Annalistes* celebrated the "science of history" but they too were remarkably reluctant to theorize about historiography. Febvre's early disinclination to deal with issues touching on the theory and philosophy of history stemmed from his training, from his conviction that "doing history" was more fruitful than thinking about history's theoretical issues, and from his antipathy to contemporary philosophers of history who—as he saw it—

accepted the traditional view of history instead of revising it. Bloch's *Historian's Craft* gained Febvre's qualified approval because of its safe distance from too much theory. Yet, there was more to the *Annalistes'* skepticism about theory. The same driving force which fueled the assault on the traditional barriers hurtled the *Annalistes* through the breach into a wide-open human realm, ready for innovative and enthusiastic exploration, analysis, and description, unencumbered by timeless features and systematic theories. Such theories, while they offered guidance, also limited the vision and the scope of the inquiry. Any structuring of the inquiry, Febvre thought, must be purely technical in nature, that is, must be the result of research techniques, requirements of teamwork, and guidance by research directors. By implication, theory belonged to the traditionalists, those lonely scholars with pencils and index cards. The historian's practice rather than the theoretician's prescription would establish what "scientific" history was. This antisystematic and antiphilosophical attitude foreshadowed recent developments in the natural sciences, where the body of past books on the philosophy of science collects dust, perceived to be of little use. The old books are replaced not by new theories or philosophies but by the pragmatic selection of topics and problems—"by kicking problems around" and defining scientific method as "doing one's damnedest, no holds barred."[8] The neat role model of the sciences still adhered to by the American New Historians was no longer available. "That science on which we as laymen relied without even having been aware of it, which was a haven and a new reason for living to the nineteenth century, has altered brutally from one day to the next and been reborn of a different existence. It is to us now honored but unstable, constantly in flux, inaccessible, and it seems certain that we will never again have the time or the opportunity to reestablish a working dialogue with it."[9] Without a binding scientific model, history could claim to be a science, although it would never be able to predict, would change interpretations with every generation, and would never break the spell cast on an objective truth by the subject/object muddle. The New American Historians still could espouse the cause of both a clearly and substantially defined science and of progress because the two drew substantial strength from each other. The *Annalistes*, lacking an affirmed *telos* of history and with it any defined historical dynamics, had no problems in adjusting to the post-1960 trend toward a greater amorphism in the interpretation of science (including that by Thomas S. Kuhn), but also were less sure about the correspondence of reality and methodology.

The common thrust of all New Historians toward a life-encompassing history of a "scientific" nature conjured up the danger of a static, descriptive historiography and forced them to resolve one of historiography's crucial issues, namely, mastering the phenomenon of time. Here both groups of New Historians embarked on a grand experiment in which they rejected, each in its own way, the centuries-old attempts to assert change while yet assuring the continuity between past, present, and future by means of timeless reference points: the stable human nature of the Ancients, the God and Divine Providence of Jews and Christians, and the ideas and world spirit of the idealists. That rejection necessitated finding new answers to the perennial questions of historical dynamics: what were the units that structured the past? the forces pushing human life on? and, finally, the nature of continuity itself?

The search for the appropriate unit of history caused the American New Historians little trouble. They saw no logical necessity for repudiating the nation-state as a convenient unit of study once the subject matter of history had been updated. The search for a unit of analysis that would structure life's complex interrelationships proved to be more difficult for the *Annalistes,* who wished to construct an abstract science of man in time. They found help in anthropology. Among American New Historians, Robinson had welcomed evolutionary views, especially for explaining the presence of "nonprogressive" elements through Edward B. Tylor's concept of "survivals." These elements were "processes, customs, opinions, and so forth which have been carried on by force of habit into a new state of society different from that in which they had their original home, and thus remain as proofs and examples of an older condition of culture out of which a newer has evolved."[10] They were obstacles to and disturbances of a rational society destined to fade. Thus, anthropology, while not needed for the search after a unit, provided support for the progressive interpretation of history.

When the *Annalistes* turned to anthropology, they too found a congenial discipline, although it had changed since the 1920s from an evolutionist to a functionalist enterprise. In it civilization became the dominant unit of life and analysis, and as early as the 1930s Febvre found it suitable for the New History. Civilization "simply refers to all the features that can be observed in the collective life of one human group, embracing their material, intellectual, moral and political life and, there is unfortunately no other word for it, their social life."[11] It became for the *Annalistes*, who shunned the nation-state, an appealing unit because of its sheer limitless opportunities for exploring human life. Braudel even grouped civilizations among the powerful forces of the *longue durée;* he saw them as quasi-stable entities, because they were extremely slow in changing. "Civilizations, like sand dunes, are firmly anchored to the hidden contours of the earth; grains of sand may come and go, blown into drifts or carried far away by the wind, but the dunes, the unmoving sum of innumerable movements, remain standing."[12] *Annalistes* also welcomed the new anthropological relativism, which put all civilizations on the same level and destroyed the concept of Civilization (substantially, Western Civilization) so dear to the advocates of progress, including the American New Historians. *Annalistes* wished to study Civilization's "autonomous provinces." Different civilizations were to be seen simply as different expressions of human life. However, accepting civilizations as the units for studying the past introduced an explicit relativism that complicated the *Annaliste's* search for historical continuity. Was history simply the record of concurrent or consecutive civilizations, governed by well-nigh imperceptible and inexplicable processes of change? Was the price of finding in civilization the unit of study a surrender to quasi-timeless anthropological theories and thus a denial of history?

With their preference for an all-encompassing history, all New Historians favored forces which effected change much more slowly than those that have prevailed in the traditional political history. They searched for history's "true" dynamics by going "below the surface" into the "depth" of history. Here they hoped to find the "true" unity and moving forces of history, which were no longer fastened to metaphysical moorings and no longer insulated from time's corrosion. Once again, the American New Historians had an easier time of it (even disregarding, for the moment, their always helpful concept of progress), since for them the active force of history remained the individual or collectives composed of individuals. Therefore, the "depth" to be probed was the realm of motives of the individual psyche, where, in the 1910s and 1920s, the economic interests were found to dominate. Robinson, acknowledging his admiration for Marx but also his distaste for simple-minded Marxists, asserted that "few, if any, historians would agree that everything can be explained economically, as many of the socialists and some economists of good standing would have us believe. But in the sobered and chastened form in which most economists now accept the doctrine, it serves to explain far more of the phenomena of the past than any other single explanation ever offered."[13] The young Beard came much closer to turning this insight into a unicausal dynamics of history when he wished to tear off the masks of ideals and traditions from the "true" reality, the world of economic interests. Eventually many progressive historians, even the older Beard, disavowed unicausalism, because it distorted the free play of forces in the human realm. In the 1930s human beings were once more seen as rational and decisive agents, moved at least as much by ideas as by interests. But for two decades, the despised hierarchy of timeless ideas seemed simply to have been replaced by a hierarchy of timeless interests.

Of the early *Annalistes* only Marc Bloch asserted the primacy of economic reality. Febvre's search for the hidden guiding forces led him away from economics, first to the structure of sensibilities, then to those of consciousness, *les mentalités*. And although economic phenomena were integrated into all three of Braudel's time rhythms, they were never seen as the determinants of history. Not even a moderate economic determinism, certainly not Marx's theory, with its production-oriented dynamics, fit into Febvre's and Braudel's view of reality as an endless interplay of forces with oscillating influences, stabilized temporarily in collective patterns of consciousness or in equilibria of time rhythms. Thus, the *Annalistes* too spoke of a continuity "beneath" the visible phenomena in an "unconscious" (or submerged) history. "One has, then, to concede that there does exist, at some distance, a social unconscious. And concede, too, that this unconscious might well be thought more rich, scientifically speaking, than the glittering surface to which our eyes are accustomed. More rich scientifically, meaning simpler, easier to exploit—not easier to discover. But the step from bright surface to murky depths—from noise to silence—is difficult and dangerous."[14] Did Braudel here sense the difference in concreteness and tangibility entailed by the step from economic motives into murky psychological undercurrents?

Finally, after having touched on history's subject matter, basic structural unit, scientific character, and dynamics, an exploratory comparison must take up the most complex problem posed for historians by the flux of time: the issue of continuity in the midst of change. In this case that means dealing with the issue of progress.

The American New Historians had enthusiastically joined the revolt against the formalist view of reality in which timeless, metaphysical entities shaped laws, institutions, and destinies, and against all stipulations of an unchanging human nature. Instead, they interpreted ideas as plans of action, institutions as products of economic or other basic forces, and history as a pragmatic tool. Yet these historians could celebrate the burial of formalism (and with it, much that had given stability and continuity to history) with joyful noises and without nagging doubts only because all change was seen as safely embedded in a general progress. "Even those of us who have little taste for mysticism have to recognize a mysterious unconscious impulse which appears to be a concomitant of natural order. It would seem as if this impulse has always been unsettling the existing conditions and pushing forward, groping after something more elaborate and intricate than what already existed. This vital impulse, *élan vital*, as Bergson calls it, represents the inherent radicalism of nature herself."[15] According to the American New Historians, this vital impulse guided history toward the maximum human mastery of the world, with its "natural" corollaries of peace, prosperity, equality, and democracy. Their pragmatism, a view with no long-range structures, was secured by Condorcet's, Comte's, and Spencer's assertions that the *telos*, immanent in the historical process, assured historians of a beneficent continuity in a world of unceasing change. That reassuring interpretation of history would be severely threatened once the Depression, totalitarian regimes, and the two World Wars weakened the belief in progress. That was why in the 1930s Beard came to deemphasize the progressive logic of history and relied on a purely voluntaristic "act of faith" in progress. And, in the 1960s, progressive history's interpretations of the past were negated by those who saw in the American past more regress than progress. But the vulnerability of American New History was really there from the start. It lay in the contradiction between the radical antiformalist denial of all metaphysical concepts and the at least quasi-metaphysical belief in progress.

The *Annalistes* consistently voiced their aversion to such metaphysical features as Reason or Progress, shunned all linear schemes that pointed toward an aim or fulfillment, and depicted the past as laid out on a plane that historians needed to crisscross over and over again in search of ever new insights. But could the assertion of a directionless history be upheld in the face of the ongoing global process of Westernization? And was history still history once time was reduced to a neutral vessel for historical phenomena, a blank sheet on which mankind could record a plotless account, where sequence was merely part of the structure, and where continuity was not essentially linked to time? In the absence of a full-fledged statement on the theory or philosophy of history by the early *Annalistes*, evidence for their views on any grand vision of history— or more prosaically, the reconciliation of the past, the present, and expectations for the future—must be gleaned kernel by kernel. The toil is hard, the harvest is sparse, but the yield is nevertheless interesting.

Febvre ridiculed the theoreticians of progress who, intoxicated by the increasing rationalization, struck up "a fine hymn of triumph."[16] Yet he spoke of the special historical sense in Western Civilization that emerged when the crushing weight of the past, in the form of a binding, deadening tradition, was replaced by the mediation of history. "History in the last resort meets the same need as tradition, whether the need is conscious or not. History is a way of organizing the past so that it does not weigh too heavily on the shoulders of men."[17] This step from tradition to history parallels the upward step that, according to Robinson (a professed evolutionist), ended the early stage of the world and human history. That stage had been governed solely by physical laws and had been transformed by unconscious changes, and was followed by the present stage, governed by mental laws and transformed by conscious changes. Was there not, for Febvre, also a progress from the habitual, unreflective tradition to a more rational, reflective history?

There were other fissures in the crust of neutral time through which again and again a whiff of the spirit of progress escaped to the surface. In *A Geographical Introduction to History* not only did Febvre speak of "relations between environment and human society in its historic evolution," but he also consoled himself that simple-minded geographic determinism only marked "a brief moment in a continuous scientific evolution."[18] And when his interest shifted first to states of sensibilities and then to states of consciousness he again discerned an upward development from one stage to the other.

> And so evolving civilizations were able to take part in that long-drawn-out drama, the gradual suppression of emotional activity through intellectual activity; having in the first instance been only elements capable of bringing about the unity of attitude and consciousness among individuals, on the basis of which intellectual commerce and its first tools were able to develop, the emotions then came into conflict with the same new instruments of communication which they alone had made it possible to create, and as intellectual operations evolved in social environments where all social relations between men were increasingly finely regulated by means of institutions and technique, the tendency grew stronger to look upon the emotions as a disturbance, as something dangerous, troublesome and ugly, at least, one might say, as something that ought not to appear naked.[19]

Although that—for some—may not seem to speak clearly enough of progress, a passage containing Febvre's condemnation of the old sensibilities does. "We have revivals of the cult of blood, red blood, in its most animal primitive aspects and the cult of the basic forces within us which reveals our lassitude, domestic animals that we are, crushed and beaten down by the frenzied noise and energy of the thousands of machines that obsess us. To compensate, we have the revival of a sort of cult of Mother Earth in whose lap it is so pleasant in the evening to stretch our weary limbs as if we were her child." Modernity paid dearly for such "exaltation of primitive feelings, going together with a rude dislocation of aim and purpose and the exaltation of cruelty at the expense of love."[20]

When even more rigorous attacks on the centrality of time were launched, they revealed the insufficiency of Febvre's dealing with the dynamics of history. While anthropology of the functional type had all along reduced time to a neutral container, structuralism insisted even more fervently on time being a useful but negligible "temporal space" for the endless and arbitrary permutations of timeless and formal structural elements. In the absence of linear schemes of continuity, such as the American New History's evolutionary progress, the *Annalistes* defended the centrality of time as well as they could. It was Braudel who pronounced with passion: "For the historian everything begins and ends with time, a mathematical, godlike time, a notion easily mocked, time external to men, 'exogenous', as economists would say, pushing men, forcing them, and painting their own individual times the same color: it is, indeed, the imperious time of the world."[21] And it was again Braudel who made a valiant effort to give the New History a theory of time that avoided those wrong images of time: as a majestically flowing "River Time," as progress, as the neutral dimension of curves of developments, or as passive, temporal space. Striving for an explanatory rather than a descriptive model, he linked time to the varied rhythms of life.

Lowest in explanatory power were the phenomena of the first level: rhythms, which governed events caused by individuals, and resulted in momentary situations. These were phenomena of brief duration, "crests of foam that the tides of history carry on their backs," "nervous vibrations," rich in passion, the stuff of journalists and chroniclers that for centuries also led historians to write *histoire événementielle* but left them unable to structure history. Braudel scolded those who built a philosophy of history on so shaky a foundation, specifically Benedetto Croce and Jean-Paul Sartre. On the second level were the *conjonctures*. These generally referred to clusters of events that formed patterns of longer duration, demonstrable in graphs of changes in production, population, monetary values, and the like. They already offered an escape from mere narration into explication and explanation. Finally, there was the third level, the *longue durée:* the slow rhythm at the "depth" of life. Its phenomena were credited with the greatest impact on history, and among them the geographical forces were seen as most prominent. The young Febvre had already proclaimed their importance along the lines of Paul Vidal de la Blache's human geography. After 1945 Braudel spoke of them with awe, first as the relationship of humankind with the inanimate and then as the human dialogue with the Earth, the most fateful of all features. In his book on the Mediterranean area, Braudel experimented with the scheme of a multileveled time and found it powerful in describing and accounting for the phenomena of each level, but nearly powerless to link the three levels of phenomena into a coherent, explanatory whole. The dominance of the *longue durée* proved difficult to expand into a systematic hierarchy of phenomena. Braudel's interpretation of time showed itself to be a morphology of time, an illustration but not a theory of the centrality of time.

How valuable was this intricate scheme of time structures for solving the problems Febvre and other *Annalistes* had encountered when trying to endow history with a discernible continuity that would at least help organize it into consecutive periods? The task became urgent when these historians rejected the progress model, which for the American historians had yielded the element of continuity.

Braudel seemed to have found a basis for establishing historical periods when he discerned temporary equilibria in which the three time rhythms coincided in a special manner, "bringing together different levels, time spans, different kinds of time, structure, conjunctures, events. These taken all together go to make up . . . a fairly precarious global balance which can be maintained only through a constant series of adjustments, clashes, and slight alterations."[22] In a reflective mood, Braudel even stated his preference among the equilibria," for when dealing with the entire world over four centuries, how does one organize such a file of facts and explanations? One has to choose. I chose to deal with long-term equilibriums and disequilibriums."[23] But none of it yielded a sense of development and Braudel himself did not rely on the equilibria of time rhythms when he ascertained periods in history. Neither did he find an adequate dynamic scheme for history in the theory of diffusion of cultural traits, even though he praised it as a key concept in historical dynamics, particularly useful as an antidote to the crypto-progressive concept of Westernization. These difficulties account for a surprising fact, namely, that despite an overt opposition to progressivist views, one can discover clear, albeit subtle traces of progressivist thinking in Febvre's and Braudel's works. Braudel used an improvement in world prosperity as a criterion for seeing at least two periods in European history. The history of Europe, he declared, "splits in two on either side of the watershed of 1608, when the whirlpool of the trend of the century changes direction, though in fact it must be said that the change did not take place in a day, or in a year, but over a long indecisive period of time strewn with illusions and underlying catastrophes."[24] After that comes an even clearer linear-progressive indicator. A unique triple revolution—scientific, biological, and industrial—gripped the West after 1750 and eventually swept over the world, changing all civilizations materially, spiritually, and intellectually, and permanently breaking the power of the previously dominant cycles.

Finally, there is the surprising affirmation of progress, tempered by the modern historian's knowledge of the shadowy sides of progress, when Braudel, the historian-turned-prophet, cited with approval the term 'modern humanism.'

> Man, civilization, must overcome the demands of the machine, even of machinery—of automation—if he is not to be condemned to enforced leisure. Humanism is a way of hoping, of wishing men to be brothers one with another, and of wishing that civilizations, each on its own account and all together, should save themselves and save us. It means accepting and hoping that the doors of the present should be wide open on to the future, beyond all the failures, declines, and catastrophes predicted by strange prophets. The present cannot be the boundary, which all centuries, heavy with eternal tragedy, see before them as an obstacle, but which the hope of man, ever since man has been, has succeeded in overcoming.[25]

Except for its cautious tone, this statement would have pleased the American New Historians. For a brief moment the abstract science of man had acquired a concrete goal and dynamics.

In sum, the two New Histories had a common root in the early 1900s, when a spirit of reform affected Western historiographies, albeit to different degrees. They shared many objectives and, during their periods of prominence, decades apart, deeply influenced their respective national historiographies. Yet, a closer look shows their specific revisionist programs differ significantly in the all-encompassing history they wished to establish, including the units of historical reality chosen and the definition of 'the people.' But their most important difference appears in the area of historical dynamics, or, in other words, in the mastery of time, which for the historian entails an examination of the forces that move history onward, their nature, relative strengths, and possible directions. It could be argued that here, too, the two New Histories shared something: an honorable ultimate failure. By means of their view of history as progress, the American New Historians achieved both an admirable congruence between their work's thrust and their society's temper as well as a superb cohesion of their methodology with their interpretation of historical continuity. But that view, although it commanded much past and present evidence, transcended all empirical boundaries with its assumption that the undoubted scientific and technological advances translated automatically into an unalterable overall direction of history toward a democratic future of perfection and the "good life" (Beard's term). That quasi-metaphysical *telos* escaped charges of radical antiformalism because its timeless character was well concealed by affirmations of incessant change. But the scope and vigor of twentieth-century tyranny, brutality, and injustice deflated the optimistic view that all evils were merely "survivals" from more primitive times and, thus, were no more than temporary obstacles on the way to the Arcadian region of full rationality. With the erosion of its quasi-metaphysical foundation, progressive history in the image of the American New History lost its magnificent unity of method and interpretation. In an ironic twist, life completed the antiformalist revolt by destroying one of its most ardent proponents, the antiformalist American New History.

Febvre bequeathed to the later *Annalistes* only unfinished business. He never succeeded in establishing a clear dynamics of history that could fuse together the past, the present, and expectations for the future; his psychological structures lacked sufficient dynamic thrust for explaining the transformation of one historical stage into the next. Marc Bloch's life was cut short. Braudel's valiant attempt to give time a greater reality and impact (and thus address continuity more seriously) ended up in a theory of time rhythms. Continuity (or in Braudel's terms, "near-permanence") was to be achieved through the phenomenon of the *longue durée*. But not only has Braudel never clearly established the linkages between the three time rhythms, he offered a continuity that anchored human phenomena in natural forces, far from the human realm. Braudel himself has admitted this with regret. "So when I think of the individual, I am always inclined to see him imprisoned within a destiny in which he himself has little hand, fixed in a landscape in which the infinite perspectives of the long term stretch into the distance both behind him and before."[26] Were Febvre and Braudel comfortable with their solutions to continuity in time? Not really. The intermittent affirmations of progress in their works, in direct contradiction to the *Annaliste* distaste for teleological history, provide an ironic illustration of the unresolved dilemma.

Notes

1. See Lawrence Stone, "History and the Social Sciences in the Twentieth Century," in *The Future of History*, ed. Charles Delazell (Nashville: Vanderbilt University Press, 1976), ch. 1; especially pp. 20–27. Also see Lawrence Stone, *The Past and the Present* (Boston: Routledge & Kegan Paul, 1981), ch. 1; especially pp. 21–30.
2. Fernand Braudel, *The Mediterranean and the Mediterranean World in the Age of Philip II*, 2 vols. (New York: Harper & Row, 1976), 1:19.
3. Frederick Jackson Turner, "The Significance of History," in *The Early Writings of Frederick Jackson Turner*, ed. Fulmer Mood (Freeport, N.Y.: Books for Libraries Press, 1969), pp. 47–48; and Edward Eggleston, "The New History," *Annual Report of the American Historical Association*, 1900, 2 vols. (Washington, 1901), 1:47.
4. Fernand Braudel, "The Situation of History in 1950," in Fernand Braudel, *On*

History, trans. Sarah Matthews (Chicago: University of Chicago Press, 1980), p. 11.

5. Braudel, *The Mediterranean,* 2:1244.

6. James H. Robinson, "The Conception and Methods of History," *Congress of Arts and Sciences: Universal Exposition St. Louis, 1904.* ed. Howard J. Rogers, 8 vols. (New York: University Alliance, 1909), 2:48.

7. Charles Austin Beard, *America in Midpassage,* vol. 3 of *The Rise of American Civilization* (New York: Macmillan, 1946), p. 912.

8. Gerald Holton, "Do Scientists Need a Philosophy?" *Times Literary Supplement,* 2 November 1984, p. 1232.

9. Braudel, *On History,* p. 7.

10. Edward B. Tylor, *Primitive Culture,* 2 vols. (New York: H. Holt Co., 1889), 1:16.

11. Lucien Febvre, "History and Psychology" in Peter Burke, ed., *A New Kind of History: From the Writings of Lucien Febvre,* trans. K. Folca (London: Routledge & Kegan Paul, 1973), p. 220.

12. Braudel, *The Mediterranean,* 1:757.

13. James Harvey Robinson, *The New History* (New York: Macmillan, 1912), pp. 50–51.

14. Braudel, *On History,* p. 39.

15. Robinson, *New History,* p. 264.

16. Febvre in Burke, *A New Kind of History,* p. 25.

17. Ibid., p. 41.

18. Lucien Febvre, *A Geographical Introduction to History,* trans. E. G. Mountford and J. H. Paxton (New York: Barnes & Noble, 1924), pp. 85 and 29.

19. Febvre in Burke, *A New Kind of History,* pp. 15–16.

20. Ibid., p. 26.

21. Braudel, *On History,* p. 48.

22. Ibid., p. 76.

23. Fernand Braudel, *Afterthoughts on Material Civilization and Capitalism,* trans. Patricia M. Ranum (Baltimore: Johns Hopkins Press, 1977), p. 5.

24. Braudel, *On History,* p. 99.

25. Ibid., p. 217.

26. Braudel, *The Mediterranean,* 2:1244.

History's Point and Subject Matter:

A Proposal

Bernard P. Dauenhauer

Many historians and not a few philosophers have long and vigorously wrestled with the thorny issue of history's point and subject matter. That struggle continues unabated today.[1] Schematically, the issue can be put as follows: Is there any sense to the longstanding traditional view that history is *magistra vitae*, the teacher of and for life? That is, is history a sort of moral science or discipline providing its students with guidance for the conduct of their lives? Or is it akin to, if not one of, the social sciences, something like a disinterested sociology of the past? Or is history perhaps a quasi-aesthetic pursuit, providing its devotees with interesting and perhaps illuminating accounts of the past but bearing no lessons for the present or future? If history either is something like a social science or is a quasi-aesthetic endeavor, then whatever its readers might take from it to guide their own lives is essentially incidental and extrinsic to its objective and cannot therefore be credited or debited to its account.

This facet of the complex issue in question here is inextricably tied to the question of the subject matter of history. Can one properly distinguish a domain of human action, a domain of performances of identifiable human beings which effect changes in the way the world is or unfolds? In other terms, is human agency irreducible to natural processes? And if so, is this agency either significant or intelligible and hence worthy of either the historian's or the philosopher's attention?[2]

A current version of this question concerning the subject matter of history is the debate devoted to the relative merits of what has come to be called social history as opposed to political history. Social history is conceived largely in terms of the social sciences. As

a science, such history is not concerned, or is concerned only pe-
ripherally, with individual persons or events. Rather, it is concerned
with structures, cycles, institutions, or "conjunctures."[3] The "entities" it takes as its subject matter perdure for long stretches of time
and generally lack well-defined points of origin or termination. Traditional political history, by contrast, has been and is concerned
with the purportedly memorable deeds and sufferings of identifiable
persons. The entities it takes as its subject matter are, at least in
principle, precisely datable. And the span of time they inhabit usually does not exceed that of the normal duration of a very few human
generations.

These intercalated questions concerning the point and the subject matter of history likewise inevitably involve the issue of how
history is to be written. This issue can be posed in various ways.
One way of posing the issue is to ask whether the historian's task is
to achieve understanding (Verstehen) or to furnish explanations
(Erklären) construed either in causal or in structural terms. Another way is to ask whether narrativity is an essential feature of
fully developed, mature historiographical practice.

The objective of my paper is not, of course, to bring definitive
resolution to any part of this multifaceted issue. Rather, it is to
shed light, perhaps obliquely, upon several parts of this issue by
proposing a coherent doctrine about the source and conditions for
the possibility of the study of history, its reading and writing, as a
senseful enterprise. This doctrine, which is distilled from the relevant themes of Martin Heidegger's Being and Time and from Paul
Ricoeur's recent studies concerning history, narrative, and time,
serves to specify history's subject matter, which in turn clarifies
history's point.[4]

In brief, the proposal I want to present holds: The possibility of the
study of history as a sensible enterprise requires the acknowledg-
ment of the persistent possibility of deliberate efficacious human
agency. This proposal does not entail that each sensible work of
historical scholarship must explicitly refer to events or actions in-
stigated or effected by identifiable human agents. It holds rather for
the corpus of historical studies taken together as a whole. Nonetheless, the proposal does imply that any single work of historical

scholarship will yield its full sense only if it refers, at least obliquely, to datable events brought about by identifiable human agents.

Heidegger on History

The basic Heideggerian thesis pertinent to my proposal is that *Dasein*, man's essential kind of being, can and does have a history precisely because one of *Dasein*'s essential constituents is what he calls historicality. Historicality is that which makes history, or historiology, a possible inquiry, a possible human enterprise.[5]

Dasein's structure is, of course, quite complex. This complexity bears upon both the subject matter and the sort of inquiry which make up history. Temporality, Heidegger says, is that in terms of which *Dasein*'s structural totality is intelligible. And *"the primary phenomenon of primordial and authentic temporality is the future"* (p. 378).

Let me spell out Heidegger's position in some detail. Heidegger maintains that "it is essential to the basic constitution of Dasein that there is *constantly something to be settled*" (p. 279). That is, *Dasein* is the sort of entity which has never reached completion. It is always ahead of itself toward its possibilities. *Dasein*'s ultimate possibility is the possibility of the impossibility of any further possiblities, namely death. Thus Heidegger can say: "Death reveals itself as that *possibility which is one's ownmost, which is nonrelational, and which is not to be outstripped*" (p. 294). Death, in this sense, is not merely some particular occurrence. It is that toward which *Dasein* is referred, or "thrown," so long as it exists. Death is certain, but when it will come is uncertain. It is possible at any moment. And by virtue of its nonrelational character, death is that which thoroughly individualizes *Dasein* (p. 308). History, Heidegger maintains, arises and makes sense only in the face of this fundamental Being-toward-death.

Just how and why is this the case? Heidegger argues that *Dasein* does not first exist as an extrahistorical subject or ego which at some moment becomes historical by becoming intertwined with circumstances and events. Rather, *Dasein* is from the outset constituted "by historizing, so that anything like circumstances, events, and vicissitudes is ontologically possible *only because Dasein is historical in its Being"* (p. 431). History, then, belongs to *Dasein's* kind of Being, which is essentially a Being-toward-death. Or, in Heidegger's own words: *"Authentic Being-towards-death*—that is to say, the finitude of temporality—is the hidden basis of Dasein's *historicality"* (p. 438).

Dasein exists futurally toward its own possibilities of existence, the ultimate one of which is the possibility of its own death. But just what specifies a particular *Dasein's* possibilities as its own is not disclosed by death. *Dasein* takes over possibilities which have been handed down to it by its predecessors. That is, *Dasein* is essentially endowed with a heritage that it always appropriates in terms of futural possibilities. This heritage, as death makes clear, is finite. *Dasein's* primordial historizing, which Heidegger calls its fate, consists, then, in a set of possibilities that it has inherited and yet has also chosen (p. 435).

Now *Dasein* is never alone. It always exists as Being-in-the-world with other *Daseins*. Thus its historizing is essentially a cohistorizing. The historizing of a people or a community constitutes, in Heidegger's terms, destiny. Destiny, he says: "is not something that puts itself together out of individual fates, any more than Being-with-one-another can be conceived as the occurring together of several Subjects. Our fates have already been guided in advance, in our Being with one another in the same world. . . . Dasein's fateful destiny in and with its 'generation' goes to make up the full authentic historizing of Dasein."[6]

Dasein, then, in its existence makes a rejoinder to the heritage which it has received and which gives specificity to its open possibilities. *Dasein's* fate, as its appropriation of its inheritance, constitutes *Dasein's* primordial historicality. And this historicality opens the way to and for *Dasein's* future. History, then, gains its essential importance "neither in what is past nor in the today and its 'connection' with what is past, but in that authentic historizing of existence which arises from Dasein's *future"* (p. 438). It is *Dasein* itself, then, which is *primarily* historical. Because of its kind of Being, *Dasein* is both the primary subject matter of history and that which makes the study of history possible at all.

Even though *Dasein* is the primary subject matter of history, it is clearly not the only subject matter of history. *Dasein* is no world-less subject. In its essential historicality *Dasein* always exists as Being-in-the-world. In Heidegger's words: *"The historizing of history is the historizing of Being-in-the-world.* Dasein's historicality is essentially the historicality of the world. . . . In so far as Dasein exists factically, it already encounters that which has been discovered within-the-world. *With the existence of historical Being-in-the-world, what is ready-to-hand* i.e., equipment *and what is present-at-hand* i.e., objectified entities *have already, in every case, been incorporated into the history of the world"* (p. 440). Or, as he puts it more clearly in his *Basic Problems of Phenomenology,* not only is *Dasein* historical, but one should also call historical "all the things that the human being, who is historical and exists historically in the strict and proper sense, creates, shapes, cultivates: all his culture and works."[7]

These things and events that go to make up the world which *Dasein* inhabits, however, can and often do disrupt *Dasein's* unity and disperse it into a sequence of objectified "experiences." The world and its constituent items, therefore, pose to *Dasein* the problem of pulling itself together out of its dispersal into a steadiness that does not consist in stringing "moments" together but rather in a unitary living out of its fate in that Being-toward-death which radically individualizes it.

Thus, history and historiology are made possible by (a) *Dasein's* fundamental way of being, (b) the world with its constituent items which *Dasein* always and necessarily inhabits, and (c) *Dasein's* proneness to lose sight of its own unity by becoming dispersed in a plethora of apparently discrete experiences, and its consequent need to establish and maintain its own unity. History, then, has something of the character of a struggle in which *Dasein* engages in order to recover its own unity.

It follows from these considerations that the theme of all historiology is not at bottom the set of unique things or events which have happened just once and are irrepeatable. Nor is it some universal scheme impervious to specific things and events. Rather, history's basic theme is the set of possibilities for *Dasein* revealed in and through what has in fact transpired in the lives of its predecessors. The point of history is not somehow to recapture moments of the past. It is rather to reveal to the presently historizing *Dasein* the possibilities already met with and lived through by previous *Dasein*s. How previous *Dasein*s have coped with these possibilities constitutes the heritage which presently existing *Dasein* can hand down to itself as its fate in the course of its own futural taking up of its own possibilities.

Thus, the records, monuments, and remains with which historiology deals are possible materials for the disclosure of previously existent *Dasein*. In Heidegger's words: "Our going back to 'the past' does not first get its start from the acquisition, sifting, and securing of such material; these activities presuppose *historical Being towards* the Dasein that has-been-there—that is to say, they presuppose the historicality of the historian's existence. This is the existential foundation for historiology as a science, even for its most trivial and 'mechanical' procedures" (p. 446).

This Being-toward the *Dasein* that has-been-there is therefore that which makes possible all three sorts of historiology distinguished by Nietzsche, namely, the monumental, the antiquarian, and the critical. Monumental historiology discloses the "monumental" possibilities of human existence. Antiquarian historiology "reverently preserves" what has previously been disclosed. Critical historiology discloses the "today" in the light of what has been and of the future. Though historiology and the history it produces can, as Nietzsche also saw, be abused, the basis for all historiological study and its ultimate objective is to disclose to *Dasein* the sense and scope of its own heritage on the basis of which it can lay hold of its own futural possibilities, including its most distinguishing possibility, namely, its Being-toward-death.[8] In summary, history deals primarily with previously lived-through human possibilities. These possibilities are all constituted by the Being-in-the-world who lived through them, with other people having distinctive possibilities of their own. And the living through of these possibilities has always been accomplished by those whose basic kind of being is primordially characterized by Being-toward-death.

For Heidegger, then, the possibility of the study of history, its reading and writing, is rooted in humanity's very way of being. We are essentially futural. We must deal with possibilities which lie before us. And these possibilities have been shaped as peculiarly ours by what we have inherited from our predecessors, who in turn dealt with a heritage they had taken over.

Heidegger's account of the source and point of history is, I think, of immense help. But one should notice that what Heidegger says about the source of history holds in some way for all positive sciences and indeed for all possible human doings.[9] One can and should press further and ask: What specifically constitutes history as a distinctive human enterprise? To pursue this issue, one does well to consider Ricoeur's recent work on narrative and time.

Ricoeur on History and Narrativity

A central thesis defended by Ricoeur is: *"Time becomes human to the extent that it is articulated through a narrative mode, and narrative attains its full meaning when it becomes a condition of temporal existence."*[10] For present purposes, I will concentrate on the first part of this double thesis.

Two of Ricoeur's somewhat earlier essays, "The Narrative Function" and "Narrative Time," provide initial guidance concerning just what the thesis in question here means. Consider first his treatment of narrativity and historicity in "The Narrative Function."[11] Ricoeur argues there that "the historicity of human experience can be brought to language only as narrativity" (p. 294). Further, narrativity itself requires the interplay of two narrative modes with two sorts of reference. One of these modes is this mode of history, the mode which chronicles events. This mode refers to these events *indirectly*, through reference to documents, monuments, archives, etc. The other mode is the fictional or configurational mode, the mode which organizes these events into stories. This second mode is characterized by what Ricoeur calls split reference. It suspends the reference involved in our ordinary experience of persons, things, institutions, relationships, etc., so that the *differences* between our ordinary sets of convictions, familiar objects and topics, and point of view on the one hand, and those revealed by the story, stand out in clear relief. Thus he can claim: "It is in the exchange between history and fiction, between their opposed referential modes, that *our historicity is brought to language*" (p. 294).

Historicity or historiological inquiry, then, brings about a dialectic between the alien and the familiar, between the far and the near. It thereby effects a confrontation between the values of the past and those of the presently real. This confrontation, in turn, opens up the real toward the possible. And so Ricoeur can conclude: "The 'true' histories of the past uncover the buried potentialities of the present. . . . *There is only a history of the potentialities of the present.* History, in this sense, explores the field of 'imaginative' variations which surround the present and the real that we take for granted in everyday life" (p. 295).

Ricoeur pursues the bearing of narrativity upon historicity and temporality more thoroughly in his essay "Narrative Time."[12] His analysis there employs three explicitly stated "working hypotheses." (1) There is a reciprocal relationship between temporality and narrativity. Temporality is that structure of existence that reaches language in narrativity and narrativity is that structure of language which has temporality as its ultimate referent. (2) Heidegger is correct in *Being and Time* both in distinguishing multiple degrees or levels of temporal organization and in maintaining that the ordinary representation of time in terms of a linear sequence of "nows" conceals the true constitution of time. (3) The temporal implications of narrativity are best revealed through a consideration of the structure of the plot. The plot is that intelligible whole that governs the succession of events in a story (pp. 169–71). Here I will concentrate on the first and third of these hypotheses.[13]

Plots, Ricoeur notes, make events into stories. Plots therefore involve both temporality and narrativity. If an event is to be historical, it must be more than merely a unique occurrence, a singular happening. It must contribute to and be incorporated within a plot. Plots, then, involve two distinct structural elements, namely, multiple episodes and a configuration of these episodes into a whole.

To explore the implications of these two structural elements of plots, Ricoeur takes as his point of departure the act of following a story. Following a story involves understanding a sequence of actions, thoughts, or feelings as having a certain directedness. Thus a story's conclusion is that toward which the whole sequence is directed. But, Ricoeur notes: "A narrative conclusion can be neither deduced nor predicted. There is no story if our attention is not moved along by a thousand contingencies. This is why a story has to be followed to its conclusion. So rather than being predictable, a conclusion must be *acceptable*" (p. 174, my emphasis).

The time of the story, the narrative, is on the one hand public time and on the other a time which is by no means indifferent to the doings and sufferings of human beings. One aspect of the story's time is that it displays the possibility of the copresence of several agents or characters. A second, no less important, aspect of the story's time is that it is incorporable into the life of its readers, its audience. "Through its recitation, a story is incorporated into a community which it gathers together" (p. 176).

Further, narratives display persons acting in circumstances they have not created and producing at least some consequences they have not intended. Narratives, then, deal with, and presuppose, "interventions." An intervention is an intersection of human powers of action with the ordered processes of the world. A narrative presents moments when an actor, aware somehow of what he can do, in fact does it. But it also presents the outcome, both intended and unintended, both patent and latent, of this intervention into processes which both antedate and outlast each intervention.

Narratives as plots, therefore, not only recount episodes or events. They also configure them as a *whole*. Part of this configuration is the imposition of some "sense of an ending" upon mere succession, whether the succession be one of events or of worldly processes.[14]

The wholeness of narratives, furnished by the configuration of events into plots, allows the narrative to be told and retold. It also permits us to see the connection between its ending and its beginning. A crucial consequence of this grasping of a temporal multiplicity as a whole is that we are enabled to establish human action in memory. In Ricoeur's words:

> By reading the end in the beginning and the beginning in the end, we learn also to read time itself backward, as the recapitulation of the initial conditions of a course of action in its terminal consequences. In this way, a plot establishes human action not only within time . . . but within memory. Memory, accordingly, *repeats* the courses of events according to an order

that is the counterpart of time as "stretching-along" between a beginning and an end. (p. 180)

These considerations lead Ricoeur to conclude that, from the outset, narrative time is the time of being-with-others and these others include predecessors and successors as well as contemporaries. If this is so, then new light is shed on the Heideggerian concept of heritage. A heritage now appears as something transmitted from generation to generation. It is a tradition. And, Ricoeur says, "it is always a community, a people, or a group of protagonists which tries to take up the tradition—or traditions—of its origins."[15]

The communal act of taking over as its own what has been inaugurated and handed down by others is, then, ultimately what makes history, and therefore its inscription, possible. Thus, Ricoeur concludes:

Historiography . . . is nothing more than the passage into writing and then to critical rewriting of this primordial constituting of tradition. The naive forms of narration are deployed between this constituting of tradition and the writing of history (for example, legends and chronicles). . . . So it is in this sense that repetition may be spoken of as the foundation of historiography. But it is a repetition that is always articulated in a narrative mode. (p. 189)

History as historiography, therefore, is what converts the initial conjunction of time and narrative into an explicit inquiry. It can do so only as a communal enterprise of readers and writers who acknowledge their own community with their predecessors. And they make this community available for their communal successors.

Ricoeur expands and deepens these considerations in his monumental *Temps et Récit* (English title: *Time and Narrative*).[16] In this work, he takes note of the attack that much contemporary historiography, particularly French historiography, makes upon the three elementary ontological presuppositions of what has been called *l'histoire événementielle*, the history of events. The history of events is taken to be political history, the history made by specific individuals. The contemporary critique displaces political history to make way for a social history whose major categories—structure, trend, cycle, growth, conjuncture—are borrowed from the social sciences, especially demography, geography, sociology, and economics. This critique challenges traditional history's assumptions that (a) history is concerned with unrepeatable, singular past events not subsumable under universal laws, (b) history is specifically concerned with the contingent rather than necessary doings of specifiable human agents, and (c) there is a gap between the event, which is always somehow strange and therefore irreducibly other, and any invariant or constructed model (pp. 95–111).

This critique of political history in favor of social history likewise effects a displacement of the point of historical inquiry. Social history is a construct. It revives nothing. Hence it is in no sense *magistra vitae*. Ricoeur cites in this context Paul Veyne's *Comment on écrit l'histoire*: " 'History,' says Veyne, 'is a bookish, not an existential, notion. It is the organization by the intelligence of givens that refer to a temporality other than that of my *Dasein*. . . . History is an intellectual activity that, through consecrated literary forms, serves the ends of *simple curiosity*' " (p. 169, my emphasis). And Ricoeur comments: "Nothing links this curiosity to some existential ground."

In opposition to this trend to eliminate or at least to depreciate the significance of events brought about by individual human agents, Ricoeur first argues that social history, no matter how radically conceived, still involves plots, that is, the configuration of elements (goals, material causes, chance, etc.) into a whole. No sort of history, he says, can sever every connection with narrative and still retain its historical character. Further, all narrative activity "has its own dialectic that makes it pass through the successive stages of mimesis, starting from the prefigurations inherent in the order of action, by way of the constitutive configurations of emplotment . . . to the refigurations that arise due to the collision of the world of the text with the life-world."[17]

These elements lead Ricoeur to defend two theses concerning the status of historical time in relation to the temporality of a narrative. First, the time spans, long or short, constructed by the historian, themselves rest upon some level of an already constructed temporality, namely the temporality of all emplotments of action. All emplotments have an ending in terms of which the story is constituted as a totality and from the vantage point of which one can both distinguish the relevant from the irrelevant and trace a sequence of moments back to a beginning. Second, and crucially, however artificial the historian's constructed time may be, it never ceases to refer back to the temporality of concrete praxis, the temporality involving determinate agents who pursue goals by assorted means in a specifiable set of circumstances with both intended and unintended consequences. These two relations, namely "constructed on x" and "referring back to y" intertwine and thus characterize all the procedures and constructs (e.g., cycles, eras, structures, conjuctures) built by history (p. 182).

This set of considerations leads Ricoeur to conclude that history, historical time, mediates between two apparently incongruent experiences of time. These two experiences confront us with a genuine paradox which he puts thus: "On the cosmic scale, our span of life is insignificant, and nevertheless this brief lapse of time in which we appear on the scene of the world is the very place whence every question of significance arises." Historical time is like a bridge which spans the gap between cosmic time and lived time. It "is constituted at the junction of our fractured concept of time."[18]

History and Human Agency

Let me begin the distillation of a coherent doctrine about the source and conditions of history's possibility as a senseful enterprise by briefly recapitulating the pertinent resources gleaned from the works of Heidegger and Ricoeur. For Heidegger, the source and condition for the possibility of history is quite simply *Dasein*'s way of being. Because man is as he is, history is possible. Man is (1) finite, (2) futurally oriented, (3) thrown toward death, (4) the inhabitant of a world of things and happenings, (5) always among other men, and (6) endowed with a heritage, (7) whence his future possibilities arise. Ricoeur basically accepts these seven features of man's kind of being. His distinctive contribution to the question of the source of history's possibility is his emphasis on (1) man's paradoxical experience of time, and (2) the possibility of narrative as a mode of discourse.

These resources allow me to propose that *history, understood as an inscribed account, is made possible as a senseful enterprise by the intersection of writers and readers, both of whom have to live out open but problematic finite futures but who find themselves set in a context including both material and cultural entities, relations, and occurrences not of their own making which they can nonetheless configure and articulate in narrative.*[19] When actualized, then, history is an elaborate mediation which both holds together and keeps distinct present people with necessarily open futures, predecessors, and a world which is in some respects common to them and in other respects peculiar to either the one or the other. On this view, Adam and Eve, or at least pre-Eve Adam, in prelapsarian Paradise, could not have written, or read, any history. They had no predecessors. Their future was neither problematic nor destined to terminate in death. And their surrounding world was, if we ignore the serpent and the tree, totally pliable to their wishes.

This means that there can be no senseful study of history unless (a) there are students, the readers and writers, capable of future agency but whose future is temporally limited, (b) these students had human predecessors, (c) these students are capable of narrative activity, and (d) these students inhabit a world which constrains as well as promotes their efficacy as agents. Taken together, these necessary conditions are sufficient for history's possibility.

The notion of agency is obviously crucial to the doctrine I am proposing. To borrow a definition from *Time and Narrative*, agents are those who learn "to 'isolate' a closed system from its environment and to discover the possibilities of development inherent to this system. The agent learns this by setting the system in motion, beginning from some initial state the agent has 'isolated.' It is this setting things in motion that constitutes interference, at the intersection between one of the agent's abilities and the resources of the system."[20] The system in question, of course, always remains affected by the environment. Its "isolation" is never complete.

When the conditions for history's possibility are in fact recognized by people, they are sufficient, though obviously not necessary, to motivate actual historical study. Students are motivated to actualize the conditions for history, acutally to study history, by the experience of their own finite freedom. Freedom, as the capacity to exercise efficacious agency, thrusts the students unavoidably toward their own open but finite future.[21] It may be that some people study history to avoid confronting their own futures. But engaging in such a dodge presupposes the recognition that one's own future is open. This recognition need not be made explicit or thematic. But it must be operative if there is to be a senseful study of history.

The recognition of the future's openness can, of course, be assessed in many ways. A student may conclude that the opportunities he has for future agency are trivial when compared to the opportunities enjoyed by some or all of his predecessors or contemporaries. But unless he sees that he can perform at least trivial action, can "butt his head against a stone wall," it would make no sense for him to study history.

Conversely, if the student were not to experience his freedom as a finite freedom, a freedom whose results he cannot confine just to his aims, he would have no reason actually to study history. Since he could do just as he pleased, he would have no reason to consult anyone, predecessor or contemporary. God has no reason to study history.

If, however, in the exercise of an unavoidable freedom one brings about unintended as well as intended consequences, then one has abundant reason to study history. One has reason to consider previous exercises of freedom to learn about one's own condition, to see how it is like and how it is unlike others' condition.

Attention to history becomes especially pertinent in view of the fact that everyone must die. Each person's freedom is finite not only in the sense that its exercise brings about unintended consequences. It is also going to end. This fact lends urgency and seriousness to a person's life. The timeliness of actions becomes important. Opportunities are either seized or missed. It makes sense, then, to attend to the whole of predecessors' lives, to their deeds as contextualized by their own deaths, in order to glimpse the inevitable contextualization of one's own deed by his own death. Again, the study of history may be abused by treating it as a way to hide from one's own death. But hiding from death presupposes acknowledging it.

This doctrine concerning the source of history's possibility and the motivation sufficient to actualize this possibility also determines history's subject matter. The subject matter for history is all previous human agency, especially that of one's predecessors.[22] Human action, as meant here, includes thought insofar as it has been transmitted. The action of transmitting thought, like any other action, is grist for history.[23] Further, since all action transpires within material contexts, then the material universe *insofar, but only insofar, as it has been intercalated with action* is also part of history's subject matter. That is, the material universe is part of the subject matter of history only insofar as it bears the mark of having been touched by human agency.

On this view, the subject matter of "natural history" is not, in and of itself, a part of the subject matter of history. A distinction can and should be made between the subject matter of any positive science and the subject matter of the history of a positive science. Astronomy, for example, has celestial bodies and their motion for its subject matter. The history of astronomy has as its subject matter the communicated thought about such bodies.[24]

Nothing, then, is subject matter for history unless it is connectable to human action. And human action, as Aristotle pointed out, has to do with that about which men can deliberate and choose. It does not have to do with necessities as such.[25]

But human action never escapes some involvement with necessities. It is always embodied, always subject to termination by death, and always tied into other actions, one's own as well as those of others. To study thoroughly the history of human action is to attend to its unrecognized conditions and its unintended consequences as well as what is recognized and intended. And the unrecognized and unintended regularly involve necessities of some sort.

The connection between history's subject matter and the source of its possibility as a senseful enterprise can be summed up in the following terms. The efficacious actions of others, especially of predecessors, in their finitude leaves room for one's own free action. And the finitude of one's own action leaves room for the free action of successors. If the study of history is to make sense, the student must recognize that not only does one have predecessors but one will also have successors.

Just as my doctrine concerning history's source specifies history's subject matter, so too does it specify the point of studying it. The point to the study of history is to uncover reasonable possibilities for future conduct, one's own or others', either contemporaries or successors.[26] It is to shed light on what people in their particular present spatio-temporal situation can and cannot reasonably contemplate bringing about.

A study of the past shows us that, whether the issues be property, power, role, or responsibility, we can hold them only because our predecessors, their previous holders, can no longer retain their hold on them. This study also shows that both the holders and their holdings changed in both anticipated and unanticipated ways during the time span of the holding.

Since the student of history, the present holder of property, power, role, and responsibility, is no less finite than his predecessors, he learns that he too will have to relinquish these holdings to his successors. But again, these holdings will bear the mark of his having held them. History instructs him how they might reasonably be held. It does so not merely by relaying facts. It relays the facts insofar as, having themselves arisen from involvement in past action, they disclose future possibilities for action. With no exaggeration, history cannot be studied, whether its students wish it or not, without its disclosing future possibilities for the exercise of efficacious freedom.

The relaying or relating of past facts, an action that is disclosive of future possibilities for actions and is thus constitutive of history, cannot be accomplished in just any mode of discourse. For such disclosure one must show multiple human agents. And to show multiple human agents, one must distinguish beginnings, middles, and endings. This is tantamount to saying that the disclosure of future possibilities for action requires that the past facts relayed must be either displayed in narrative or be linked in some recognizable way to a narrative of human agency. Only narrative presents action as marked by endings and beginnings and therefore attributable to specific agents.[27] It also shows action to be shaped by circumstances which both are distinct from it and make it possible.

Implications of This Proposal

I do not claim to have proven the truth of my proposal. But I do claim that I have shown it to be coherent and nontrivial. I want to buttress it by pointing briefly to some of its salient consequences, as a means of illustrating its fruitfulness.

I should point out at once that the proposal that I have set forth does not imply that the human agency with which history deals is either of great worth or highly effective. The study of history might indeed show that human agency is insignificant, having only trivial consequences. Natural processes and forces might be shown to circumscribe or overwhelm human agency to such an extent that the interruptions of or interventions into these processes attempted by human beings scarcely leave a trace. Nonetheless, the study of history cannot avoid dealing with the question of human agency. It cannot avoid referring to that agency precisely as agency. Even if human actions are trivial, they are nonetheless actions. It is the task of history to assess these actions. History cannot perform this task if it dismisses them. The proposal I offer does not attempt to preempt the assessments which properly belong to historical studies. But it does insist that there are necessarily assessments of this sort for history to make.

One of the strengths of my proposals is precisely that it requires the student of history to distinguish the trivial from the nontrivial. Nothing in my proposal suggests that one can achieve apodicticity concerning these discriminations. The finitude of the student, among other factors, points to the impossibility of apodicticity in these matters. But the question of triviality or nontriviality remains insistent.

One would be hard pressed to show how the question of triviality could make sense with *absolutely* no reference to subsequent human thought and action. How, without reference to humans, would one determine that natural process A was trivial in comparison with natural process B? Whether in the case of the positive sciences or in that of some sort of history, matters are either trivial or nontrivial only with reference to people. My proposal accounts for the persistence of the issue of triviality in history by emphasizing that the student of history necessarily lives an open future which is, however, always marked by death.

My proposal, then, is squarely at odds with the view of history's point espoused by Paul Veyne. For Veyne, as I mentioned above, history does no more than serve the ends of simple curiosity. The study of history can, of course, spring in particular cases simply from curiosity. But sheer curiosity, as Heidegger has shown, is fundamentally evasive. He who indulges his curiosity is evading the seriousness of his own finite freedom. As evasive, curiosity presupposes at least an implicit recognition of that which it seeks to evade.[28]

In attempting to distinguish the trivial from the nontrivial, the student of history assesses not only the significance of several natural processes and their influence upon human agency. He also attempts to distinguish the more from the less efficacious agents. Does one look to kings or to commoners for exemplary efficacy? Does one look to the clearly named individual persons or to the anonymous individuals or groups? Again, my proposal does not pretend to settle these matters. That is a task for history's students. But my proposal does account for the persistence of this issue. Each student of history both presently bears a name and is headed for a death after which he will soon be either unknown or quite possibly misknown. He studies history to discover possible ways of sensible living under such conditions.

It is worth repeating at this point that my proposal does not require that each and every piece of historical scholarship deal explicitly with the questions of triviality and relative efficacy of either natural processes or human agency. Rather, it claims that the corpus of historical studies as a whole necessarily involves these matters. It further claims that each work of historical scholarship gets its full sense only when it is referred to the corpus as a whole and is thereby referred to the issue of human agency.

The proposal I offer thus shows the pertinence of both political and social history, of histories of both the short and the long *durée*. Conversely, it shows the pointlessness of attempting to consign the field to only one of these or even of attempting to assign unequivocal primacy of one over the other. To fill out political history with accounts of material resources and cultural conditions always makes sense. Demography, economics, psychology, and sociology are never irrelevent. But, likewise, social history, no matter how far reaching, cannot make attention to political interventions or interruptions pointless. These latter may indeed be trivial. But it is no small matter to note and detail that triviality.

History, then, on my proposal remains *magistra vitae*. The student of history is instructed about the sense and scope of his own finite existence and action. My proposal does not indicate the nature of this instruction. It does not determine whether the lesson will be one announcing human strength or admitting its weakness. But it does show why and how history necessarily proffers instruction to its students concerning the sense and thrust of their own lives.

Notes

1. Among recent philosophers who have dealt with this issue let me mention particularly R. G. Collingwood, W. B. Gallie, Georg H. von Wright, Arthur Danto, William H. Dray, Hans Jonas, Hannah Arendt, and Paul Ricoeur. Among contemporary historians who have addressed this issue are Fernand Braudel, Philip Arias, Ernst Breisach, Lawrence Stone, Paul Veyne, and, of course, Michel Foucault.

2. See Hannah Arendt, "What Is History?" in her *Between Past and Future* (New York: Viking Press, 1968); and Paul Ricoeur, *Time and Narrative*, vol. 1, trans. Kathleen McLaughlin and David Pellauer (Chicago: University of Chicago Press, 1984) pp. 54–55 and 132–43.

3. See in this connection the collection of essays by Fernand Braudel, *On History*, trans. Sarah Matthews (Chicago: University of Chicago Press, 1980). Of special interest for present purposes are: "The Situation of History in 1950," "History and the Social Sciences: The *Longue Durée*," and "On a Concept of Social History."

4. Heidegger deals with the topic of history in several of his other, later writings. There are noteworthy shifts in what he later says. The proposal I am offering, though, is heavily indebted to *Being and Time*. Ricoeur had addressed the question of history in earlier works. Here I draw exclusively on his very recent writings. It should also be mentioned that in distilling my proposal I have ignored his critique of the doctrine of temporality found in *Being and Time*. Thus, though my proposal owes its existence to Heidegger and Ricoeur, it is in the final analysis my proposal. It does not claim the sanction of either of them.

5. Martin Heidegger, *Being and Time*, trans. John Macquarrie and Edward Robinson, (New York: Harper and Row, 1962), pp. 41–42. Of "prehistorical" peoples Heidegger says: "If historiology is wanting, this is not evidence *against* Dasein's historicality; on the contrary as a deficient mode of this state of Being, it is evidence for it. Only because it is 'historical' can an era be historiological" (p. 42). Two excellent discussions of Heidegger's treatment of history and historicality are: David Hoy, "History, Historicity, and Historiography in *Being and Time*," in *Heidegger and Modern Philosophy*, ed. Michael Murray (New Haven: Yale University Press, 1978), pp. 329–53; and Joseph J. Kockelman's chapter entitled "History and Historiography," in his *Heidegger and Science* (Washington: University Press of America, 1985), pp. 190–209.

6. P. 436. As Heidegger had said earlier in this text, "not only is Being towards Others an autonomous, irreducible relationship of Being: this relationship, as Being-with, is one which, with Dasein's Being, already is" (p. 162).

7. Martin Heidegger, *The Basic Problems of Phenomenology*, trans. Albert Hofstadter (Bloomington: Indiana University Press, 1982), p. 169.

8. Pp. 448–49. See, on the significance of historicality, Charles B. Guignon's stimulating if controversial essay, "Heidegger's 'Authenticity' Revisited," *The Review of Metaphysics* 38 (December 1984): 321–39, esp. 334–38.

9. See Heidegger, *Basic Problems of Phenomenology*, pp. 320–22 concerning the objectification of beings in the positive sciences and the basis for this objectification.

10. Ricoeur, *Time and Narrative*, 1:52.

11. Paul Ricoeur, "The Narrative Function," in his *Hermeneutics and the Human Sciences*, ed. and trans. John B. Thompson (Cambridge: Cambridge University Press, 1981), pp. 274–96. Ricoeur uses the term 'historicity' in the same way that Heidegger does. Historicity or historiological inquiry and research, according to Heidegger, is a kind of Being that *Dasein* may have because historicality is one of *Dasein*'s determining characteristics. See *Being and Time*, pp. 41–42.

12. Paul Ricoeur, "Narrative Time," in *Critical Inquiry*, 7, no. 1 (Autumn 1980): 169–90.

13. To deal also with the second hypothesis would require me either to repeat what I have said in the first section or to take up Ricoeur's critique of Heidegger's account. Neither course would advance the project I have undertaken here.

14. P. 179. Ricoeur borrows the phrase "sense of an ending" from Frank Kermode.

15. Pp. 188–89. Ricoeur suggests that he is rectifying Heidegger on this point. A good argument can be made, though, that Ricoeur is rather filling out what is already delineated in Heidegger's work. Guignon's essay, mentioned in n. 8 above, is pertinent to this matter.

16. Paul Ricoeur, *Temps et Récit* (Paris: Editions du Seuil, 1983–85), 3 vols. The English translation of vols. 1 and 2, by Kathleen McLaughlin and David Pellauer, have been published by the University of Chicago Press in 1984 and 1985 respectively under the title *Time and Narrative*. All references to this work here are to vol. 1. Page numbers in my text refer to this translation of vol. 1.

David Carr has published a valuable review essay on vol. 1 in *History and Theory* 23, no. 3 (1984): 357–70.

17. P. 180. Ricoeur distinguishes a threefold mimesis. Mimesis$_1$ consists in a pre-understanding of the semantics, symbolic systems, and temporality involved in human acting. Mimesis$_2$ consists in the configuration of diverse elements, e.g., agents, interactions, circumstances, unexpected results, into a whole. This whole is one which can be followed from a determinate beginning to a determinate ending. It makes possible the telling and retelling of a story as the sort of whole in which the initial conditions of a course of action are seen as recapitulated in its final consequences. Mimesis$_3$ refers to the effect which the story has upon the subsequent life of its hearers or readers. Narrative, then, is fundamentally diachronic (pp. 54–87).

18. Ricoeur, "Le temps raconté," p. 441.

19. Oral history, like written history, is inscribable. And all writers started out, of course, as readers. Many even continue to read, though perhaps only what they themselves write.

20. P. 135. Ricoeur is here following the lead of G. H. von Wright. See von Wright's *Explanation and Understanding* (Ithaca: Cornell University Press, 1971) esp. pp. 58–64.

21. On the connection between freedom and efficacy, see my "Relational Freedom," *The Review of Metaphysics* 36, no. 1 (1982): 77–101.

22. Both autobiography and "contemporary" history are notoriously troublesome. There is always the danger that, with insufficient counterweights, they will degenerate into special pleading.

23. By no means do I want to suggest that there is some thought which is in principle nontransmissible. But clearly some has not been transmitted: my paternal grandfather's, for instance.

24. See in this connection Heidegger, *Basic Problems of Phenomenology*, pp. 164–70. It is worth noting that Heidegger denies, as Hegel would also, that a similarly sharp distinction can be made between philosophy and the history of philosophy (pp. 20 and 23).

25. Aristotle, *Nicomachean Ethics*, 1111b4 ff. See in this connection Charles Taylor, "Foucault on Freedom and Truth," *Political Theory* 12, no. 2 (May 1984): esp. 168–70.

26. See in this connection *Time and Narrative*, esp. pp. 70–71 and 182.

27. My account here is not self-referentially inconsistent. But my claims would be empty if there were not already narratives in existence. It is these narratives which alone are able to provide the material evidence for my view.

28. Heidegger, *Being and Time*, pp. 214–17.

Michel Foucault and the Career
of the Historical Event
Thomas R. Flynn

French historians in the last few decades have commonly distinguished "history of events" (*histoire événementielle*) from "non-event-oriented history" (*histoire non événementielle*) and have focused their attention on the latter. This "new" history of the nonevent relies explicitly on the methods of the social sciences, especially as they express comparativist or structuralist insights and exploit the possibilities of statistical arguments and computer techniques. This is the realm of serial history and history of the long term (*la longue durée*). Its practitioners tend to publish in the journal *Annales: économies, sociétés, civilisations,* founded by Marc Bloch and Lucien Febvre; they have become known as the "Annales" school of historiography. Perhaps the leading work to emerge from this distinguished group thus far is Fernand Braudel's massive study *The Mediterranean and the Mediterranean World in the Age of Philip II.*[1]

The inevitable polemics surrounding the rise of the new history tended to dichotomize the field of historiography into the chronological and the achronological and to belittle the former as interested merely in "battles and treaties," as being political and nationalist in origin, and lately, in France at least, as having devolved into a kind of "Stalino-Marxist historicism."[2] One of the casualties of this conflict has been the "responsible agent" of classical humanism and recent existentialism. In its place these historians favor anonymous forces and impersonal constraints, glacier-like movements, demographic tables and economic curves. Little wonder, then, that they should be linked with the structuralists, whose fashionability in the '60s they shared. Small wonder, too, that Foucault's "histories" of madness, of clinical medicine, and of the epistemic shifts between the classical, modern, and postmodern world-views should place him in their number in the eyes of many.

I wish to discuss an aspect of Foucault's thought in light of this controversy. Philosophers in particular should not lose sight of the fact that Foucault was a historian. Indeed, he christened his position at the Collège de France, "Chair in the History of the Systems of Thought." The very title sounds structuralist. He gained notoriety in the sixties by arguing against the historicist pretensions of the modern *episteme* and its humanism. Foucault's neo-Nietzschean proclamation of the "death of man," that is, that the concept of the individual, finite subject had lost its centering function with the passing of modernism, raised a barrage of antistructuralist fury in the name of humanism and of history itself.[3]

But the fire was misdirected. Foucault had long since left the target area, if indeed he had ever stood there. With typical acerbity he reviled his critics for locating him among the structuralists. In fact, by characterizing structuralism in *The Order of Things* as "the troubled consciousness of modern thought" (p. 208), he seemed to assume a poststructuralist stance even in his most "structuralist" book.[4]

In fact, Foucault's relationship with structuralism and with the new history as history of the nonevent is ambiguous. But this very lack of definition affords him the *Spielraum* to develop his own approach to the history of discourse and practices. By focusing on the concept of the historical event as exemplified in *Discipline and Punish* in particular, I intend to show how the very meaning of "event" has been broadened by Foucault so as to span the chasm marked by New Historians between the "eventworthy" and the "noneventworthy."

Because *Discipline and Punish* appears after Foucault has elaborated both his "archaeological" and his "genealogical" approaches to history, we should first explain his use of these two terms, especially as they bear upon the meaning of 'event' in his historiography.

Foucault called his first three major works "archaeologies." The term denotes the uncovering of those cognitive and evaluative limits that map the region in which certain kinds of discursive and nondiscursive practices can take place. But these limits are also conditions that make such practices possible. Archaeology is not interested in the persons involved or their history, but, for example, in how it was possible to conceive of both "physiocratic" and "utilitarian" knowledge in interlocking and simultaneous forms—a question Foucault addressed in *The Order of Things*. His concern is with practices, not actions, and this Wittgensteinian term, Gallicized by Pierre Bourdieu,[5] immediately directs him away from the "battles and treaties" of event history toward such nonevents as madness as a practice of exclusion, and clinical medicine as following a certain perceptual code. In *The Archaeology of Knowledge*, where he presents his "discourse on method" for these archaeologies, Foucault's aim is to define "a method of analysis purged of anthropologism" (p. 15). In that work he proceeds to evict a host of notions dear to event-oriented historians, including the theme of continuity with its attendant concepts of origin, tradition, influence, development, and evolution. In their stead he gives us discursive regularities which will emerge from the "pure description of discursive events" that he proposes as an initial phase of his archaeological project (see p. 27). As the vocabulary suggests, Foucault's thought takes a decidedly linguistic turn in *The Archaeology of Knowledge*.

For our topic, two aspects of archaeology are especially relevant: Foucault's interest in the statement/event, as he calls it, and his questioning, not the grammar of the statement, but "how it is that *one* particular statement appeared rather than another" (p. 27).

The statement (*l'énoncé*) for Foucault is the basic unit of communication. Though it need not be verbal (consider forms of aesthetic communication), it is an ordering of material traces and hence, though unique as event, is repeatable as thing. (A suggestive analogy might be the type-token relationship in aesthetics.) Without pursuing the obscure track of the Foucaultian *énoncé*, let us merely note his reason for speaking of the statement as event, namely, to restore the specificity of its occurrence and show that discontinuity characterizes the simple fact of the statement (p. 28). The discontinuity of events is also difference. With statements as with all differential events, individuation consists in a differential relation to other events in a series. Though I used the word 'unit' to describe the statement, neither it nor any event is an atomic entity.[6] Events are relative and susceptible to a merely differential analysis, as Saussure argued.[7] The series in which the statement/event gains its differential identity is called a discursive practice.[8] It is discursive and nondiscursive practices such as the separation of the mentally ill from the healthy and its concomitant adoption of the medical model and vocabulary for communicating with and about the insane that has captured Foucault's attention from his first major work to his very last.

Still, discursive practice, especially in the *Archaeology,* enjoys a "relative" autonomy, as the Marxists would say, vis-à-vis non-discursive phenomena. In words of caution that some of his commentators have failed to note, Foucault warns that archaeological description of discourses "is deployed in the dimension of a general history; it seeks to discover the whole domain of institutions, economic processes, and social relations on which discursive formations can be articulated; it tries to show how the autonomy of discourse . . . [does] not give it the status of pure ideality and total historical independence" (p. 165). The inscription of discursive and nondiscursive practices in a broad general history is most evident in his histories of madness, the clinic, and the prison.

Since discourse has "its own forms of sequence and succession" (p. 169), discursive events, whether statements or practices, need not be confined to the linear time of traditional history. Like a comparative social scientist (one thinks of Weber's study of the city through the ages)[9] the archaeologist brings to light the fissures, the breaks, the contrasts—in effect, "events" at right angles to the temporal line of evolution or development.

The second aspect of Foucault's archaeology of importance to the topic of the historical event is his question of how one statement appears rather than another. I take this to be a form of the search for objective possibility that has interested social theorists since Marx and Weber. But the arbiter of possibility for Foucault is neither social nor economic. It is what he calls the archive, "the general system of the formation and transformation of statements," whether as events or as things (p. 130). Archaeology, in Foucault's mind, is not a form of mental geology, much less a search for begin-

nings (*archai*), but the description of the archive, the historical a
priori of a given period which conditions the practices of exclusion
and inclusion that are ingredient in all social exchange: the true
and the false, the normal and deviant, the evident and the un-
thinkable, and so forth.

Although one's own archive remains invisible, being the necessary condition for describing other archives, these others are available for comparison and contrast. Indeed, of all the "events" the
archaeologist describes, the most important and the rarest are what
Foucault calls transformations or ruptures, of which the most radical bear on the general rules of one or several discursive formations
(p. 177). The famous epistemological "breaks" analyzed in *The
Order of Things* are examples of such ruptures. But the point is that
he refers to these radical breaks as "events" even as he allows that
"archaeology distinguishes several possible levels of events within
the very density of discourse" (p. 117).

We gain an insight into Foucault's understanding of the relation
between his archaeological description of events and the so-called
New History, if we consider his inaugural lecture at the Collège de
France. After noting the logophobia that marks our society, its fear
of the proliferation of disorderly discourse, he suggests three reme-
dies, the third of which is "to restore to discourse its character as
event" (p. 229). As befits an inaugural address, he elaborates the
point in programmatic fashion: "We frequently credit contemporary history with having removed the individual event from its
privileged position and with having revealed the more enduring
structures of history." But he cautions: "I do not think one can
oppose the identification of the individual event to the analysis of
long-term trends quite so neatly." In fact, he thinks it is by
"squeezing the individual event" that those massive phenomena
emerge. "What is significant," he continues, "is that history does
not consider an event without defining the series to which it belongs, without specifying the method of analysis used, without
seeking out the regularity of phenomena and the probable limits of
their occurrence, without enquiring about variations, inflexions,
and the slope of the curve, without desiring to know the conditions
on which these depend." History has long since abandoned its attempt to understand events in terms of cause and effect in the

formless unity of some great evolutionary process, he assures us. Still, its search is not for structures alien and hostile to the event. Rather, it seeks to establish "those diverse converging and sometimes divergent, but never autonomous series that enable us to circumscribe the 'locus' of an event, the limits to its fluidity and the conditions of its emergence" (p. 230). The series and the event emerge as the pivotal concepts on which Foucault's "histories" will henceforth turn. The "series" will establish the intelligible contours, a certain regularity without continuity. Foucault admits it is a paradoxical concept, this discontinuous systematization (consider the image of dot matrix printing!). It is the sheer positivity of the event, its factical occurrence as incorporeal yet material, that requires Foucault to appeal to the concept of chance in the production of events. So Foucault's necessities are hypothetical: *if* an event occurs within a series, it must be of this character and not of that; but whether it occurs or not is quite unpredictable. And since the series itself is a higher-level event, this relationship obtains among series-events as well. This is hardly rationalism, yet neither is it the irrationalism with which Foucault had been branded over the years. Antifoundationalist? Yes, we are *in medias res.* Methodological anarchy? No, if we decide to sweeten our coffee, we must all wait for the sugar to dissolve.

It is in this same inaugural lecture, delivered 2 December 1970, that Foucault distinguishes the critical from the genealogical "ensembles" of analysis that he proposes for his subsequent work. In fact, his next essays and major works constitute "genealogies" whose Nietzschean inspiration he freely admits. Let us briefly characterize genealogy before turning to its application in *Discipline and Punish.* Three features are relevant to the historical event.

First, genealogy as a method is concerned not with origins, which Foucault sees as linked with Platonic essentialism, but with the course of descent *(Herkunft)* of a series of events. Unlike the continuities of a theory of origins, genealogy stresses the jolts and surprises of history, the chance occurrences, in order to "maintain passing events in their proper dispersion."[10] In this it resembles archaeology.

The second and third points are that genealogy "poses the problem of power and of the body (of bodies), indeed, its problems begin from the imposition of power upon bodies."[11] As Foucault notes in *Language, Counter-Memory, Practice*, "*Herkunft* attaches itself to the body and all that touches it: diet, climate, soil" (p. 146). His genealogy of the "carceral system," as we shall see, centers on the way "the body as the major target of penal repression disappeared" at a certain point in history. Likewise, chapter two of the second volume of his history of sexuality, which appeared just before he died, is entitled "Diététique" and underscores the concern of the classical Greeks for matters of diet and physical regimen; sex is placed in that context, rather than in a primarily moral sphere.[12] Its question is to determine precisely the conditions for the transformation of sexual practice and its problematic in the classical, Hellenistic and Patristic eras.

Power relations underwrite all Foucault's genealogies. This translates "history" from the realm of meaning and communication toward a "micro-physics of power," in Foucault's telling phrase. Though he never accords us a definition of power, as befits a self-proclaimed historical nominalist, he does characterize it as all-pervasive, positive, productive, and operating through "capillaries" in the social body. Though elusive as such—indeed one can only conceive of it within some relation or other—"power" serves several functions for Foucault's genealogies, of which the most important for us is methodological: mechanisms of power constitute a "grid of intelligibility for the social field."[13] Specifically, the concept of power enables us to understand relations in history in terms no longer of knowledge and meaning but of strategy and tactics. In *Language, Counter-Memory, and Practice*, history is thus seen as the locus of the "hazardous play of dominations" (p. 148), where war, not law (*le droit*) is the fruitful model of intelligibility.

If the historical "documents" are now to be read in terms of strategy and tactics, the historical event assumes the guise not only of chance discontinuity but of "opportunity," or better, "occasion." (Of course, the "strategist" of history has been relieved of duty; the events are differentials of practice.) To the "what" of the superficial occurrence, such as the torture of a regicide or the building of a reformatory, must be added the strategic or tactical question of the form of subjection operative here. It is that question which he poses with regard to the penal system in *Discipline and Punish.*

With accustomed irony, Foucault is said to have referred to this as his "first book," though it ranks rather far along the line of his published works.[14] It is a "genealogy," that is, an uncovering of the basis (*Herkunft*) of nineteenth-century penal reform, not in the high-minded humanitarianism of its proponents, but in a entire "carceral system" which included military training, scholastic discipline, and the organization of individuals in factories and hospitals. As with its predecessors, the book centers on a crucial transformation, this time in the practice of legal punishment, beginning in 1790.

But the work is also an "archaeology" of those impersonal relations that make it possible, indeed natural, to speak of surveillance, reeducation, and training—words from the military and scholastic vocabulary—in the context of judicial punishment. As with his earlier archaeological studies, a new object appears for a new science; the science is criminology, the object is the delinquent.

The descriptive aspect of his enterprise reveals a rather rapid and wide-spread change in the penal practices of the European and North American communities between 1791 and 1810.[15] Prior to that, governments inflicted on criminals any of a vast array of punishments, most of them corporal. These ranged from flogging and the pillory to the gruesome torture and execution of a regicide, an account of which opens Foucault's book. Yet within two decades this multiplicity of punishments had been reduced to one: detention. Foucault asks why.

Traditional social history would examine the historical period in great detail, describing precisely the ideological movements, economic conditions, political changes, and, of course, the individual agents, that influenced this dramatic shift in practice. Foucault, in contrast, is concerned, not with a period (e.g., penal reform in early nineteenth-century France) but with a problem: what made this transformation possible? Why was it so quickly and so thoroughly adopted? Description has yielded a radical break, the kind that in-

186 : Thomas R. Flynn

terests the archaeologist, who will analyze it to discover a transformation of discursive and nondiscursive practices. But the nature of the evidence in relation to the questions asked warrants the method of the genealogist as well, who seeks a new economy of power relations beneath the surface of this penal reform.

The Roman historian Paul Veyne, Foucault's colleague at the Collège de France, remarked that the New Historian should question what a particular society takes for granted, what its own chroniclers believe "goes without saying."[16] This is especially true of the archaeologist/genealogist, who queries the very normality of a practice as well as, in the present case, the practice of normalization itself.

What people came to take for granted during this crucial twenty-year span was a new rationale, what in *L'Impossible Prison* Foucault terms "punitive reason," as well as a new set of practices of surveillance and punishment (p. 33). Rationale and practice reenforced each other as knowledge and power respectively. Indeed, it is one of Foucault's recurring theses that the social sciences, which rose to prominence after this break, are themselves tactics of normalization and control.[17]

Two terms from Foucault's analysis are of particular import for our discussion because they are each forms of the historical "event," namely, 'transformation' and 'displacement.' In *The Archaeology of Knowledge* Foucault had pointed out that he "held in suspense the general, empty category of [historical] change in order to reveal transformations at different levels" (p. 200). His opposition to traditional history is in part the rejection of a uniform model of temporalization. In the present case, Foucault is noting a transformation in the way the body itself is related to power. What had made penal incarceration and its panoply of public apologists and social and psychological "experts" so natural an option in the early nineteenth century was an unconscious but real shift in what Foucault terms the "political technology of the body" (*Discipline and Punish*, p. 24). Such a transformation is a radical event in the language of the *Archaeology*. It is not attributable to any one agent, such as a founder or a reformer, and yet its temporal parameters can be charted with relative precision.

This new "political anatomy" which expressed itself by the ease with which incarceration and the disciplinary motif were accepted by the greater public also appeared in the numerous petty forms of coercion that gradually took root in society in the previous century. Typically, Foucault cites examples from eighteenth-century military training, scholastic discipline, and worker regimentation on which to map this "micro-physics of power." What we may term micro-events of coercive behavior "converge and gradually produce the blueprint of a general method" (*Discipline and Punish*, p. 138). Alongside this political anatomy another, ideological view was forming that was to gain prominence in the history of ideas, namely, that of the perfect society of eighteenth-century philosophers and jurists, based on some form of social contract. But the political anatomy that genealogy reveals had its own ideal. Foucault calls it the "military dream society," and observes the convergence of the two visions in the Napoleonic regime with its double Roman allusion: citizens and legionnaires, guided by law and tactical maneuvers (p. 169). Again, this transformation is "an event of a quite different type" (*Archeology*, p. 172) which confers a new intelligibility on the political and social occurrences of early nineteenth-century France.

Foucault joins his former teacher, Althusser, in employing the Freudian term 'displacement' to characterize this new "economy of power." Althusser had observed an epistemological break between the early and the later works of Marx, wherein the discourse ceased to be philosophical and humanistic and became scientific, and where the earlier terminology, even if it persisted, assumed a new meaning.[18] Foucault, who disagrees with Althusser concerning Marx, notes in *Discipline and Punish* a similar displacement of the vocabulary and the very objects of practical and theoretical concern by the "punitive reason" that become operative in the early nineteenth century and the "carceral system" which it served to legitimate. What he calls the "technology of power" mediates the humanization of punishment and the rise of the social sciences. As before the displacement, the object is ostensibly the body of the criminal, but now it is confined for the sake of discipline. It is the individual's body as social instrument that must be rendered a docile and pliable tool of social productivity (a "productive member of society" is the phrase); this, rather than the vengeance of the sovereign, is the goal of the techniques of punishment.

The architectural figure for this displacement of punishment is Bentham's Panopticon. Symbol and instrument of constant surveillance, it assured the automatic application of power by rendering the prisoner perpetually visible; and since the overseers could not be seen, the inmates became their own guards—the ideal of a carceral society. Panopticism, Foucault concludes, "is the general principle of this new 'political anatomy' whose object and end are not the relations of sovereignty [as before the break], but the relations of discipline" (p. 208).

After extended descriptions of disciplinary techniques in the army, the workshop, the hospital, and the school, where their similarities are striking, Foucault asks: "Is it surprising that the cellular prison, with its regular chronologies, forced labor, its authorities of surveillance and registration, its experts in normality who continue and multiply the function of the judge, should have become the modern instrument of penalty? Is it surprising that prisons resemble factories, schools, barracks, hospitals, which all resemble prisons?" (pp. 227–28).

Given Foucault's previous analysis, it is anything but surprising; indeed, it is "obvious" with that clarity of something that "goes without saying." And that is Foucault's point in his struggle against the "optics of the sources," namely, to point out the all-too-obvious and the radical events of transformation and displacement that make it so. But these events themselves, while they make possible a profusion of disciplinary practices and a science to perfect them, are not themselves causally linked to a previous system. It did not have to happen that way. The rules come into play only if chance throws the dice.

Nowhere does the centrality of "event" for Foucault's historiography come more clearly into view than in a formal discussion he had with a group of professional historians on the theses of *Discipline and Punish*. For in defending himself from the old charge of a structuralist neglect of history, he insists that he has always tried to work in the direction of an "eventalization" (*évènementialisation*—eventfulness?). A neologism in French and a barbarism in English, "eventalization" denotes a procedure very much like the archaeology and genealogy we have just described. As the word counsels, this method stresses the "singularity," the rupture with accustomed interpretations of the evidence. Thus it is not so obvious (or should not be) that delinquents be incarcerated, that the mad are mentally ill, or that the causes of illness are to be found by "opening up a few bodies." These are indeed the common sense of the period, the "taken for granted" of the sources. This initial phase is a rupture and reversal of the evidence on which our received understanding and practices rely. In *L'Impossible Prison* Foucault terms this the theoretico-political function of eventalization (p. 44).

The next step, which he calls causal "gearing down" (*démultiplication*), though complex, is really a continuation of the methodology with which we are now familiar. It consists of "rediscovering the linkages, encounters, dependencies, blockages, plays of force, strategies and the like, that at a given moment have formed what will subsequently function as evidence, universality, necessity" (p. 44). Translated into the vocabulary of *The Archaeology of Knowledge*, 'gearing down' implies uncovering those conditions, practices, and chance events whose conjuncture at a certain point constitutes the archive, the historical a priori, of a given period.

This concept of a down-shift reveals how radically antifoundationalist Foucault really is. In the face of his frequent references to the event as differential within a series, it would seem reasonable to ask whether the event or break does not presuppose a continuity as its prior condition. But he urges that gearing down is centrifugal, that it multiplies rather than reduces aspects of intelligibility in endless profusion. So let us follow Foucault as he pursues this second phase of eventalization.

Causal "gearing down" means analyzing an event according to the multiple processes that constitute it. Thus penal incarceration, for example, if considered as an event and not as an institutional fact or an ideological effect, entails defining the processes by which previous practices of incarceration were progressively inserted into the forms of legal punishment, and this, in turn, entails analysis of such constitutive processes as the establishment of closed educational spaces, their function as reward and punishment (e.g., sitting in the corner), and so forth.

In *L'Impossible Prison*, harkening back to the logophobia of his inaugural discourse, Foucault speaks of inscribing, around the singular event analyzed as process, a polyhedron of intelligibility, the number of whose sides is necessarily without limit. He advises us to proceed "by progressive and necessarily unfinished saturation" (p. 45). As we have seen in the case of the "carceralization" of the penal practice, the more closely you examine it, the more you are led to correlative practices such as that of the school or the military barracks. As a rule of thumb, Foucault observes that "internal decomposition of the process and multiplication of analytical 'salients' go hand in hand" (p. 45).

One is left with an increasing polymorphism as the analysis advances. Foucault notes a threefold polymorphism, viz., of elements, of relations, and of domains of reference. Regarding the prison again, we must consider such elements as pedagogical practices, the rise of professional armies, British empiricism, the techniques of firearms, a new division of labor and the rest. As for the relations themselves, we can focus on the transfer of technical models such as the architecture of surveillance, or examine the tactics of response to a particular situation like the disorder provoked by public torture, or examine the application of such theories as utilitarianism regarding behavior, and so forth. Finally, we encounter a polymorphism in the very domains of reference—their nature, generality, and the like. Here, Foucault points out, it is not merely a matter of technical changes regarding details but "involves *new techniques of power* which are coming to play in a capitalist economy and all that they require" (p. 45).

The point of this typically Foucaultian schema is precisely to counter the "structuralist's" insistence on a single mechanism, a nonevent which is as unitary, necessary, and inevitable as possible, like a demographic scale or an anthropological schema. As Foucault explains, his methodological program offers the new historians too much and too little: too many diverse relations, too many lines of analysis; but not enough unitary necessity. We are left with a plethora of intelligibilities and a lack of necessity. But he resolutely refuses, as he puts it, to place himself "under the sign of unique necessity" (p. 46).

We now have a better understanding of the place of Foucault's "histories" and the events they constitute in the debate between the old historians and the new. From the start he has distanced himself from the former. His rejection of the concepts of consciousness, of underlying continuity, and of historical progress seem to leave him nothing but the nonevent. Indeed, the archaeologies of mental illness, medical perception, and political economy seem to avoid prominent roles for the "great initiators" of these disciplines. It is now evident, with the retrospective insight that history affords, that Foucault's studies have always tended toward the proliferation of "causes" which he is calling "eventalization" and which *Discipline and Punish* so well exemplifies.

Finally, his reference to the event is an appeal to chance over necessity in historical "explanation."[19] In a pivotal essay written several years before *Discipline and Punish*, and included in *Language, Counter-Memory, Practice*, Foucault discusses Nietzsche's "effective" history (*wirkliche Historie*) in terms that anticipate the process we have just described. "Effective history," he writes, "differs from traditional history in being without constants." It transposes the relationship ordinarily established between "the eruption of an event and necessary continuity" (p. 153). Regarding our general topic, he argues: "An event consequently is not a decision, a treaty, a reign, or a battle, but the *reversal of a relationship of forces*, the usurpation of power, the appropriation of a vocabulary turned against those who had once used it, a feeble domination that poisons itself as it grows lax. The forces operating in history . . . always appear through the singular randomness of events" (pp. 154–55, my emphasis). This final sentence could well serve as the motto of Foucaultian historiography: to search for the "forces of domination" operating in history by a painstaking and inventive analysis of innumerable heterogeneous events.

By concentrating on the event, Foucault has succeeded in underscoring the weakness of structuralist "accounts" of historical real-

192 : Thomas R. Flynn

ity. But by giving 'event' a rather uncommon meaning, he has avoided reviving the shopworn battles-and-treaties understanding of traditional historians. We are now in a position to summarize the foregoing by addressing the problematic Foucaultian event and its role in historiography.

As should now be clear, the Foucaultian event is a multifaceted concept which accounts for its theoretical versatility. In an interview published in 1977 and reprinted in *Power/Knowledge* he states the issue well:

> One can agree that structuralism formed the most systematic effort to evacuate the concept of event, not only from ethnology but from a whole series of other sciences and in the extreme case from history. In that sense, I don't see who could be more of an anti-structuralist than myself. But the important thing is to avoid trying to do for the event what was previously done with the concept of structure. It's not a matter of locating everything on one level, that of the event, but of realizing that there are actually *a whole order of levels of different types of events* differing in amplitude, chronological breadth, and capacity to produce effects.

In this, he resembles Braudel, who insists on diverse historical "times," or rhythms, including that of the long term. But Foucault reveals his characteristically Nietzschean pedigree when he adds:

> The problem is at once to distinguish among events, to differentiate the networks and levels to which they belong, and to reconstitute the lines along which they are connected and engender one another. From this follows a refusal of analyses couched in terms of the symbolic field or the domain of signifying structures, and a recourse to analyses in terms of the genealogy of relations of force, strategic developments, tactics. . . . The history which bears and determines us has the form of a war rather than that of a language: relations of power, not relations of meaning. (p. 114)

We have noted the differential nature of events, their intrinsic reference to a series, and we have remarked their discontinuous and aleatory nature. We observed that the materiality of the statement-event was constituted by being the relation of material "traces." We can now say that this holds true for the concept 'event' in general as we consider Foucault's attempt to define the concept in his inaugural lecture: "An event is neither substance, nor accident, nor quality nor process; events are not corporeal. And yet an event is certainly not immaterial; it takes effect, becomes effect, always on the level of materiality. Events have their place; they consist in *relation* to . . . material elements" (*Archaeology of Knowledge*, p. 231).

Recalling Foucault's claim that there are different types of event, let us offer a brief typology of Foucaultian events as we bring our discussion to a close.

We should mention first the micro-events (the term is not Foucault's, though he does speak of a micro-physics of power). These would denote the dust of the historical cosmos—transfers or blockages of power, for example, which would scarcely be noticed except that they are where we normally leave off in giving a historical account. Since Foucault is no foundationalist, these are neither ultimates nor are they building blocks of some total account. As we noted, the intelligibility of the event is in principle without limit.

Next we must mention the statement-event discussed earlier, which figures so centrally in the *Archaeology of Knowledge*. This is the most elusive of the set. In *Language, Counter-Memory, Practice* Foucault describes it as the meaning-event when discussing Gilles Deleuze's writings on a similar topic. As meaning-event it exists "at the limit of words and things, . . . as neutral as the act of dying, and as singular as a throw of the dice" (pp. 174, 179). In this respect, the meaning-event avoids the pitfalls of three recent attempts to conceptualize the event. Neopositivists, failing to grasp the distinctive level of the event (as a relation between material traces), misread it as a material process, as a kind of physicalist phenomenon. Phenomenologists, by insisting that meaning is only for consciousness, concluded that meaning never coincides with the event. Finally, the philosophers of history, by claiming that events exist only in historical time, enclosed the event in a cyclical pattern or some other solidly centered order. Inspired by Deleuze, Foucault counters that the meaning-event is incorporeal, although it is the relation of material traces; it is a meaning, but without reference to an intending subject; and it is free of that temporality which understands the future as rising out of a past essence. Like any Foucaultian event, the meaning-event is incorporeal, but material, anonymous, and aleatory.

Major portions of Foucault's books are devoted to a class of events that we have called *practices*, whether discursive or nondiscursive. The discourse of mental illness or sexuality, the various disciplinary techniques—these are so many practices, events of a different amplitude and capacity to produce effects than either the statement or the micro-event. These are the objects of the descriptive phase of Foucault's method.

Generally, we may say that a practice is a preconceptual, rule-governed, socially sanctioned manner of acting.[20] In *L'Impossible Prison* Foucault offers a characteristically spatial metaphor in describing a practice as "the place of linkage between what one says and does, between the rules one imposes and the reasons given, between projects and evidences" (p. 42). Obviously, this description promotes that unity of theory and practice, or, in Foucault's case, of knowledge and power, that Marxists and pragmatists have likewise valued. A practice is neither a private quality like a habit nor an individual ascription like an act. What we may now term a practice-event constitutes the intelligible background, i.e., the serial unity, for micro-events by its two fold character as "judicative" and "verdicative." As "judicative," practices establish and apply norms, controls, and exclusions; as "veridicative," they are productive of truth, that is, they render true/false discourse possible. So the practice of legal punishment, for example, entails the interplay between a "code" which regulates the ways of acting—how to discipline an inmate, for example—and the production of true discourse that legitimates these ways of acting (see p. 47). The famous power/knowledge tandem in Foucault's overall schema simply extends these judicative and veridicative dimensions of the practice-event respectively.

Passing over the "initiatory" event of someone like Marx or Freud,[21] and the "dynastics" (as Foucault terms it) of those solemn events by which traditional historians canonize the national biography (Veyne), let me complete this table by mentioning those radical events which Foucault describes variously as epistemological breaks, transformations of practice, and displacements of vocabulary, meanings and objects. We know the interest these events carry for the Foucaultian historian. It is to reach them that he "reverses evidence" and questions the obvious. They account for why it was natural to incarcerate in the nineteenth century while in the eighteenth the practice was relatively rare; why pathologists *saw* differently in the classical and in the modern periods; and why sexuality, far from being repressed, was never so discussed as in the Victorian Age—and why we have wanted to believe the opposite. These macro-events, as we might term them, reveal a shift in strategy, the advent of a new differential lending definition to a plurality of other events. In sum, an event of the greatest amplitude, if not of the widest chronological breadth, and of the most far-reaching capacity to produce effects—such is the archive as macro-event.

If the model of the carceral society is Bentham's Panopticon, the instrument of total and unblinking surveillance where each inmate becomes his own guard, the model of Foucault's histories could well be the kaleidoscope.[22] Each particle-event, though discrete, is identified by differential relation to every other. The pattern is aleatory. Whatever permanence a pattern may assume is limited by a spatial "before" and "after" the turn of the instrument (like the "here" and "there" of a trajectory). Each transformation is a new creation. No theme or subtext perdures. There is sequence but not causal influence. (Even the unity of the question posed in a Foucaultian "history" is merely apparent, since its meaning adjusts with each transformation.)

Several French historians have spoken recently of the "return of the event." Indeed, Jacques Le Goff has remarked that the "structure *versus* event" contrast is a false dilemma. And Paul Veyne, as Ricoeur notes, has "undramatized" the contrast.[23] My thesis has been that Foucault's "event" confirms Le Goff's suspicion, that it is a functional concept which serves to introduce differential relations and chance occurrences into the very core of historiography. The structure/event distinction is simply replaced by the series/event relationship, and series are conceived as events of a higher level, enjoying their own duration and succession.

If his differential analyses and decentering of the subject have linked Foucault with the new historians, his insistence on "eventalization" and on the possible service of archaeology and genealogy to a number of broad historical processes reminds us of his ties to the old. (Recall his remark about the nonevent being "squeezed" out of quite common events like birth and death.) As we have seen, Foucault's practice confirms his claim that the event/nonevent dichotomy is exaggerated.

But what, then, is the relation of Foucault's kind of history to the tradition of historiography as an evidential account of the past? Does it revolutionize our reading of history, as Deleuze and Veyne suggest? Or is it an important moment in the history of historiography but not the start of a new era? Or finally, should Foucault be simply dismissed as a brilliant, erudite curiosity in the history of ideas?

His achievement is too formidable and his thought too resonant with recent intellectual movements to warrant bald dismissal. Despite criticism by specialists in the various fields Foucault has sought to diagnose, no historian working in these areas can now ignore the problems he has raised in their regard. At the very least, they must be aware of the epistemic assumptions and the corresponding political (i.e., the power-oriented) dimension of their undertaking as never before.

Yet the fundamental role of lived experience (*le vécue*) and its temporality to historiography seems too obvious to allow its "flattening" in a total Foucaultian revolution. After all, even "slow motion" (*la longue durée*) is still motion. So I choose the second alternative for the following reasons.

My basic philosophical difficulty with Foucault centers on his nominalism, a position that I find destructive of the philosophical enterprise at its roots. The issue has been debated for centuries and there is no need to discuss it here, except to note that the elusiveness of Foucault's pivotal concept of power stems from his nominalist claims, and that its inadequacy as an historical explanation is likewise a function of the indefinite nature of the term. If power is everywhere then it would seem it is nowhere; if everything, including resistance, is power, then nothing is power.

Fully consonant with Foucault's nominalism is the aestheticism, if not nihilism, implicit in his diagnosis of logophobia and his championing of a proliferation of discursive practices. If there is anything positive in his uncovering of the strategies of subjection and subordination that honeycomb a society, it is an implicit appeal to style, a term which figures centrally in his two most recent volumes on the history of sexuality. In *L'Usage des plaisirs* Foucault scarcely conceals his approval of the "aesthetic of existence" that distinguished the classical and Hellenistic attitude toward sexual conduct from the "hermeneutic of desire" introduced by Christian moral teaching (p. 103). When one examines his writings and charts their course, one is led to conclude that the positive "moral" value being propounded by him, as by the classical Greeks he most recently studied, is a "stylization of freedom" (see p. 111). Although Foucault was committed to political action, especially during the gestation period of *Discipline and Punish*, it is difficult to see his theory justifying more than politico-moral "happenings."

My third reason for not joining the Foucaultian revolution is that I am convinced that historiography is a human enterprise and, further, that it is the prolongation of our native ability to follow and to recount stories, as Paul Ricoeur has argued.[24] This does not mean there is no place for impersonal forces, formal structures, or chance events in history, but it does imply that these are derivative phenomena, that their properly "historical" character depends on their inclusion (or includability) in the human narrative. As historian Michel de Certeau has observed, the challenge Foucault leaves us is precisely to show how "a narrative theory [of historiography] would be indissociable from any theory of practices."[25]

Furthermore, Foucault's significant contribution to historiography can be acknowledged short of turning the enterprise on end. In fact, his statement of the question at each crucial juncture, his "eventalization" (or, as he later called it, "problematization") contributes to the only kind of progress that history allows, namely, the "lengthening of the historian's questionnaire," as Veyne would say.[26] Each shift of the kaleidoscope, in so far as it is faithful to the "documents" it arranges, yields a new perspective on the subject matter. Without resorting to hermeneutical procedures that some

198: Thomas R. Flynn

would find invalid, Foucault too could justify the claim—paradoxical as it would sound on his lips—that we understand the historical agents better than they understood themselves.

But the chief obstacle to my accepting Foucault's kaleidoscopic history as an alternative to history as it is commonly pursued, and the reason that tells against the adequacy of the New History in general, stems from the fact that the lived, experienced time of the responsible agent is too firmly entrenched, to speak like a nominalist. It is an essential ingredient in our human condition, to use more comfortable terms. Casting suspicion on that experience demands that it be more nuanced than we have heretofore required but not that it be replaced. To paraphrase a moral from Hannah Arendt: "Kaleidoscopically speaking, man is insignificant," says the archaeologist; "Kaleidoscopically speaking, man holds the kaleidoscope," replies the poet. Perhaps Aristotle stands vindicated yet again: we continue to learn more about human nature from the poet than from the (New) historian.

Notes

1. Fernand Braudel, *The Mediterranean and the Mediterranean World in the Age of Philip II*, trans. Sian Reynolds, 2 vols. (New York: Harper and Row, 1972–74). Paul Ricoeur calls it "the real manifesto of the Annales school" in his *Time and Narrative*, trans. Kathleen McLaughlin and David Pellauer, 2 vols. (Chicago: the University of Chicago Press, 1984–85), 1:101.

2. Paul Veyne, *Writing History*, trans. Mina Moore-Rinvolucri (Middletown, Conn.: Wesleyan University Press, 1984), pp. 216, 282; François Furet, *In the Workshop of History*, trans. Jonathan Mandelbaum (Chicago: The University of Chicago Press, 1984), p. 3.

3. Michel Foucault, *The Order of Things* (New York: Vintage Books, 1973), p. 342. For examples of the outcry attending Foucault's proclamation, see Mikel Dufrenne, *Pour L'Homme* (Paris: Editions du Seuil, 1968), pp. 37–47; and "Jean-Paul Sartre Répond," *L'Arc*, no. 30 (1966), pp. 87–96.

4. See Michel Foucault, *The Archaeology of Knowledge* and *The Discourse on Language*, trans. A. M. Sheridan Smith (New York: Harper Colophon Books, 1976), pp. 200–201. On the "structuralism" of *The Order of Things*, see Dominique Lecourt, *Marxism and Epistemology: Bachelard, Canguilhem, Foucault*, trans. Ben Brewster (London: New Left Books, 1975), p. 189.

5. Pierre Bourdieu, *Outline of a Theory of Practice*, trans. Richard Nice (Cambridge: Cambridge University Press, 1977).

6. In fact, Foucault prefers to treat the statement as a function rather than as a unit (see pp. 86–87). Nowhere is the problematic nature of his *énoncé* more evident than in those pages of the *Archaeology*.

7. See Ferdinand de Saussure, *Cours de linguistique général* (Paris: Payot, 1978), p. 166.

8. Foucault defines 'discursive practice' as "a body of anonymous, historical rules, always determined in time and space, that have defined for a given period and for a given social, economic, geographical or linguistic area the conditions of operation of the enunciative function" (*Archaeology*, p. 117, translation emended).

9. See Max Weber, *General Economic History*, trans. Frank H. Knight (Glencoe, Ill.: The Free Press, 1950), especially chapter 17.

10. Michel Foucault, *Language, Counter-Memory, Practice*, trans. Donald F. Bouchard and Sherry Simon (Ithaca: Cornell University Press, 1977), p. 146.

11. François Ewald, "Anatomie et corps politique," *Critique* 343 (1975): 1229.

12. Michel Foucault, *Discipline and Punish: The Birth of the Prison*, trans. Alan Sheridan (New York: Pantheon, 1977), p. 8. Idem, *Histoire de la sexualité*, vol. 2, *L'Usage des plaisirs* (Paris: Gallimard, 1984), pp. 109 ff.

13. Foucault, *Discipline and Punish*, p. 139; idem, *Histoire de la sexualité: La volonté de savoir* (Paris: Gallimard, 1976), 1:122.

14. Michelle Perrot, ed., *L'Impossible Prison* (Paris: Éditions du Seuil, 1980), p. 26.

15. The *terminus ad quem* is the French penal code of 1810. Foucault notes that penal reformers before that period had opposed incarceration as being a practice "directly bound up with arbitrary royal decision and the excesses of the sovereign power." See *Discipline and Punish*, p. 119.

16. Veyne, *Writing*, p. 223.

17. See Foucault, *Order of Things*, ch. 10; and *Discipline and Punish*, pp. 182–94, 210–28, 295–96.

18. See Louis Althusser, "On the Evolution of the Young Marx," *Essays in Self-Criticism*, trans. Grahame Lock (London: New Left Books, 1976), pp. 151–61.

19. In fact, it is doubtful that Foucault's "histories" claim to be "explanations" in the historical, much less in any "scientific" sense. Regarding the *régimes* of *The Order of Things*, for example, he has observed: "I wasn't for the moment trying to explain them"; see *Power/Knowledge: Selected Interviews and Other Writings*, trans. Colin Gordon et al. (New York: Pantheon Books, 1980), p. 113. His "archaeologies" as well as the first phase of "eventalization" are descriptive analyses. The "genealogies" may be construed as explanations by virtue of their appeal to "power" as an axis of intelligibility, but the elusive character of that term as well as Foucault's avowed "nominalism" in its regard, leaves its "explanatory force" questionable.

20. Pierre Bourdieu places "practice" midway between *habitus* and field. See his *Outline*, pp. 78 ff. See also idem, *Le Sens pratique* (Paris: Editions du Minuit, 1980), pp. 87–114.

21. The "initiatory event" (my term, not Foucault's) constitutes a special challenge to Foucault, in view of his suspicion of "origins" and his decentering of the

subject and author from the historian's repertoire. He sees Homer, Aristotle, and the Church Fathers, for example, as authors of a special magnitude, occupying a "transdiscursive" position vis-à-vis the discursive realm that succeeds them. Yet among these, a distinct position is occupied by "initiators of discursive practices" such as Marx and Freud. They produced not only their own work "but the possibility and the rules of formation of other texts." Foucault claims that the initiation of a discursive practice is "heterogeneous to its ulterior transformations." (See *Language, Counter-Memory, Practice*, pp. 131, 133.) Though it would take us too far afield to consider the nature of these "authors" and the consistency of the concept with the rest of Foucault's thought, the point is that the transformation which their work entails is what we may term an "initiatory" event. They are like the macro-events we shall now discuss, except that they are attributable in some noteworthy fashion to specific "authors" whose names they bear. The nature of this attribution remains obscure.

22. It is Paul Veyne who suggests the image in the appendix to the French edition of his *Writing*, "Comment on écrit l'histoire suivi de Foucault revolutionne l'histoire" (Paris: Seuil, 1978), pp. 225–26.

23. See, e.g., Pierre Nora's "Le retour de l'événement" in *Faire de l'histoire*, ed. Jacques le Goff and Pierre Nora, 3 vols. (Paris: Gallimard, 1974), 1:210–27; and Ricoeur, *Time and Narrative*, 1: 207 ff., 249, n. 36, 217–18, 170.

24. That is a major thesis of his *Time and Narrative*. See especially chapters three and six of volume one.

25. Michel de Certeau, "Micro Techniques and Panoptic Discourse: A Quid Pro Quo," *Humanities in Society* 5, nos. 3 & 4 (Summer & Fall 1982): 265.

26. See the interview with Foucault, "Le Souci de la vérité," *Magazine littéraire* 207 (May 1984): 18: Problematization is "the ensemble of discursive or nondiscursive practices that brings something into the play of the true and the false and constitutes it as an object of thought (whether in the form of moral reflection, scientific knowledge, political analysis or whatever)." Veyne, *Writing*, p. 226.

Habermas and History: The Institutionalization of Discourse as Historical Project

A. Anthony Smith

A fully adequate historical perspective must have two components. It first must be retrospective, and make our present historical context intelligible in light of past development. It also must be prospective, and establish the direction our future historical development should take. Jürgen Habermas's most recent and most comprehensive work, *The Theory of Communicative Action*, attempts to fulfill both tasks. In the first section of my paper I shall present Habermas's account of the historical processes which have brought about our contemporary situation and his argument for the direction future development ought to take. In part two I critically evaluate the goal for our future history that Habermas advocates. In the final section I defend an alternative goal for historical praxis which I contend is more compatible with Habermas's principles than Habermas's own proposal.

Habermas's Theory of Communicative Action

For our purposes here we can summarize the position defended in *The Theory of Communicative Action* in five theses. The first four attempt to make our present historical context intelligible through a retrospective reconstruction of the essential processes of modernity. The fifth, with which we shall be especially concerned, argues that the central problems of modernity can only be resolved through a future "institutionalization of discourse."

Thesis 1. Underlying modernity is a process of rationalization in which the subsystems of political administration and economic production and distribution have broken off from the life world. These subsystems now provide for the material reproduction of the life world. In doing so, however, they now function independently from the life world. They are fuelled by means of power and money, whereas the life world is bound together by the medium of communication. Habermas is especially interested in the four social roles formed at the intersection of the subsystems and the life world: that of wage laborer, who provides input (labor) into the economic subsystem from the life world; consumer, who receives output (goods and services) from the economic subsystem; citizen, who provides the political subsystem with inputs—legitimations and taxes—from the life world; and client, who receives outputs from the political subsystems provided to the life world in the form of services.[1]

Thesis 2. Economic and political subsystems functioning independently according to the media, money, and power can set off crises in the life world. These economic and political crises affect primarily the social roles of wage laborer and citizen. Left unattended, these crises would set off struggles, especially class struggles, in the life world. In principle, however, these crises can be defused if compensations are provided to the life world. The "social state" (Sozialstaat) of developed industrial societies has the function of providing such compensations.[2] Specifically, the social state first offers compensations for the risks inherent in owning nothing besides one's labor power. As a result of these compensations, class conflict has been "pacified."

> The legal institutionalization of wage conflicts has become the basis of a reformist politics which has brought forth a pacification by the social state of class conflict. Essential to the enterprise are labor laws and social legislation which provide for the basic risks of wage labor and compensates for the disadvantages resulting from structurally weak market positions (laborer, renter, consumer, etc.). Social policy does away with extreme injury and insecurity without of course touching the structurally unequal relations of property, income, and dependency. (pp. 510–11)

Second, just as compensations to the consumer smooth over the insecurities of the labor market, so services provided to state clients compensate for the lack of effective participation by citizens of the state: "For the neutralization of the generalized role of state citizen, the social state also pays in the coin of use-values which the state citizens receive as claims on the bureaucracies of the welfare state . . . the role of clients is the pendant that makes acceptable a political participation damned to abstraction and robbed of its effectiveness" (pp. 514–15).

Thesis 3. System complexity tends to increase as networks bound together by money and administrative power expand. As system complexity increases, more social compensations are required to "pacify" social relations.[3] But as more and more compensations are provided, the independently functioning systems now determine not just the material reproduction of the life world, but its social reproduction as well. Habermas terms this process the colonization of the life world.[4]

Thesis 4. Habermas claims that social reproduction (i.e., the processes of cultural reproduction, social integration, and socialization) must take place through the medium of communication in the life world. If it is instead subjected to the imperatives of power and money due to the expansion of political and economic subsystems, then social pathologies will inevitably break out; for "these media break down in the realms of cultural reproduction, social integration, and socialization; in these functions they cannot replace the action-coordinating mechanism of understanding. . . . In distinction from the *material* reproduction of the life world, its *symbolic* reproduction cannot be transformed by monetarization and bureaucratization without pathological consequences in the basis of systematic integration" (pp. 476–77). These pathological consequences are built into the very form in which expanding compensations are provided:

As the social state expands beyond the pacification of the class conflict that immediately arises in the sphere of production, and extends a net of client relationships over the realm of private lives, the expected pathological consequences of state regulations step forth all the more strongly, representing simultaneously a monetarization and bureaucratization of core realms of the life world. . . . The guarantees of the social state ought to serve the goal of social integration and yet simultaneously they lead to the disintegration of those life contexts which are dissolved from the action-coordinating mechanisms of understanding and transformed by such means as money and power.[5]

Thesis 5. The above presents Habermas with the following dilemma. He wishes to maintain the increase in technical efficiency resulting from economic and political subsystems that function independently from the life world. He agrees with systems theorists that any attempt to reincorporate these subsystems back into the life world would lead to a regress in the level of technical rationality, and this must be avoided. Further, Habermas feels that practical rationalization in the life world can be successfully accomplished only when the life world is set free from the necessity of concerning itself with its material reproduction.[6] On the other hand, however, it is also the case that Habermas wishes to end the colonization of the life world and the social pathologies that stem from subsystems encroaching upon the life world. Habermas's general answer to this dilemma is to insist that practical rationalization in the life world and technical rationalization in the subsystems must be somehow joined: "After we first differentiate in social action between action oriented to understanding and action oriented toward success, we can then grasp as *complementary* developments the communicative rationalization of everyday action and subsystem formation for purposive-rational economic and administrative action" (1:457).

Before proceeding we must first define the notion of "communicative rationality." The social life world, for Habermas, is constituted by networks of communication. In the course of communication certain types of validity claims are continually being made. Here we shall be concerned exclusively with practical validity claims, i.e., claims that the social interactions constituted through speech acts are justified. The communicative rationality of a society is measured by the degree to which practical validity claims are subjected to full testing to see if they are warranted. Practical claims regarding the correctness of a particular policy are today necessarily couched in terms of the general interest of the community. Testing these claims therefore means attempting to discover whether the proposals are indeed compatible with the general interests. Habermas asserts that this can be done only within a special sort of communication. He terms this a "discourse which anticipates an ideal speech situation." This discourse is characterized by two features: (a) the speech is potentially unrestricted, i.e., in principle it may include all who are affected by the proposal; and (b) no coercion is exercised upon any of the participants in the discourse. Only proposals which are truly in the general interest would be agreed to in an uncoerced and unrestricted speech situation; a consensus would not be attained for any proposal which is not generalizable.

We can now describe the model for future historical development within which communicative (practical) rationality and technical rationality can be joined. Habermas argues that the economic and administrative subsystems ought to be allowed to function independently according to the media of money and power as long as they are fulfilling the conditions for the material reproduction of the life world. Past this point they cannot be allowed to go. If they begin to spread further, something along the lines of what Habermas terms "counterinstitutions" must intervene. Counterinstitutions are organizations within the life world, functioning according to the medium of communication, whose task is to protect the life world from infringement. As soon as subsystems transgress their proper limit and begin to affect the process of *social* reproduction, i.e., as soon as signs of a colonization of the life world appear, the counterinstitutions would intervene to prevent social pathologies from being set off. "The life world develops out of itself counterinstitutions in order to limit the autonomous dynamic of the economic and political-administrative systems" (2:582). As these counterinstitutions are established, then, "a preview of a post-traditional, everyday communication arises, which stands on its own feet, which sets limits to the autonomous dynamic of independent subsystems . . . which works against the combined danger of reification and devastation" (p. 486). Rather than being organized by the exchange of power or money, the counterinstitutions would function along participatory lines: "Procedures of conflict resolution must arise which are appropriate to the structures of action oriented to understanding: discursive processes of will formation and procedures for deliberation and decision oriented toward consensus" (p. 544). In other words, a discourse anticipating an ideal speech situation is to be institutionalized in the counterinstitutions, whose task it is to protect the life world from colonization by the economic and political subsystems.

Evaluation

Habermas's theory of discourse is, I believe, one of the most significant contributions to social theory made in the twentieth century. And I accept that the task of institutionalizing discourse is the most profound historical challenge facing humanity today. Nonetheless it is my view that Habermas's own working out of the implications of this perspective is inadequate.

Habermas's position represents a rejection of Marxism that cannot be defended. In the Marxist perspective an economic sphere functioning exclusively according to the medium of money ("generalized commodity production") necessarily undermines social relations in the life world. Marx concludes that the processes of production and distribution must be subjected to the decisions of men and women in the life world. Regarding the subsystem of political administration, Marx insists that the social body must take back all the forces absorbed by "the state parasite" and that all political officials be elected, subject to recall at any moment, and paid only average workers' wages. These proposals are ways of subjecting political administration to the imperatives of the life world.[7] In sharp contrast to the classical tradition of Marxist theory, Habermas insists that the independence of these subsystems from the life world is an intrinsic feature of modern societies.[8] He combines this view with a belief that the integrity of the life world can be maintained if discourse is institutionalized in something along the lines of "counterinstitutions." My central contention is that counterinstitutions cannot fulfill the tasks Habermas assigns them when subsystems are allowed to continue to function autonomously from the life world. One or the other must be given up. Habermas's insistence that political administration and economic production and distribution should function exclusively by means of power and money guarantees, unfortunately, that it will be the institutionalization of discourse that is sacrificed. Habermas fails to see this, due to his rigid separation of the material reproduction of the life world (entrusted to the economic and political subsystems) and its social reproduction. There are three areas where this undialectical separation breaks down in ways Habermas does not take into account: (1) the formation of the capacity to participate in discursive situations; (2) the continued generation of class conflict in the life world; and (3) the dynamics of the new forms of conflict set off by social pathologies in the life world.

1. The functioning of the economic and political subsystems, concerned with material reproduction, directly determines the sorts of communicative interactions possible in the processes of social reproduction. A first connection is the direct correlation between one's position in the process of material reproduction and one's ability to take part in a process of social reproduction along the lines Habermas advocates:

> The objective situation of alienation at the workplace has deleterious consequences for other spheres of life. The worker who is denied participation and control over the work situation is unlikely to be able to participate effectively in community or national decision making, even if there are formal opportunities to do so. This is because effective participation in decision making requires certain skills (keeping oneself informed, understanding the issues, presenting one's viewpoint clearly and forcefully) and certain attitudes (a motivation to participate, and the self-confidence to do so) which a worker shut off from decision making at work has little opportunity to develop. In other words, participatory democracy at the workplace appears to be an essential prerequisite for meaningful democracy in community and national affairs.[9]

If this is the case then it may be naive for Habermas to think that participatory counterinstitutions can be established in the life world without transforming the economy and political administration along participatory lines.

A second connection is that the process of political will formation, a central part of social reproduction, cannot occur along the rationalized lines Habermas proposes—i.e., political discourse cannot be oriented toward the attainment of uncoerced consensus—if the public's material interests can be manipulated to prevent this. Political will formation cannot be rational in Habermas's sense if there exists a bureaucratic administration which, through its power of allocating services, can channel will formation in a particular direction. This means that there must be some sort of check on those who exercise administrative power. It is difficult to see what could attain this other than measures along the lines proposed by Marx: the election and recall of, and lack of bureaucratic privileges for, those who administer. Likewise the formation of a public will cannot be rational in Habermas's sense if economic decisions regarding investment can be used to threaten a community with disinvestment were it to form a political will of a particular sort. And this means that there must be some sort of democratic, public control over the making of investment decisions. It is difficult to see what this could be other than the socialization of the means of production along the lines Marx recommends. What is common to these proposals is the insistence that material reproduction not occur independently from the life world. The economic and political subsystems must be subordinated to the life world if discourse is to be institutionalized in any meaningful sense.

2. Habermas would grant that in the early stages of capitalism, setting up economic and political subsystems apart from the life world was ultimately incompatible with adequately institutionalizing discourse in the life world. That is because these subsystems set off class conflicts in the life world. The fundamental antagonism of class conflict is incompatible in the medium to long term with attaining a rational consensus uniting all the interests of the community, and this is the goal of discourse. Habermas asserts, however, that the compensations provided by the social state of late capitalism prevent these sorts of conflicts from arising:

> The pacification by the social state of class conflict comes about under the condition of the continuation of a process of accumulation whose capitalistic motor mechanism is protected by state intervention, but in no way changed. . . . Namely, with the institutionalization of class conflict, the so-

cial opposition, which is set off by private control over the means of the production of social wealth, increasingly loses its power to form structures for the life world of social groups, although it remains, as before, constitutive of the economic system. . . . The class structure, transferred from the life world to the system, loses its historically graspable form.[10]

This supposed success of the social state is one significant factor in Habermas's belief that retaining economic and political subsystems that function according to the means of money and power can in principle be compatible with institutionalizing discourse.

A great number of points could be made here. First of all, one might question Habermas's restriction of his analysis to countries of the first world. Even if he were correct regarding the accomplishments of developed capitalist countries, setting off an economic subsystem that functions exclusively by means of money involves a global system. If the compensations paid to inhabitants of the first world are directly connected to the superexploitation of workers and peasants in third-world countries, then it can hardly be argued that class struggle has been pacified on the global scale.[11] Secondly, even within developed capitalist countries Habermas may be accused of confusing the buying off of the most organized sectors of the working class with the pacification of class struggle as a whole. The major beneficiaries of the social state were white males within unions, the most politically powerful sector of the working class. Women, people in unorganized sectors, and people of color have benefited far less from the social state.[12] A third point is that the compensations provided for those not working ultimately must be kept low enough and be tendered in a form demeaning enough so that a system based upon the compulsion to sell one's labor power is not threatened.[13] Can speech situations without coercion be institutionalized when such compulsion remains? Further, it is true that along with other superexploited groups the unemployed possess relatively little political power. But from the fact that they lack the ability to threaten the equilibrium of the established order it does not follow that this order has been successful in resolving distributional conflicts, as Habermas concludes. Finally, Habermas's account is formulated in subjectivist

terms. But the category of class struggle has an objective component to it. From the fact that those within the social state may not
use the category of class struggle to interpret their social world, it
does not follow that that category is inapplicable to that social
world objectively.

These replies to Habermas's position raise issues which he does
not consider. But I shall concentrate on an internal difficulty within
his position. Habermas notes that the compensations provided by
the social state to smooth over class conflict require revenues. With
any given level of revenues, the more that is spent on social compensations, the less remains for expenditures necessary for the further-
ing of capital accumulation. Therefore, given a fixed amount of
revenues, social state policies set off a zero-sum game in which class
struggle is not at all pacified, but merely continued on the political
level.[14] The social state cannot increase its revenues by lessening
significantly the share of social wealth of working men and women,
since this is the group which is to be compensated. Nor can the
share appropriated by the wealthy be lessened significantly, since
this would provoke an investment strike. The only way out of this
impasse is for revenues to increase as a result of growth in the
economy. Only if the economic pie is expanding can the social state
appropriate revenues for social compensations without provoking
class conflicts. "Interventions in the patterns of distributions [made
through] social compensations in general do not set off reactions on
the side of priviledged groups only when they can be paid for from
the growth of the social product and do not touch property already
held; otherwise they cannot fulfill the function of limiting and put-
ting to rest class conflicts" (p. 511). Yet there are good reasons to
think that the dream of uninterrupted growth in capitalist economies is just that, a dream. Habermas himself asserts that "crisis
tendencies . . . spring from the indigenous breakdown of the process of accumulation" (p. 565). In the short run the state may step in
to fill the gaps in the market. But in his own discussion of state
interventionism Habermas mentions that eventually this just shifts
the form taken by the crisis from an economic to a political one,
which in turn eventually leads the state to attempt to shift the
burden of the crisis back to the economic sphere.[15] There is thus an
internal tension in Habermas's argument. If the social state is to

accomplish the task of pacifying class conflict it requires continuous capitalist growth, a continuous growth which Habermas's own discussion of crisis suggests is impossible. Instead of attempting to resolve this tension, he simply proceeds as if the difficulties here could be overlooked: "If one disregards the disequilibrium of a crisis-laden system, which is given again to the life world in an administratively processed form, [then] capitalist growth resolves conflicts within the life world" (p. 516). This is analogous to asserting that if one disregards the deadly side effects of a drug, it is quite effective in curing disease. In both cases one is disregarding what is crucial.

It is astonishing that Habermas could suggest that this sort of disregard is legitimate today. It is true that rebuilding after the horrible devastation of World War II set off a tremendous period of economic expansion. In his early writings, impressed by this growth, Habermas speculated that perhaps the key to smoothing over economic and political crises had been found (albeit at the cost of setting off cultural crises). But by the time Habermas came to write *The Theory of Communicative Action* in the late seventies and early eighties, this period had been over for quite some time.[16] Today few pretend that the capitalist state can simultaneously provide compensations to those in weak market positions and further the accumulation of capital. And since it remains a capitalist state, it is the latter which is selected when a choice has to be made. In a period of all-out assaults upon the social state Habermas praises its stability—in a period where, throughout the developed capitalist world, the state institutes austerity measures, provides tax breaks to the wealthy, encourages wage cutbacks for workers, cuts back social services, and oversees a restructuring of the labor process in the interests of capital.[17] Habermas speaks of class conflict as "pacified." Given that economic and political subsystems set off class conflicts in the life world which the social state has failed to pacify, and given that such conflicts are in principle incompatible with institutionalizing discourse in the life world, we have a second reason for concluding that these subsystems must be subordinated to the life world if discourse is to be institutionalized in any meaningful sense.

3. We have just examined Habermas's argument that the specific

conflicts arising from the wage labor–capital relationship have been "pacified" under the social state of late capitalism. Habermas, however, does not conclude from this that late capitalism is without conflicts. Conflicts remain inherent in this society, but they are located elsewhere than where Marxists root them: "The more the class conflict which is built into the private-economy form of accumulation in society can be dammed up and held latent, the more problems press to the foreground which do not injure immediately ascribable class specific interests" (p. 513).

These are the problems of social pathologies that stem from the colonization of the life world.[18] Like class conflicts, the social conflicts resulting from social pathologies are also incompatible with institutionalizing unrestricted and uncoerced discourse in the life world. And so, as we have seen, Habermas advocates something along the lines of counterinstitutions to check the rise of these conflicts. Unfortunately, there is no reason to suppose that these counterinstitutions will be any more successful in pacifying conflicts arising from social pathologies than the social state has been in pacifying class conflicts.

Habermas points out that the new movements responding to social pathologies all share a common focus in the critique of growth: "The themes of the critique of growth are the sole bonds between these heterogeneous groups" (p. 577). But on his own account there is a yet deeper principle unifying the different conflict forms. He asserts that these are "conflicts which do not arise primarily in class-specific forms and yet go back to a repressed class structure that is expelled into systematically integrated realms of action" (p. 515). In other words, all the new forms of conflict resemble each other in being at least partially determined by underlying class relations. The fact that there are a number of mediations between the class structure and the conflicts which "do not arise primarily in class-specific forms" does not lessen the fact that on Habermas's own account the causal chain moves from the class structure generated in the economic subsystem, through the social state and its compensations, through the colonization of the life world and social pathologies, to its culmination in the social conflicts which arise in response. This reading is further confirmed in Habermas's closing summary of the new forms of conflict:

The alternative praxis directs itself against the profit-dependent institutionalization of vocational work, against the market-dependent mobilization of labor power, against the extension of the pressures of competition and achievement to grade schools. It also moves against the monetarization of services, relations, and time, against a consumeristic redefinition of private life spaces and personal life styles. Further, the relationship of clients to public social-service agencies ought to be broken up and made to function in a participatory manner, according to the paradigm of self-help organizations. Finally, these forms of protest negate the definition of the state-citizen role and the routine of the purposive-rational carrying through of interests. (pp. 581–82)

The first sentence of this passage is interesting in that it seems to contradict Habermas's claim that the wage labor–capital relation has been "pacified." But the point I wish to stress here is that from this perspective the conflicts Habermas discusses are responses to the generalization of the commodity form and a corresponding lack of participation in the control of one's own destiny, as more and more social relations are submitted to the commodity form (including the services provided by the state to its clients, the spreading of special interest politics, campaign contributions, lobbying, and the like). Neither of these factors is changed if one allows the economic system to continue functioning autonomously according to the medium of money.

Habermas himself asserts that "the thesis of the inner colonization states that the subsystems of the economy and the state become ever more complex as a result of capitalist growth and penetrate ever deeper into the symbolic reproduction of the life world" (p. 539). And the search for growth in a money economy by definition involves the extension of the commodity form into more and more realms of life. Habermas's proposal leaves all this intact. His model leaves the counterinstitutions with the task of addressing a problem without being able to address the underlying cause of that problem. They are in the same situation as a doctor who is forced to treat only the symptoms of a disease, not its cause. This is clearly not a very effective way of guaranteeing the institutionalization of discourse. The only effective way of guaranteeing this is, once again, to reincorporate the subsystems within the life world.

An Alternative Model

From our account above it follows that the institutionalization of discourse cannot be done half-way. Attempts to institute it only in counterinstitutions and not in the main institutions of society are ultimately doomed to failure. Someone convinced by Habermas's arguments regarding the connection of independent subsystems with social pathologies therefore must make the institutionalization of discourse throughout the society the goal of future historical development.

Habermas himself is sympathetic to instituting worker control over production, communal control of investment decisions, and so on,[19] and these are the sorts of things we have in mind. But if workers are controlling the production process and the community is controlling investment decisions, and—we may add—those exercising administrative authority are elected, subject to recall, and not granted special material privileges, what remains of the "independence" of the political and economic subsystems? In certain circumstances democratic political will formation in the life world certainly may approve setting up an administrative apparatus functioning exclusively by means of power (e.g., militia forces) and economic institutions functioning exclusively by means of money (perhaps "farmers' markets" for the exchange of food grown locally in small gardens). But generally speaking it is not possible to attain rationalization of the life world in its social reproduction without subordinating political administration and economic action (i.e., material reproduction) to the articulated desires of men and women in the life world. What would this look like?

It obviously is impossible to offer a complete blueprint for a future institutionalization of discourse. But whatever the details might turn out to be, it is possible to state that the institutionalization of discourse must involve the organizational structure of council democracy defended in the classical Marxist tradition. In conclusion I would like to sketch briefly a model of council democracy, state why this model fulfills the project of institutionalizing discourse, and reply to some objections that might be made against it.[20]

In this model the basic units are worker councils and consumer councils, at both local and regional levels. Local worker councils are self-managing units of production organized at the workplace. Within them workers themselves formulate proposals regarding what is to be produced, how the production process is to be organized, who among them is to oversee the production process, and so on. These decisions, like the decisions in all the councils to be discussed, are made democratically. They are based on a principle of consensus, with majority vote being resorted to only if time constraints demand. Higher-level worker councils will be made up of democratically elected representatives from local worker councils. Their tasks will include deciding on questions regarding production which cannot be made at a local level.[21] They also will have to ensure that the plans of local worker councils ultimately fit together coherently. Local consumer councils are to be organized at the neighborhood level. Their tasks would include articulating the needs of their members, formulating requests that items of consumption be produced to satisfy these needs, and formulating principles for the distribution of such items. Higher level consumer councils have the task of ensuring that the requests of the various local councils ultimately cohere, and also of dealing with consumer goods that transcend the local level.[22]

This model would function as follows. Everyone would be both a member of a worker council and of a consumer council. As such, everyone would have an opportunity to present his or her ideas regarding what should be produced and how, and what should be requested for consumption. After a period of discussion the local worker councils would democratically agree on a proposal to produce so and so many units of various sorts of goods or services, while the local consumer councils would agree on a proposal to request to consume so and so many units of various sorts of goods and services. These plans would then be punched into a local terminal connected by a main computer to the terminals of every other local council. Once armed with the information regarding the decisions of every other council, each local council would then voluntarily adjust its proposals to better match future production with articulated social needs. This process could be repeated a number of times within a given time period, with the higher-level councils having the final responsibility of matching production plans with consumers' needs to the greatest extent possible at the given level of productive capacity.

This model, brief as it is, may be sufficient to establish what council democracy is. Can the model serve as an example of the institutionalization of discourse? To do so, two conditions must be fulfilled. The speech leading to decisions must be unrestricted and uncoerced to the greatest possible degree. Under council democracy each individual within the various councils would have an equal access to speech, an equal opportunity to propose different claims, to question the claims of others and to defend one's own claims. In this manner the speech within councils is in principle unrestricted (subject, of course, to time constraints). Next suppose that some individual within a worker or consumer council proposes that she or he perform significantly less labor or receive significantly more goods than the other members of the council. Short of extenuating circumstances, it is most unlikely that those who are required to do more or receive less would agree to this proposal. The proposal would be voted down. In this manner anyone who tries to exercise a freedom not compatible with the freedom of others will not be able to coerce others into accepting this. Thus council democracy allows for uncoerced decision making. We may therefore conclude that council democracy is based upon institutionalizing an approximation of an ideal speech situation as described by Habermas.

One last point remains to be considered. Ought not council democracy be rejected on the grounds of its technical inefficiency? The first thing to be pointed out is that council democracy does not imply that everyone gets to decide about everything all the time. All higher-level councils are representational bodies, and even on the local levels many decisions regarding the day-to-day management of worker and consumer councils can be delegated whenever that furthers efficiency. Nor does the institutionalization of discourse in this full sense imply that systemic considerations ought never to be considered independently from the life world. For example, advanced mathematical techniques have been developed which can be used to calculate input and output requirements for vastly extended series of possible production processes. These calculations fix what sorts of production outputs are possible with different possible sets of inputs. The set of technically possible combinations of inputs and outputs is, of course, completely independent from social relations in the life world. There is certainly no reason why rational techniques allowing calculation of different possible combinations could not be fully appropriated within council democracy.

Finally, there is a good deal of evidence to suggest that subordinating the subsystems to the control of the life world would not result in increased inefficiency. Limiting our remarks to the economic sphere, there are two separate questions to consider here. Is an independent economic system functioning exclusively according to the medium of money truly efficient? And are there convincing arguments for the claim that subordinating this aspect of the material reproduction of the life world to institutionalized discourse would be inefficient? Regarding the former, there are a great number of inefficiencies built into an economic system held together by money transactions. It would take at least another paper to establish this adequately; here I can only present a partial list of factors that suggest this is the case. In the course of the economic cycles that are an inherent feature of economics based on money transactions, a good deal of productive capacity is unused.[23] Those who are unemployed and underemployed are prevented from making productive contributions to society. Many of those who are employed are in jobs which do not allow or do not encourage the further development of their physical and mental potentialities. Many resources are wasted and many potential resources are destroyed, as social costs which are not monetary in form are mostly ignored in profit calculations. Items that are necessary to meet basic human needs are not produced or are wasted if those who need them lack sufficient purchasing power. In an economy functioning according to the medium of money, whenever investors can maximize their return by buying other companies, by speculating on commodities, or art, or gold, rather than by investing in new productive buildings and equipment, they will do so. None of these factors should lead one to deny the dynamism of money-based economies or the ability of such economies to foster the development of productive capacity. But they at least provide a reason to question Habermas's assumption that this sort of economic arrangement has attained the highest degree of efficiency that humankind can reasonably hope for.

The question of the efficiency of institutionalizing discourse with regard to decisions about the production and distribution of goods and services remains to be considered. There is some empirical evidence that the council democracy model could function in an efficient manner. Many corporations, seeking to increase worker productivity, have experimented with greater worker participation in management decisions, greater variety in workers' tasks, and the like. No matter how the experiments were organized, changes which provided workers with more power in production than they normally enjoy all increased worker productivity.[24] These experiments have been kept within strict limits and remain far short of anything approaching council democracy. In all cases management retained ultimate control over production decisions. Nonetheless, the available evidence strongly suggests that a thorough institutionalization of discourse can occur without a loss in productive output. I conclude that on Habermasian grounds institutionalizing discourse along the lines discussed above ought to be the goal of our praxis in history.

Notes

1. "The economic system exchanges wages for rendered labor (as an input factor), as well as goods and rendered services (as output of its own production) for the demand from consumers. Public administration exchanges organizational achievements for taxes (as an input factor), and political decisions (as output of its own production) for mass loyalty. . . . From the perspective of the life world the social roles of employees and consumers, on the one hand, and clients and state citizens, on the other, crystallize around these exchange relations" (Jürgen Habermas, *Theories des kommunikativen Handelns* [Frankfurt: Suhrkamp, 1981], 2:472; all translations from this work are my own).

2. "When one proceeds from a model of the exchange between formally organized spheres of action in the economy and the polity on the one hand, and communicatively structured spheres of action in the private sphere and the public on the other, one must account for the fact that the problems which arise in the

work world are transferred out of the private and into the public spheres of life and are there changed under conditions of competing democratic will formation into mortgages on legitimation. The social, i.e., initially private consequences of class conflict cannot be kept apart from the political public. Thus the social state becomes the political content of mass democracy. This shows that the political system cannot be emancipated from the use-value orientation of state citizens without effect; it cannot produce mass loyalty to any degree it wishes, but must rather also make testable offers of legitimation by means of social state programs" (p. 510).

3. "The politically propped-up internal dynamic of the economic system results in a more or less continuous increase in the system's complexity, which means both the extension and the internal concentration of formally organized realms of action. At first this holds for relations within the subsystems of the economy and public administration and for the interactions of the subsystems between each other. . . . But the growth of the whole complex affects just as greatly the interchange of the subsystems with these spheres of the life world which have been redefined in the system-world. Chief among these redefined spheres are, on the one hand, the private households which are redefined by mass consumerism and, on the other hand, coordinated client services that are redefined by bureaucratic concerns" (pp. 515–16).

4. "The thesis of the inner colonization states that the subsystems of economy and state become ever more complex as a result of capitalist growth, and penetrate ever deeper into the symbolic reproduction of the life world" (p. 539).

5. P. 534. Habermas discusses the pathological consequences of state legislation regarding the family and schools (pp. 41 ff.), social insurance (p. 531), bureaucratically administered therapy programs (p. 533), and manipulation of public opinion (p. 507).

6. "The life world unburdened from the task of material reproduction can . . . multiply its symbolic structures and set free the unique development of cultural modernity" (p. 564).

7. For Marx's proposal for the life world to reincorporate the economic subsystem, see his "Critique of the Gotha Program." His most explicit remarks regarding the reincorporation of the subsystem of political administration are to be found in "The Civil War in France." Both works can be found in *The Marx-Engels Reader*, ed. Robert C. Tucker (New York: Norton, 1978). Regarding the former, Habermas correctly writes that the goal of the praxis Marx advocates is "to destroy the institutional foundation of the means through which the capitalist economy is differentiated [from the life world] together with private ownership of the means of production, and to incorporate the systematically independent process of economic growth back within the horizon of the new life world" (2:500). This goal is common to the classical contributors to Marxist theory, including Lenin, Luxemburg, Trotsky, Gramsci, Marcuse, and Mandel.

8. "Thus Marx's starting point of interpretation does not let the question arise whether the systematic connection of the capitalist economy and the modern state does not *also* present a higher and evolutionarily privileged level of inte-

gration. . . . Marx grasps capitalist society as a totality to such an extent that he misses the unique evolutionary *value* which subsystems directed by means such as money and power possess. Marx doesn't see that the differentiation of state apparatus and economy *also* presents a higher level of systems differentiation, which simultaneously opens up new steering capacities *and* demands a reorganization of the old, feudal class relations. . . . [He] deceived himself over the fact that *every* modern society, no matter how its class structure is constituted, must show a high degree of structural differentiation" (pp. 499–500). Also note Habermas's comment, "Bureaucratization must count as a normal component of the modernization process" (p. 471).

9. *The Capitalist System*, ed. Richard C. Edwards, Michael Reich, and Thomas E. Weiskopf, (Englewood Cliffs, N.J.: Prentice Hall, 1978), p. 267. Carole Pateman's *Participation and Democratic Theory* (London: Cambridge University Press, 1970) develops this point both theoretically and through a number of empirical studies.

10. P. 512. Habermas gives this as a further reason to distance himself from Marxism. He writes, "Marxist orthodoxy has difficulty formulating a plausible explanation of state interventionism, mass democracy, and the welfare state. The economistic beginning fails vis à vis the pacification of class conflict and the long-term success which reformism has achieved in the European countries since the second world war, under the banner of a social democratic program in a broader sense" (p. 505). Whether Habermas is correct in his estimate of the achievement of the social state is discussed in the text. But here it should be pointed out that Marx does have an explanation for the strategies of class pacification pursued by the social state. Similar strategies were proposed by the "democratic petty bourgeois" of his own day, which Marx explained as follows: "As far as the workers are concerned, it is certain above all that they are to remain wage-workers as before; the democratic petty bourgeois only desire better wages and a more secure existence for the workers and hope to achieve this through partial employment by the state and through charity measures; in short, they hope to bribe the workers by more or less concealed alms and to sap their revolutionary vigour by making their position tolerable for the moment." See "Address of the Central Authority to the League" in Karl Marx and Frederick Engels, *Collected Works* (New York: International Publishing Co., 1975–82), 10:280.

11. For an overview of the various arguments for this view, see Anthony Brewer's *Marxist Theories of Imperialism: A Critical Survey* (Boston: Routledge & Kegan Paul, 1980).

12. See David M. Gordon, et al., *Segmented Work, Divided Workers: The Historical Transformation of Labor in the U.S.* (New York: Cambridge University Press, 1982).

13. "Just as the recipients of stock dividends often choose not to work, so too might others if welfare benefits, unemployment compensation, etc. were adequate and readily available. After all, capitalist ideology glorifies the pursuit of self-interest and provides little concept of social obligation. Moreover, in a system of

alienated labor, individual material rewards (rather than, for example, the social necessity of production or the intrinsic rewards of the job) are the chief motivation to work; if an alternate means of livelihood are provided, large numbers of people might well quit work. "Decent" welfare benefits would thus come into serious competition with low-wage, boring, exhausting, and dangerous wage-labor" (Richard C. Edwards, "Who Fares Well in the Welfare State?" in *The Capitalist System*, [p. 308]).

14. "Of course the politics directed toward the building of the social state stands before a dilemma that expresses itself on the fiscal level in the zero-sum game of public expenditures for sociopolitical projects on the one hand, for expenditures for anticyclical and growth-aiding infrastructure policies on the other" (p. 511).

15. "Economically conditioned crisis tendencies are not only administratively worked on, flattened, and braked, but also are invisibly transported into the administrative system. They can appear in different forms there, e.g., as conflicts between its goals in compensation policies and its goals in infrastructure policies, as an excessive claim on the resource time (state debt); as excessive demand upon bureaucratic planning capacity; etc. This can in turn call forth unburdening strategies with the goal of transferring the burden of problems back to the economic system" (p. 506).

16. Among the extensive literature on this topic see *The Economic Crisis and American Society* by Manuel Castells (Princeton: Princeton University Press, 1980); *The Deepening Crisis of U. S. Capitalism* by Harry Magdoff and Paul M. Sweezy (New York: Monthly Review Press, 1981); and, especially, Ernest Mandel's *Late Capitalism* (London: Verso, 1978).

17. Habermas writes, "In the social state the roles which the occupational system offers are normalized, so to speak" (p. 514). This is certainly news to the corporate community, which is presently instituting a massive restructuring of the labor process with the goal of increasing their profits. *Business Week* (16 May 1983) lists some of their strategies: "Cutting the size of crews; enlarging jobs by adding duties; . . . giving up relief and wash-up periods; . . . working more hours for the same pay" (p. 100).

18. "In the developed societies of the West, conflicts have developed in the last one to two decades which in many respects deviate from the social-structure paradigm of institutionalized distributional conflicts. They no longer flare up in the realms of material reproduction, they aren't channeled in political parties and associations and they also won't be made to disappear by system-conforming compensations. The conflicts appear much more in the realms of cultural reproduction, social integration, and socialization; they are borne by subinstitutional or at least extraparliamentary forms of protest; and the basic shortcomings they point to mirror a reification of communicatively structured realms of action, which can't be overcome through the means of money and power. It is not primarily a matter of compensations which the social state can guarantee, but of the defense and restitution of endangered modes of life, or the carrying through of new ones" (p. 576).

19. See "A Reply to My Critics," in *Habermas: Critical Debates*, ed. John B. Thompson and David Held (Cambridge: MIT Press, 1982), p. 312. Regarding worker control of the production process he writes: "The justification of normative regulations that help this repressed interest obtain its rights follows the logic of practical discourse."

20. This model is taken from Michael Albert and Robin Hahnel's *Socialism Today and Tomorrow* (Boston: South End Press, 1981).

21. For example, the question whether one large steel mill should be built to take advantage of economies of scale as opposed to building a number of small mills close to places of production could not be answered appropriately on the local level.

22. An example of the issues that would arise here would be those involving public goods such as regional parks and cultural centers.

23. "All these wasted resources add up. We can compute how much output—measured in terms of goods and services in the market—the economy *could* have produced if our resources were used in their fullest potential. During the last completed business cycle from 1973 to 1978, according to the government's fairly conservative methods for computing potential output, the economy produced at an average of 13% below capacity. This means that production in 1978, a year of peak prosperity during the business cycle, could still have been almost $300 billion more than it was. *The economy wasted nearly one-seventh of its potential output during the mid-70s.* Conditions have not improved since" (Institute of Labor Education and Research, *What's Wrong with the U.S. Economy?* [Boston: South End Press, 1982], p. 161).

24. For a summary of these studies see Paul Blumberg, *Industrial Democracy: The Sociology of Participation* (New York: Schocken Books, 1973), pp. 124–28.

The Contributors

Richard J. Bernstein is Wistar Brown Professor of Philosophy at Haverford College. He has written widely on pragmatism, critical theory, and hermeneutics.

Ernst A. Breisach is a professor of history at Western Michigan University. His publications include works in Renaissance and Reformation history and studies in historiography.

Bowman L. Clarke is a professor of philosophy at the University of Georgia. His research has been focused upon logic and metaphysics.

Bernard P. Dauenhauer is a professor of philosophy at the University of Georgia. He has published regularly on the theory of human agency and topics in political philosophy.

Louis Dupré is Lawrason Riggs Professor of Philosophy of Religion at Yale University. In addition to his publications in the philosophy of religion, he has written extensively on both Marxism and phenomenology.

Thomas R. Flynn is an associate professor of philosophy at Emory University. His works in large measure have dealt with phenomenology and contemporary French thought.

Ofelia Schutte is an associate professor of philosophy at the University of Florida. Her works include studies of Nietzsche and contemporary Hispanic thought.

A. Anthony Smith is an associate professor of philosophy at Iowa State University. His research has been centered on critical theory and contemporary German thought.

Nancy Streuver is a professor of history and member of the Humanities Center at Johns Hopkins University. Her works have emphasized the rhetorical tradition in intellectual history.

Kirk Willis is an assistant professor of history at the University of Georgia. His research is centered on recent British intellectual history.

Richard D. Winfield is an assistant professor of philosophy at the University of Georgia. He has published on Hegel and topics in social and political philosophy.